W9-DJA-136

MANUAL FOR
GROUP PREMARITAL
COUNSELING

MANUAL FO

GROUP PREMARITAL COUNSELING

By Lyle B. Gangsei

ASSOCIATION PRESS

NEW YORK

CARL A. RUDISILL LIBRARY
LENOIR RHYNE COLLEGE

MANUAL FOR GROUP PREMARITAL COUNSELING

Copyright © 1971 by Association Press
291 Broadway, New York, N. Y. 10007

All rights reserved. No part of this publication may be reprinted, reproduced, transmitted, stored in a retrieval system, or otherwise utilized, in
any form or by any means, electronic or mechanical, including photo-
copying or recording, now existing or hereinafter invented, without the
prior written permission of the publisher.

Standard Book Number: 8096-1807-9
Library of Congress Catalog Card Number: 78-129435

PRINTED IN THE UNITED STATES OF AMERICA

301.414
D15m
92939
april 1975

To my wife, Virginia, whose love, support and constant encouragement have made this work possible, I dedicate this book.

Contents

Preface

The material in this manual has been shaped and reshaped as I have used it over the past six years with a number of young engaged couples who were members of the college community in which I work. The eight chapters explore the areas which have been of the greatest concern to them, and which are among the most significant for the marriage relationship. Each chapter begins with expressions of a wide range of viewpoints from the writings of some of the foremost authorities in marriage counseling. There follows a discussion which seeks to sort out and assess the issues raised in the opening section. The chapter then closes with a list of suggestions for discussion. It is the purpose of this book to provide not only the members of the group but also the non-professional counselor-leader with the tools needed to enter into a serious discussion of marriage.

The Introduction provides, in brief compass, some general background information covering the contemporary situation, and also some specific suggestions on ways in which this manual may be productively used. All group participants are urged to read at least the first half of the Introduction even if they do not choose to read it all. The latter sections, however, are particularly recommended for those who will be leading groups in the use of this manual.

Many people have helped in the preparation of this manual. I owe a special debt of gratitude to the couples with whom I have worked, and whose response has encouraged me to refine and redraft the material into its present form. They have given me confidence that the project as a whole has authentic value.

I wish to acknowledge the considerable financial assistance to this project which has been provided by the Board of College Education and Church Vocations of the Lutheran Church in America, the Board of Education of the American Lutheran Church, and California Lutheran College.

I express my sincere appreciation to Dr. Paul Vahanian and Dr. Philip H. Phenix, both of Teachers College, Columbia University. Their constant stimulus to restudy, rethink, and to rewrite has had much to do with the form which the work has finally assumed.

I wish to thank my secretary, Mrs. Dorothy Wilson, who has typed, read copy, checked references, proofread, and prevented many an error from appearing in the final manuscript. Without the loyal and efficient help which she has given, the completion of this book would have been long delayed. I also wish to thank Mrs. Pauline Johnson for her invaluable assistance in the same area.

Any errors in style or any mistakes in content, however, are to be attributed solely to the author.

California Lutheran College   L.B.G.
Thousand Oaks, California

Introduction

In his preface to *Neurotic Interaction in Marriage,* Eisenstein writes:

> Statistically, there are some 400,000 divorces [over 580,000 in 1969 [1]] and annulments granted in this country each year, about 40 per cent of which involve children. The official figures, however, do not begin to convey the true picture. We would have to add a far greater number of separations and desertions in order to appreciate the widespread consequences of broken homes in our society, where daily the courts, social agencies, mental hospitals and penal institutions bear witness to the ultimate effects of disturbed marital interaction.[2]

Sociologists Bossard and Boll estimate that from one-third to one-half of the married population are finding the restraints and responsibilities of marriage burdensome. Values once generally accepted, though not always implemented, are being set aside. Almost every aspect of marriage and family life from the most basic definition to the most extended activity is being questioned. Currently, marriage is in the process of being re-evaluated, redefined, and perhaps even reshaped. Many persons within marriage and many persons approaching marriage lack the sense of sureness which once prevailed. Roles have changed, and are changing, so rapidly and so completely that it is difficult for those most personally involved to know what is expected from them today.

Some professional observers optimistically believe that the increased number of divorces indicates that the level of marital expectation has been raised and that people will no longer go through life trapped in intolerable relationships. The movement out of one marriage and into another, they say, is simply the process of exchanging sick marriages for whole ones.

While this may be an accurate description of the motivation of many who bring their marriages to an end, yet the story does not always end happily. Six out of seven divorced Americans eventually remarry, but about 40 per cent of these end up with yet another divorce. A third marriage is even less apt to succeed. The cost in unhappiness, in the "deep psychological scars" of marital failure, is enormous and the totals continue to rise.

The Concerned

More and more institutions, agencies, groups, and individuals are seeking solutions to this critical situation. Increasingly, the focus is on preventive action, attempting to get to the cause of the problem before it develops. In recent years there has developed a growing emphasis on premarital education and counseling with the hope and goal of preventing marital problems and of establishing strong family relationships.

Many educational institutions are vitally involved. Enrollments in "marriage and family" courses are growing each year. First offered in 1922 at Boston University, these courses have grown in popularity until today hardly a major college or university operates without offering such classes. More and more high schools are beginning to do the same. Even elementary schools are experimenting with sex education down through the kindergarten level. In each case the goal remains the same—to strengthen the family structure through increased knowledge and understanding of what is involved in marriage.

The church is among the many institutions and groups concerned with the problem. Since each year more people are married under the aegis of the church than all other agencies put together, it has an obvious interest in the state of marital and family health. The active concern of the church is seen in the type of training now being given in the seminaries to candidates for the ministry, in the growing number of parish pastors who provide premarital education for their parishioners, in statements by official boards which speak of the religious and social implications of the changes in American marriage, and in the rethinking of theological positions as they relate to marriage. Some of this new thinking is reflected in this manual.

In addition, there are many people who are specifically trained to do marriage counseling. These, in turn, are joined by concerned persons from many different professional fields. Social workers, college and high school teachers, clergymen, counselors, lawyers, medical personnel, along with many others, are entering into the current discussion determined to search out both the essence of the problem and possible solutions.

Loss of Values

Part of the problem is the loss of a stable definition of love and marriage. More and more options seem available. A couple about to be married must make many basic decisions without benefit of the old, more stable guidelines of the past: Shall we engage in premarital intercourse? Shall we have a religious or civil ceremony? Shall we have a child soon, later, or never? Shall we create an authoritarian or an equalitarian relationship? Shall we both work? Shall we establish a church home? How shall we relate to our in-laws? Do we really mean to be faithful to one another? In times past a man or woman had some rather clear patterns as to what was expected before and within marriage; today it is more difficult to be sure. Many things previously held to be of value have been discounted. Philosopher Abraham Edel has summed up the dilemma in the words of a simple poem:

> It all depends on where you are,
> It all depends on when you are,
> It all depends on what you feel,
> It all depends on how you feel,
> It all depends on how you're raised,
> It all depends on what is praised,
> What's right today is wrong tomorrow,
> Joy in France, in England sorrow.
> In all depends on point of view,

Australia or Timbuctoo,
In Rome do as the Romans do.
If tastes just happen to agree
Then you have morality.
But where there are conflicting trends,
It all depends, it all depends . . .[3]

If the absolutes and near absolutes of the past are no longer being accepted, then a number of alternatives confront the concerned person. He may let the situation run its course and wait until the dust settles to see how things work out, or he may move in with the hope and intent of helping to create or re-create a value system that can furnish some essential stability in the unstable marital situation of the day.

Currently, the pace of change has increased to the point where the editors of *Newsweek* commented in 1967 that there have been more changes in the ethical-moral atmosphere of the United States in the last year than in the previous fifty.[4] The rapidity and extent of these changes has led some observers [5] to conclude that marriage, as it is now practiced, is a hopelessly outworn and insufficient answer to the needs of the day and that some new form of cohabitation and child-rearing must be provided. That the value of marriage as it has been known in the past is no more and that it may as well be discarded.

Many others regard this as a weak and cowardly response to a difficult problem. They believe that the shifting ideas and attitudes, the changes in social outlook, the experimental forms of living together, the doubt and confusion regarding values—all call for a most serious re-examination of the nature and forms of marriage. Even if the answers will only be partial ones, without encompassing all the factors involved, nevertheless the attempts must continue.

Purpose of the Manual

This manual is part of the response being made to the basic problem. It is intended to be a means whereby some of the underlying values of marriage can be re-examined. It is the author's contention that there are sufficient values of real worth to be found in the traditional monogamous form of marriage to justify such study. Little is gained by believing that marriage as we know it is over and done with. As long as children are conceived by two parents, marriage and the family will persist. Over fifty years ago Malinowski observed that marriage is always in the mores of even the most primitive tribes.[6] It will undoubtedly remain in the mores of less primitive people, too, since its roots are deeper than at first they may seem to be. It is these roots that the chapters of this manual will display for critical, searching examination.

The manual provides a considerable amount of value-oriented material for discussion from which individuals and couples may draw in developing or stabilizing their own marital value systems. The discussion of the material will allow people to think through, in a concrete way, some of the implications of marriage before they actually are involved in it. Baber is undoubtedly right when he says:

> Marriage would be immeasurably strengthened, and the frequency of divorce correspondingly reduced, if couples would thoughtfully and honestly work out their philosophy of marriage before they embark, deciding what they can reasonably expect from it and what they can not, how much failure they can have in some lesser aspects of it without losing the greater, basic values, which inevitably would bring collapse.[7]

The central purpose of this manual is to assist couples to "thoughtfully and honestly work out their philosophy of marriage."

Use of the Manual

This manual is designed for use in small-group discussion sessions with engaged couples as the prime participants. These sessions may be organized and conducted by agencies such as congregations, colleges and universities, YMCA organizations, youth camps, counseling centers, and the like. They may be led by the professional counselor trained in the techniques of marital and premarital counseling, or by the interested nonprofessional counselor—the professor, the lawyer, the pastor, the youth leader, the physician. Many of these persons will have already demonstrated both interest and competence in dealing with people's problems so as to qualify them to lead groups in the discussion of some of the more significant aspects of marriage.

This is not a how-to-be-happily-married book. It does not contain a listing of tried and true formulas for marital problem-solving. Rather, in the compass of its eight chapters it lays before the reader a wide variety of fact, opinion, and judgment dealing with eight areas related to marriage, each of them a potential problem area. Each chapter concentrates on one subject, but in the chapter a number of different and sometimes conflicting points of view are stated. These points of view, made up of excerpts from the writings of recognized experts, are drawn from a great variety of sources. They make up the body of the manual and constitute the material for discussion. The purpose of these discussions is to both prod and guide young adults into thinking and talking about their values and concepts as related to marriage. If small but significant changes can be effected in an individual's outlook on marriage, all of his subsequent marital life may be modified to a marked degree.[8]

Goller describes the need and suggests a possible solution in the following paragraphs:

Many newlyweds have had little or no experience in practical matters, such as budgeting and household management. More important, though, are the areas of relationship which are new and at times difficult. Important among these are the reality of the marriage as compared with the premarital fantasy, getting to know another adult's special characteristics as they are revealed in daily intimate living, the altering of each mate's pattern of daily living in relation to the needs of the other as well as of himself.

Some of the facts about these aspects of marriage can be obtained from the literature. But what many people need, along with the facts, is the opportunity, through a shared experience with other couples in similar situations, to see all aspects of what is involved in these problems. Among other things, they need help in understanding how their feelings about money, about changes in the nature of their personal freedom, about family planning, can affect their handling of these facets of their marriage.

The educational groups for engaged couples have anticipatory guidance as their primary purpose.[9]

Content of the Manual

Something needs to be said about the materials in use in this manual. The eight themes were chosen because they deal with areas of marital experience which are common to most marriages in this country. There are, of course, many others which might also have been included. The five professional fields from which excerpts have been chosen were selected as being those most deeply involved with the problems of contemporary marriage in the United States. The writings studied were those of men recognized as leaders in these professions. The specific excerpts were chosen for a number of reasons, the chief ones being that each excerpt met the criterion of presenting, defending, or attacking a significant position or judgment, or of being provocative, informative, or definitive in relation to the values under discussion. The entrance of the United States into World War II in 1941 marked the beginning of a time of significant change in the marital structure in the United States. Therefore, all material selected for use first appeared in book form or in professional journals at some time during or after that year.

Each writer quoted speaks for himself in his own words, and is agreed with or disagreed with by other writers quoted in that section, and may be engaged in conversation by the participants and the leader. The attempt is to simulate, to a limited degree, a panel discussion in which everyone has the privilege of the floor. What Hoffman and Plutchik believe about the readings suitable for a college orientation program applies equally well to this marital orientation situation. They write:

Readings should provide the student [participant] with motivation for thinking; they should excite, stimulate and even startle him. This can best be done through a confrontation of opposites, through a controversial approach to important questions of life. . . . In summary, then, readings provide both background and stimulation for significant group discussions.[10]

Groups and Group Dynamics

There are many good reasons for working with groups. One of the more obvious is the time factor. If one leader can meet with ten people together for one hour instead of with ten people for one hour each separately, much time is conserved.

But another and more significant reason is that group work can be highly effective. Recognizing this, Peterson says that group premarital counseling is "one of the most promising movements to aid young people to prepare more adequately for marriage." [11] Group membership allows each participant to proceed at his own pace, employing his defenses as long as it seems necessary, emerging and retiring at will, talking to himself or others, and exercising some control over the intensity of his own therapeutic involvement. "Each group member not only presents his own problems, his own thinking and feeling about himself, but responds to what others say about themselves. He learns by vicarious living in others' experiences . . ." [12]

A number of significant things can happen within groups. The principles of group dynamics have been identified and labeled. The following have been selected from Strang's list as being especially significant for the purposes of this manual. She writes:

Some of these principles relate to attitudes toward people and their needs; some to the behavior and responsibility of group members; others to the formation, composition, and activities of groups; still others to the group process and the role of adult leaders. Among the many principles of group dynamics and group work are the following:

1. Respect for the individual member and concern for his best development underlie effective group work. This respect stems from a belief that each person has resources within himself that can be released in response to group stimulation.
2. The group experience is a means for meeting individual needs for recognition, for new experiences, for approval, for security, for perspective.
3. Each member tends to assume certain roles that affect the group process.
4. Each member should feel responsibility for the group activity;

leadership responsibility may be assumed at times by any member of the group as well as by the official leader; maximum participation will be encouraged by adult leaders or consultants who support and guide but do not dominate.

5. Each member should listen to others, identify himself with other members and recognize and appreciate their contributions.

· ·

7. While recognizing that a certain amount of homogeneity is necessary for stability, the leader should also value heterogeneity of personality and background, and create conditions in which each member can make his best and most appropriate contribution.

· ·

10. The feeling tone of the group and emotional security of individuals grow out of the pattern of responses encouraged in the group.

11. Psychological principles of learning apply to the group situation.

12. Co-operation is strengthened when a group tries to attain both group goals and the "hidden agenda" of individual goals.[13]

The first principle stated above calls for some elaboration. Therapists like Sullivan and Rogers have a rather optimistic view of the human personality. Both believe that something which can be generally defined as a "drive for health" is basic to the human personality. Though employing totally opposite methods, both men have a strong belief that given guidance (Sullivan) or freedom (Rogers) the human personality will grow toward wholeness. In short, the person is of great worth and must be respected. Rogers puts it this way:

The primary point of importance here is the attitude held by the counselor toward the worth and significance of the individual. How do we look upon others? Do we see each person as having worth and dignity in his own right? If we do hold this point of view at the verbal level, to what extent is it operationally evident at the behavioral level? Do we tend to treat individuals as persons of worth, or do we subtly devaluate them by our attitudes and behavior? Is our philosophy one in which respect for the individual is uppermost? Do we respect his capacity and his right to self-direction, or do we basically believe that his life would be best guided by us?[14]

The Group Leader

It is important that the leader should have done some serious thinking about his own faith and values, standards and goals.[15] These should be strong enough and clear enough for him to use in developing his own style of life, but he should be willing as a matter of principle to respect the rights of others to hold differing opinions. This does not mean that in seeking to deepen and root the convictions of his group members he cannot challenge the validity of a point of view. Not to do so may mean that he is not making the contribution of honest candidness which each member should contribute to the group process. His problem will be to avoid establishing himself as the authority figure before the group, the one who has already thought this subject through and has come up with the right answers to all the questions. This latter creates a group dependency on the leader as the "expert." On the contrary, there should be a "willingness on the part of the leader to have every individual in the group express any fact, feeling, or opinion he may wish to." [16]

The experience and skill of the leader and the needs of the group will usually determine the use to which group methods will be put. Almost any combination seems possible. A leader may choose to follow the discussion suggestions at the end of each chapter, or he may let those items which seem most significant to the group come up for review on their own.

The best leader is the one who gradually gets the group to assume the leadership. Perhaps the single most important thing which the leader can do is to provide a permissive atmosphere within which judgment is suspended and free expression is encouraged. He should allow the participants to ventilate their anxieties, antagonisms, guilt, and other repressed feelings. He should allow and encourage questions of every kind. He should be ready to generalize and universalize what may be revealed so that feelings of isolation, awkwardness, worthlessness, and fear are reduced to the point of toleration. When this has been done, the minimum conditions have been established which allow for the development of insight and the healing of inner hurts.

There are no rigidly defined standards which a potential group leader must meet before he may dare to begin group premarital counseling. Needless to say, the better training he has in basic human psychology, in marital relationship problems, and in counseling techniques the better equipped he is. But the processes which may go on in a group range from the passing of information from leader to participant to relationships of therapeutic transference with deep involvement. Each leader must look at himself first and then determine what he can realistically expect to do. The leader does not operate purely out of a theoretical position but rather out of his own background, competence, and integrity.

And, of course, any counselor owes it to his counselees to develop his knowledge and his competency as thoroughly and as rapidly as possible. But as Luckey and Neubeck point out: "The instructor's philosophy of the subject, his own hierarchy of values, as well as his personality, strength and limitations determine what any one instructor will be able to use as his teaching tools." [17]

The format of the manual seeks to provide a relatively safe starting point for a nonprofessional counselor with only a minimum of professional counseling training. He may begin at the point of an objective academic discussion of the value judgments expressed and feel that he is making a contribution. However, the leader can make his most effective contribution to the group by helping the members personalize their reactions to the material. As he grows in knowledge, competency and confidence, the leader can begin more and more to help the group members bring out and deal with the attitudes and feelings which they may have and which should be discussed before a marriage takes place. Perhaps the best preparation for this approach is for the leader to work through the manual *before* he uses it, seeking to rethink, re-evaluate, relive, and perhaps even to reorganize his own marriage in order that he may encourage the participants to do the same rethinking and re-evaluation in anticipation of their own marriages.

It is possible to come up with oversimplified judgments about marriage and about people who have marriage problems, or people who have problems with marriage. The group leader should inform himself of the many powerful, subtle forces which are currently affecting the American cultural scene. He must remind himself that people are not just being bad when they go counter to or refuse to accept some of the values of the past. He must realize that a value system which may seem of prime importance to a married couple in their forties may be regarded as ancient and therefore obsolescent by a person in his twenties.

The threat of the H-bomb is not spoken of openly very much among college age students, yet Graham B. Blaine, psychiatrist in the Harvard University Health Services, recently stated that this threat is very evident in the dreams which students report. Why go slow? Why wait? Why deprive yourself of today's gratification if there may be no tomorrow? These are not necessarily questions of bad people; these are the questions of a generation faced with death before they have had their share of life.

The war in Vietnam is also an important part of the context within which counseling takes place today. To speak of morality to those who perceive it as both a norm and a practice of the society around is one thing. To speak of sexual or social, or marital, morality to many young people who consider that the nation is involved in a totally immoral war venture may be a total waste of time. As they first reject and then protest against the morality of a society that will support such a venture, they also reject many of the other values which are considered almost sacred by the same social order.

Still another factor is the sensual milieu created and fostered by advertising, cinema art, the television industry, and the stage. This may well be as much a product of the times as a contributing factor but it obviously is helping to shape new approaches to traditional values.

Organization and Orientation of a Group

The leader has several responsibilities. The first is to bring together a group of young adults who are either engaged or at least seriously considering marriage. Preferably, a group should consist of five to seven couples, all involved on a voluntary basis. Attention should be given to such seemingly simple things as the room location, room atmosphere, amount of privacy provided, temperature, and type of furniture used. While people can talk almost anywhere, still a quiet, comfortable, informal atmosphere will speed up the process of relaxing defenses and tensions within the participants. The small volume by Hoffman and Plutchik already referred to contains a wealth of information about the entire process of group discussion from the practical matters mentioned in this paragraph to the types of interchange and the varieties of roles which may be found in the average group.

A nine-session schedule is recommended. At the first session time should be allotted for such things as introductions, preferably by the future spouse in each case. The leader should also participate in this. Copies of this manual should be distributed to those who have not already received them and its format and intended use explained. If there is a desire to gather individual, family, and personal relationships data, a simple but rather complete form produced by Rutledge, "Individual and Marriage Counseling Inventory," may be used.[18] An agenda of questions for which answers will be sought may be put together by the group before the first session is over. A "diary of feelings" may be part of the assignment for the series. This would be a record in which each participant is asked to honestly record what happens to him at the feeling level during this period of time.

Session Format

The session format is flexible, but it is recommended that each session should be about 90 minutes in length. One leader may want to open with a 10- to 15-minute presentation of some of the issues as he sees them. This would allow 75 to 80 minutes for discussion, summary, and assignments. Another may choose to allocate all the time for discussion.

At the close of the nine sessions some evaluation may be desired. This can be secured from the participants through the use of questionnaires, private interview sessions, reaction-type papers, reports to be returned two to six months later, or any combination of these. This is left up to the discretion of the leader. The question as to whether personal interviews should be held with each of the participating couples at the close of the series is also dependent upon the individual leader's preference.

One final opportunity may present itself. If, in his evaluation of the separate couples, the leader sees problems of such a nature that he believes their marriage would be seriously handicapped if it were to be consummated at this time, he should seriously consider sharing his judgment with the couple, encouraging them to seek further help, either before or after their proposed marriage. He may accept them into a counseling relationship if he is qualified, or he may refer them to another therapist. But unless his involvement has been on a very superficial level, he will almost certainly wish to assist the persons concerned in whatever way he can.

NOTES

1. In 1969 there were 582,000 divorces and 2,059,000 marriages. U. S. Bureau of the Census. *Statistical Abstracts of the United States: 1969.* Table 54: "Live Births, Deaths, Marriages and Divorces: 1910–1968," p. 47.

2. "Introduction," *Neurotic Interaction in Marriage,* ed. Victor W. Eisenstein, M.D. (New York: Basic Books, Inc., 1956), pp. vii–viii.

3. Abraham Edel, *Ethical Judgment* (Glencoe: The Free Press, 1955), p. 16.

4. "Anything Goes: Taboos in Twilight," *Newsweek,* November 13, 1967, p. 74 ff.

5. Among them George Bernard Shaw, Bertrand Russell, Max Lerner.

6. Bronislaw Malinowski, *The Family Among the Australian Aborigines: A Sociological Study* (London: University of London, 1913), p. 60 ff.

7. Ray E. Baber, *Marriage and the Family* (New York: McGraw-Hill Book Company, Inc., 1953), p. 492.

8. Leona Tyler, "Minimum Change Therapy," *The Personnel and Guidance Journal* XXXVIII (February, 1960), p. 475.

9. Gertrude Goller, "Group Education," in *Neurotic Interaction in Marriage,* ed. Victor W. Eisenstein, M.D. (New York: Basic Books, Inc., 1956), p. 294.

10. Randall W. Hoffman and Robert Plutchik, *Small Group Discussion in Orientation and Teaching* (New York: G. P. Putnam's Sons, 1959), pp. 70–71.

11. James Peterson, *Education for Marriage,* 2nd ed. (New York: Charles Scribner's Sons, 1964), p. 221.

12. Sanford N. Sherman, "Sex Therapy in Group Counseling," mimeographed monograph privately circulated, p. 2.

13. Ruth Strang, *Group Work in Education* (New York: Harper & Row, 1958), pp. 30–31.

14. Carl R. Rogers, *Client-Centered Therapy* (Boston: Houghton Mifflin Co., 1951), p. 20.

15. See Paul Halmos, *The Faith of the Counsellors* (New York: Schocken Books, 1966).

16. Randall W. Hoffman and Robert Plutchik, *op. cit.,* pp. 37–38.

17. Eleanore Luckey and Gerhard Neubeck, "What Are We Doing in Marriage Education?" *Marriage and Family Living* XVIII (November, 1956), p. 351.

18. Aaron L. Rutledge, "Individual and Marriage Counseling Inventory" (Detroit: Merrill-Palmer Institute).

CHAPTER **1**

The Meaning of Marriage

The Experts Speak

[BASED ON BIOLOGICAL DRIVES]

Sexual Urges and Reproductive Processes *

Since marriage is a social institution founded upon sex and reproduction, it is inevitable that the sexual function in human life will be the major theme of this book. Appropriately, sex will be accorded its wider meanings in respect to complete personality development and the social values of marriage.

It is well to bear in mind that sex has a biological history of several hundred million years, while the social institution of marriage is, like civilization itself, an infant phenomenon that began only a few thousand years ago. Through all its long history the

* From Walter R. Stokes, *Married Love in Today's World* (New York: The Citadel Press, 1962), pp. 10–12.

27

sexual urge has tended to increase in power, since it has had the highest of values in the biological struggle for survival. By the law of natural selection, those individuals with the strongest sexual drive have most tended to perpetuate their species, at the same time passing on their strong sexual drive. And nowhere in nature is the sexual drive stronger or more continuously active than in the human species. Indeed, we are almost unique among living things in displaying a relatively constant readiness for sexual response that shows little of the fixed cyclic tendency of other forms of life.

When humans first emerged as a biological species it seems unlikely that they knew anything of marriage. But as they banded together for greater security, family units were increasingly held together by ties of safety and convenience. Mutual gratification in sexual intercourse and the protective tenderness of mothers toward their children were the positive satisfactions from which marriage appears to have taken root. Precisely how our ideas of marriage evolved in prehistoric times is necessarily open to conjecture. Many significant inferences may be drawn from recent studies of the family life of existing primitive peoples. From all that is known it seems that our concepts of love and marriage have been arrived at through a long, tedious struggle against want, ignorance, fear and superstition. The more we have advanced in the social sciences the more we have found occasion to reject unquestioning acceptance of traditional patterns of family life. Our inherited cultural ideals are likely still to contain undesirable elements and should be regarded as open to progressive improvement. To adopt a static, unalterable philosophy of love and marriage would be to deny the reality and usefulness of those forces of change which have brought us the best we possess today.

Our heritage of ideals of the past surely deserves close study and appreciation, but we shall be wiser than some of our ancestors if we will employ these ideals as useful tools, susceptible of improvement, instead of setting them up as unalterable rituals to be obeyed at any cost in human misery.

WALTER R. STOKES
Behavioral Sciences

[SHAPED BY SOCIAL FORCES]

Feminine Influence in Control of Sex *

. . . The thought of marriage is natural for a woman; she takes to it as a duck to water; but there is something alien in the idea of marriage to men. Men are marriage-shy. Imagine that drakes are at first water-shy; then you have the full analogy.

Logan Clendening gives the male viewpoint in his book, *The Human Body.* Man, says this physician, "is expressly made to roam over the earth impregnating as many females as he possibly can." It is "simply silly" to pretend that this is not the case or to try to control this desire by moral admonitions. The one thing that can control the male is common sense of the female, the sense "to lead him to the altar or to the Justice Court, the sense her old mothers fashioned for her to bind him with hoops of steel."

Man will bow his neck to matrimony only if there is no other way out, and "he wonders all the rest of his life why he did." Clendening emphasizes that the average man lies, coaxes, fawns in order to make woman give in to him, that he promises to love her forever to have his way. After it is accomplished, "he is alertly ready for the next candidate, and to remind him of the means he used to accomplish it or to call him names for using them is as unworldly as to rebuke the flowers for blooming or the bees for visiting them." Here is the biological truth, plainly spoken.

Let's see what Bernard Shaw has to say on the subject. Tanner, in *Man and Superman,* asserts it is "a woman's business to get married as soon as possible and a man's to keep unmarried as long as he can." Marriage is for this bachelor "apostasy, profanation of the sanctuary of my soul, violation of my manhood, sale of my birthright, shameful surrender, ignominious capitula-

* Reprinted with the permission of Farrar, Straus & Giroux, Inc. from *Of Love and Lust* by Theodor Reik, copyright © 1941, 1944, 1957 by Theodor Reik, copyright 1949 by Farrar, Straus & Company.

tion, acceptance of defeat." A married man is to him a man with a past while a bachelor is a man with a future. When Anne reminds him that he need not marry if he does not want to, he answers, "Does any man want to be hanged? Yet men let themselves be hanged without a struggle for life, though they could at least give the chaplain a black eye. We do the world's will, not our own."

Shaw believes that a mysterious Life Force, operating irresistibly, pulls man into this mantrap. Nothing of such a biological necessity can be discovered by science. The sexual drive is certainly not tied to marriage. Marriage is an institution which civilization imposed upon men, a result of the organic evolution of mankind under the influence of certain cultural factors. (pp. 391–392)

For women marriage is a question of legitimacy; it is a bond acknowledged and approved of by convention and society. For men marriage is connected with associations like the thought of duty, obligation, responsibilities. It is a moral problem. For women duty is something which has to be done because society wants it. For men it is the voice of the daughter of God, whom you could not forget even if you were an atheist. Women act often because they feel affectionate, men oftener because they are under the pressure of duty. Obligation, duty, responsibility— these words have for male ears an undersound which is for women as little audible as are, for male ears, the emotional undercurrents which women feel when they think of kindness, tenderness and affection. (p. 396)

It is this high sense of responsibility, the unconscious foreknowledge of what marriage might mean to them, which often makes men—and the best of them—afraid of marriage.

Their lust for conquest, their spirit of adventure, their love of freedom, their sexual instability make them shy away from the idea of marriage.

But what really makes them afraid is just this: they know they have to fulfill their obligations, that they must and will take their responsibilities seriously to the end.

They are afraid of the high price they have to pay, not forced by authorities outside but by something within themselves which they have to obey whether they want to or not, even if it means misery, death and self-destruction. Psychoanalysis has a name for this unpitying factor within oneself: it calls it the superego. The superego is more severe, makes higher demands, on men than it does on women, who seldom have this terrible feeling of duty and guilt when obligation is not fulfilled. (pp. 397–398)

Women should understand this and comfort men, not emphasize that being married means more duties and responsibilities. It is not necessary to make him take it easy but to make him take it easier, to reassure him that he is quite capable of doing what will be necessary, that married life means not only heightened burdens, increased responsibilities, but also *shared* responsibilities, that there will be a companion at his side able and willing to carry the burden with him and—above all—that the burden will not be as heavy as he anticipates. (p. 399)

THEODOR REIK
Behavioral Sciences

Community Sanctioning of Mutual Consent *

. . . The offer of marriage itself is a proposal to establish the common life which love demands as the condition of its fulfilment and creativity, and acceptance should theoretically lead straight to the consummation by which that common life is initiated. That this does not happen so simply in practice is because not even in this most intimate and personal of all transactions are man and woman independent of the community to which they belong; indeed, the community nowhere concerns itself

* Reprinted with permission of The Macmillan Company from *Sexual Ethics: A Christian View* by Derrick Sherwin Bailey. Copyright © by Derrick Sherwin Bailey, 1962, pp. 107–110.

more with the private business of its members. The reason for this is obvious; marriage means the emergence of a new social unit, and probably the birth of children who will be the citizens of the future. Therefore society has both the right and the duty to ensure, as far as it can, that the couple act responsibly and in a manner not likely to prejudice their own interest or those of their fellows; and the couple, in turn, are bound morally to honor their obligations to society by submitting to its lawful and reasonable requirements. Hence the institutional formalities which attend the making of a marriage.

In the past these formalities were often twofold—and sometimes still are. First came betrothal—a solemn promise made before witnesses, to enter at some future time into a regular and complete marriage. Betrothal was a contract—a contract to marry, and like other contracts had to be performed. This performance, the second part of the process, was and is effected in two stages. By another solemn pledge or exchange of consent, again before witnesses, the parties there and then take one another as husband and wife, thus making their union regular; then, by consummating it in coition, they make it complete (and, according to one view, indissoluble) by becoming one-flesh. Thus the contract is discharged in full, and marriage, a state of life, takes its place.

. . . .

Of the formalities which belong to the making of marriage, then, only the second, the public exchange of mutual consent, now survives in general use—and this, in one form or another, is compulsory. In the civil ceremony it stands plain and unadorned; in the Marriage Service it is finely elaborated in the context of a rite which declares its theological meaning; but in both cases its institutional purpose is the same. It enables the couple to declare publicly that they intend forthwith to enter upon a relationship recognized and approved by the community, and it enables the State (and where the religious ceremony is used, the Church also) publicly to sanction their intent. Thus they act responsibly towards society, and society in turn accords them the status and security which they need in order to work out their common life.

But mutual consent has a deeper ethical significance. As love tends towards a point of moral decision, so also it requires lovers to bear witness to their choice and its implications; and for this the wedding provides the opportunity. Then, as bride and bridegroom, they exchange their consent to marriage in the form of specific promises, one being a promise of mutual love. By this we should understand, not love in the comprehensive sense described in the preceding chapter, but that element in it which was defined as tender, warmhearted affection—for love in its full meaning is not simply one part of their mutual pledge, but the whole of it. Comfort, honor, "to have and to hold . . . for better, for worse; for richer, for poorer; in sickness and in health; to love and to cherish, till death us do part"—all these are but different expressions of the one fundamental love which husband and wife seek to fulfil in the common life upon which they now enter. Thus their consent is also a public affirmation of that love in all its range and depth, and a public acknowledgment of the obligations and duties which it lays upon them.

SHERWIN BAILEY
Theology

[MODIFIED BECAUSE OF PERSONAL CONCERNS]

Happiness as the Chief Goal of Marriage *

What are the values of marriage today? There are two which may be considered basic. The first and no doubt the most important value sought is *happiness*. Is this a worthy goal? Many cultures have not considered it so. A hundred years ago in the

* From Paul H. Landis, *For Husbands and Wives* (New York: Appleton-Century-Crofts, Inc., 1956), pp. 5–7.

United States it was far from the primary concern of marriage. A person was more likely to be concerned about the practical aspects of the marriage and to pick a mate for qualities that wore well. But people also worked fourteen or sixteen hours a day in order to make a living. They struggled for the conquest of a frontier. Life was rigorous and serious. The stakes were often survival itself. A puritanical attitude prevailed toward all levity. Pleasure seeking as such was condemned, no less in marriage than in other aspects of life.

The material aspects as well as the values of life have changed since that time. A rigorous life demands a special breed—serious, work-minded, self-disciplined, and stoic. Life today would be a perpetual holiday in the eyes of our ancestors. But the basic change has not been in people but in conditions. For the first time in history the masses of people have time for laughter and leisure, so both have grown in our esteem. As basic comforts and luxuries come within the reach of every man, we accept them as our natural rights—free time for recreation, and education, and a comfortable dwelling place.

The fact that youth can make happiness the first demand of marriage testifies to the luxury enjoyed today, both in material blessings and spiritual values. On the material side, the human spirit has been freed from the overwhelming burden of incessant work and duty. On the spiritual side, the modern concepts of progress provide a culture in which man dares dream that he can be happy.

Pleasure has gradually become more than merely acceptable; it has taken on a quality of sanctity in our eyes. Like a healthy body or a religious spirit, it is thought to produce a finer race of people than would otherwise exist.

In terms of such contemporary values, who is to say that this goal of marriage happiness is a spurious one? Most students of American marriage prefer to accept the contemporary values, holding not only that happiness in marriage is a worthy goal, but also that it represents a new and higher level of human aspiration than men of earlier generations dared hold.

It is doubtful that humanity has ever sought a goal in marriage so difficult to realize and yet so worthy of attainment as "happiness."

More than half of married couples live out their life span without completely shattering their dream of happiness. One cannot claim that all who remain loyal to their marriage pledge realize it fully, but many studies have measured the happiness of married couples. These show that of those marriages that last, two-thirds are either happy or very happy.

To those who would challenge such research and say that one cannot depend on people's ratings of their own happiness or success, there is the evidence of studies using not only self ratings, but the opinions of friends. Self ratings and ratings by others have been found to generally agree. This suggests that a couple knows whether or not their marriage is happy, and that the great majority of marriages which last actually do realize happiness. Three generations ago no one would have thought of asking couples whether or not their marriages were happy.

Even legal grounds for divorce today indicate how seriously we consider "happiness" as a goal in marriage. Many divorces are granted for "mental cruelty," an intangible quality but one which well expresses the opposite of happiness. The Mosaic Law recognized no such reason for dissolving marriage, nor did the customs and laws of 1890.

PAUL H. LANDIS
Social Sciences

[DEFINED BY UNCONDITIONAL COMMITMENT]

Commitment of All to One *

The sacredness of marriage as it has been developed in the Judeo-Christian pattern of human life is best understood by

* From *The Recovery of Family Life* by Elton Trueblood and Pauline Trueblood. Copyright 1953 by Harper & Row, Publishers, Inc., pp. 43–46.

emphasis on three main features. *The first of these is the notion of commitment as against mere contract.* The point that marriage is more than a contract needs to be given the widest possible dissemination, because many marriages owe their failure to a misunderstanding of this point. The first essential of marriage is the advance acceptance of the family relationship as *unconditional.* The father's responsibility to the child does not depend upon the child's health, his success or his character. The two participants in the marriage service pledge themselves, "for better and for worse." Frankly recognizing the dangers and pitfalls in advance, our religion tends to be intensely realistic rather than sentimental. The standardized service recognizes the strong possibility of economic difficulties, including real poverty, so the participants take each other "for richer, for poorer." One partner may become ill, one may be unable to become a parent, but this eventuality is recognized too; they take each other "in sickness and in health." Far from being a temporary affair, we pledge our troth "so long as we both shall live." If it were a contract it would have an escape clause.

It is this mood of commitment which distinguishes the family from worldly institutions and makes it intrinsically a religious institution. Commitment is the crucial step in religious experience. Faith, we know, when we think about it, is not merely intellectual assent to a set of propositions, but the supreme gamble in which we stake our lives upon a conviction. It is closer to courage than it is to mere belief. In this profound sense, marriage is an act of faith. Undoubtedly some dim understanding of this is very widespread, even in our highly secularized society, and this accounts for the fact that so many, who have no connection at all with any organized religion, turn to the church when marriage is planned. They sense, somehow, that the highest things belong together; they are sufficiently sensitive to realize that there is at least one human undertaking that is debased if it is wholly secularized. We may be a pagan generation, but it is highly revealing that we are not willing to take our paganism straight.

The commitment we call marriage is not a bargain! It is a situation in which each gives *all* that he has, including all his devotion and all of the fruits of his toil. "With *all* my worldly goods I thee endow." There is something extremely moving about the concept *all*, as everyone recognizes when he reads the gospel story of the widow's mite. This is part of the reason why almost every marriage ceremony is profoundly moving. The charming young woman gives *all* to this young man. The result is that marriage is an amazing relation in which the ordinary rules of business, with its contracts and escape clauses and limited liabilities, are despised and set aside. Marriage is no marriage at all if it is conditional or partial or with the fingers crossed. There must be, on both sides, an uncalculating abandon, a mutual outpouring of love and loyalty in a prodigal way. The best-loved story of the New Testament is a family story, the story not primarily of the prodigal son, but of the father who was prodigal in his affection, and the story of every truly married couple is the story of the prodigal pair. The enduring rule of marriage is "Love one another with all your mind and heart and body." The truly married person, finite though he be, is more interested in his mate's happiness than in his own, and his desire is to be to the other a constant delight. The fact that we do not achieve this ideal does not invalidate it.

The family is much older than our religion, and, as a natural grouping, would undoubtedly go on if our religion should come to an end, but the natural urges need a great deal of help and direction. The Judeo-Christian conception does not create the natural institution, but vastly improves it. It is like the Sabbath, in that it is a deliberate effort to facilitate holiness in the natural order. Marriage, as we have received it, is an attempt to produce a sanctuary out of a natural need. It is monogamy, but *monogamy plus*. It is the effort to make a holy path, not in separation from sex and work, or in seclusion, but in the midst of ordinary life. It thus maintains an ideal higher than that of the ascetic or monastic person. Marriage is the attempt to return man and woman to Paradise where they can live without sin. Such is our frailty, that this attempt does not wholly succeed, but the very effort is one of the noblest aspects of our common life. So long as marriage is seen as a holy commitment there is hope for our confused civilization.

ELTON and PAULINE TRUEBLOOD
Philosophy

Commitment as Creating Uniqueness *

. . . God has given me a *human being,* not merely someone who performs the *function* of a human being. So in marriage it is not merely a matter of another person's performing certain functions for me, perhaps the function of erotic satisfaction of physical intercourse, or perhaps also merely the function of providing for me as a money-earner, or of acting as a contributing honorary member of my family or—from the husband's point of view—of furnishing a cheap housekeeper. If the other person is only good for performing such functions for me, then I really have no fellowship with him of the kind that God wants. And then too, he is "finished" as far as I am concerned as soon as he can no longer perform his functions.

How many marriages there are which end in divorce for this very reason, because the other person has become unattractive to me and his erotic "function" no longer clicks. Then I look for a younger partner who can better perform the function.

God does not will that this should be so and he binds me to the *person,* not merely to his functions. This is clearly expressed in the ancient order for marriage, for in the vows it employs the words: "till death us do part."

. . . .

Is there any certainty at all that this particular man or this particular woman is the only possible choice given to me by God? Is this so sure after all? If man must not put asunder what God has joined together—yes, but *was* it God who joined them together or was it not all too often just two deluded persons, who

* From Helmut Thielicke, *How the World Began* (Philadelphia: Muhlenberg Press, 1961) [trans. 1960 by John Doberstein], pp. 95–99.

for a moment were filled with a lot of airy dreams and thought they were Romeo and Juliet, but after a short time simply choked with boredom and disgust whenever they looked at each other? . . .

But even if there are not such rude disillusionments, are there not in almost every fateful relationship between two people moments when the question arises whether I should not have made a different choice, and thus whether the other person is really the 100 per cent complement for me, the flesh of my flesh of which this simile of the rib speaks.

. . . .

Or perhaps the crisis may come because another fascinating person crosses our path and sets to ringing sides of our personality which we never knew were in us. And then the question always arises: "Was it really true in my case—what according to this ancient story ought to be true—that I was assigned by a higher hand to the one person who really is suited for me? Or when I chose him back there did I make a wrong turn and am I now doomed to travel for the rest of my life in a direction which is alien to me and which leads me farther and farther away from my real self and all the fulfilments I dreamed I would have?"

Now, this question cannot be dismissed with a wave of the hand or with a cheap pious consolation. . . . I am convinced of one thing, and that is that nobody who is caught in this difficulty and does not know whether he should find his way back or be divorced, dares to ignore these two thoughts. One way or another he will get it all wrong if he does not face them.

The first thought is this: It is in any case utterly foolish to brood over the question whether the other person is the one conceivable partner for me. Perhaps I *really* could have married another man or another woman! That this particular person is the only person for me is not the thing which creates the foundation of marriage. It is the other way around: it is marriage that makes him or her the only one for me. Let me give the reason for this briefly.

Now that God has brought me together with this other person

I have a life and a history with him. The other person has revealed to me his secret in his psycho-physical wholeness. We
have gone through many trials and vicissitudes together. Perhaps
we have been refugees together. Perhaps we have been hungry
together, been homesick for each other in long years of military
service, built up an existence for ourselves together, seen our
very being reproduced anew in our children—and so put our
stamp upon each other, each has become a part of the other. Has
become! We no longer are what we were in the beginning; we
each bear the mark of the other.

This is what I meant when I said: That the other person is the
only person for me is not the thing which creates the foundation
of marriage; it is rather the other way around. For this uniqueness
of the other person, this unrepeatable belonging together, this
business of your being cut out for me is not all something that
is there beforehand. Rather we *become* unique and irreplaceable
for each other only when God brings us together, gives us a life
and a history together, and blesses us, if we will only trust him
and watch for his directions. Anybody who does not trust that in
everything God works for good with those who love him, and
that his life partner is also included in this plan for his good is a
poor sight indeed. For then there is nothing left but to try to
puzzle out with his reason whether or not he has caught the
right man or the right woman. (I say "caught" intentionally, because he is delivered over to chance or his own dubious calcula-
tions and now he must constantly compare his partner with
others, incessantly comparing and never getting away from his
uncertainty and his everlasting testing.)

And then the second thought. It is the more important and
serious of the two.

In order to determine whether my life partner is really the
right one for me, I would have to be able to ascertain objectively
—in a clinical diagnosis as it were—who or what this other
person is, and besides this, who or what I am, in order to com-
pute by exact calculation whether we best complement each
other.

I should think that one would need to go through this experiment of thought only once to find out how absurd it is.

HELMUT THIELICKE
Theology

[ESTABLISHED AS A DIVINE ORDER OF CREATION]

Marriage as a Product of God's Creative Will *

... In marriage we have the exemplary form of the encounter of the sexes. Here all the lines intersect which elsewhere only converge and in many instances break off without reaching this point. Here everything becomes actual which elsewhere is only potential and may often remain potential. Here is fulfilled and disclosed the structure of the relationship of the sexes, their characteristics and the order of their relations in the serious instance which basically is always in question wherever they meet, if not always realised in practice. Here is the natural home of every man and woman even though they may have good reasons not to settle in it. The exemplary character of marriage necessarily means that—from the standpoint of our previous reflections and insights—we must now be prepared to break quite new ground again.

We may review, if only for the moment in outline, the concepts, ideas and realities which both individually and together, as elements in an inseparable whole, make up marriage. Marriage may be defined as something which fixes and makes concrete the encounter and interrelation of man and woman in the form of the unique, unrepeatable and incomparable encounter and relationship between a particular man and a particular woman. Their encounter and relationship signifies in this context

* From Karl Barth, *Church Dogmatics,* Vol. III, Part 4: *The Doctrines of Creation,* trans. A. T. Mackay *et al.* (Edinburgh: T. & T. Clark, 1961), pp. 182–183.

a life-partnership. This partnership is not partial but complete. It extends over the whole area of the human existence of both participants. It is on both sides a total receiving and giving. Again, it is not inclusive but exclusive. No third person can share in it. Again, it is not temporary but permament. It lasts as long as the life of both concerned. And its establishment corresponds to its nature and constitution. As this concrete life-partnership between two distinct individuals marriage does not simply exist, nor do they create it of themselves, nor does it spring from somewhere above them, but it takes place in the form of a free resolve and act on the part of both with a view to this lasting fellowship. And the characteristic motive for this resolve and act is on both sides a choice of love, a *di-ligere,* in which man recognises woman and woman man as the one and final partner in this fellowship, and they may and must desire and affirm each other, in this special sense and with this special intention. Finally, this life-partnership on the basis of this resolve and act is characterised as marriage by the fact that as an event and relationship which has significance for others, *i.e.,* a wedding, it is accomplished in a definite responsibility to them and with their acknowledgment. These are the elements which together constitute marriage and mark it out as something special and exemplary within the totality of the relations of man and woman. Marriage is exemplary because in all its elements it may be seen that there is here ventured, performed and achieved something which outside of this *telos,* this centre of the whole complex, is certainly suggested, is more or less closely envisaged, and may even be possible, but is not actually ventured, performed and achieved.

KARL BARTH
Theology

Commitment, Consummation and the "One-Flesh" Union *

When Jesus was asked whether divorce is lawful he went behind the Mosaic law with which he had been confronted and appealed to the law of God governing the relations between men and women:

Therefore shall a man leave his father and his mother, and shall cleave unto his wife: and they shall be one flesh. [Genesis 2:24]

St. Paul used the same words, both to explain the analogy between marriage and Christ's union with the Church and to show the momentous consequences which attend even casual or mercenary sexual transactions. These references to Genesis were more than formal citations of a convenient proof-text; they were affirmations of a principle in sexual relation which, although never precisely defined, was clearly held to be of fundamental importance. This principle is expressed in the term "one flesh", the meaning of which must first be considered.

The emphasis in "one flesh" is primarily upon the *henosis* which results from the sexual union of man and woman. In Scripture "one" is a rich and suggestive word. In the Genesis passage it may at first have meant simply that husband and wife become "one" in relation to the community—that through marriage a new social unit emerges—but when taken into the context of the New Testament it gains greatly in significance. It implies the resolution of discord, the transcending of superficial differences and antagonisms at a new and deeper level of existence or experience; not an amalgamation in which the identity of the constituents is swallowed up and lost in an undifferentiated unity, nor a mere conjunction in which no real union is involved. The singleness for which "one" stands, in its most pregnant use, is organic, not arithmetical, and has a suggestion of uniqueness; it is exemplified at its highest in the mysterious triunity of the

* From pp. 43–45, 49–50 in *The Mystery of Love and Marriage* by Derrick Sherwin Bailey. (Harper & Row, 1952.) Reprinted by permission of the publisher.

one God, of which the biunity of husband and wife is an analogue.

In marriage man and woman become "one *flesh*". This means that through the sexual intercourse in which they consummate their love they restore the original pattern of human unity. The older of the two Genesis creation myths describes how God took one of Adam's ribs and built it into a woman. Male and female are thus shown to have a common origin; they are not independent but complementary, and individually incomplete until they have achieved the union in which each integrates and is integrated by the other.

Although the union in "one flesh" is a physical union established by sexual intercourse (the conjunction of the sexual organs) it involves at the same time the whole being, and affects the personality at the deepest level. It is a union of the entire man and the entire woman. In it they become a new and distinct unity, wholly different from and set over against other human relational unities, such as the family or the race; to bring into existence the "one flesh" a man must leave his father and his mother. Yet husband and wife in their union remain indissolubly one with all "flesh"—with the things which are passing away, and this "fleshly" character of the *henosis* sets a term to its life; it endures until death, but in heaven there is neither marrying nor giving in marriage. (pp. 43–45)

In determining the constitutive factor in marriage, however, there is no need to oppose intercourse to consent; like the institutional and ontological aspects of sexual union, they are really complementary. Consent is the basis of the public exchange of vows which expresses the intention of the parties and provides the only satisfactory *terminus a quo* for the recognition of their union by the community; it may therefore properly be said to effect marriage on the institutional level. But the mere exchange of vows, whether in public or in private, does not and cannot bring about any essential change in the character of the personal relation between man and woman. That is to say, consent by itself has no ontological connexion with marriage and is powerless to effect a union in "one flesh"; it is simply the precondition of the establishment of that union by sexual intercourse. (pp. 49–50)

DERRICK SHERWIN BAILEY
Theology

Exploring the Issues

"Marriage is an institutionalized mating arrangement between human males and females." [1] "Marriage is that order of creation given by God in love which binds one man and one woman in a lifelong union of the most intimate fellowship of body and life." [2] "Mating is a biological matter, while marriage is a social affair. Marriage implies a ceremony, a union with social sanctions, a recognition of obligations." [3] "Marriage is an institution which civilization imposed upon men." [4] "Marriage is a holy estate, ordained of God, and to be held in honor by all." [5] There is no end to the number and diversity of definitions of marriage that have been formulated. This manual begins with still another:

Marriage is a relationship of commitment between two persons, male and female, who live together in a sexual union, in a mutually sustaining state intended to be permanent, and who assume together the pleasures and responsibilities which may be present or which may ensue, including the conception and rearing of children.

Within each marriage there are factors of many kinds—economic, cultural, ethnic, emotional, religious, to name a few—which affect each relationship and provide each with its own distinctive character. But the most significant factor of all is that of personal commitment expressed in sexual love. It is this commitment with all the consequent ramifications that, in essence, defines and constitutes the nature of marriage.

This manual contains, among other things, the observations of the anthropologist, the statistics of the social scientist, the canons of the church, the descriptions of the hedonist, and the concepts

of the theologian. All these deserve to be examined and they
will be. For until marriage has been seen at both the widest and
the deepest levels of human experience and meaning, any conclusion reached will be only of limited value to those intent upon
finding and developing workable solutions to the problems which
may arise when two people enter into this partnership.

This first chapter presents five viewpoints concerning the
nature of marriage, none of which necessarily contradict the
others. The first three follow the general pattern of social evolution, each containing the content of the previous stage but adding
new dimensions. These are mainly descriptive in nature. The
last two more directly present philosophical interpretations which
attempt to encompass the essence of marriage. These are intuitive
and reflective and stem primarily from theological thought.

These five viewpoints approach the nature of marriage from
different theoretical positions. Simply stated these regard marriage as a relationship which primarily is:

I. Based on Biological Drives (survival)
II. Shaped by Social Forces (society)
III. Modified Because of Personal Concerns (self)
IV. Defined by Unconditional Commitment (service)
V. Established as a Divine Order of Creation (sacred)

I. *Based on Biological Drives*

The first is rooted in the biological-psychological make-up of
man. It deals with the basic concept of racial survival. Van de
Velde wrote in *Ideal Marriage,* "Life is dominated by the urge
of self-preservation and by the sexual urge. The former preserves
the individual; the latter the race. For biological purposes racial
preservation is more urgent than individual survival; therefore
the urge of sex is stronger than hunger, stronger than fear." [6]
This statement goes a long way in explaining why lovers risk, and
sometimes lose, life and limb in search of each other's love. It
also explains how and why people are drawn out of shy retire-
ment from involvement with others to seek a mate and to establish families in the midst of a society.

Marriages take place because of sexual needs. In fact, sexual union is the *sine qua non* of marriage. It is possible to have too little sex expression in marriage or too much, but it is impossible to have no sex at all and speak of a marriage. Ecclesiastical and civil courts are agreed that where there is no sexual consummation there is no marriage. Such a legal relationship may be ended by annulment, but no divorce is called for since no marriage existed. La Piere [7] posits that the first family was built upon a compromise. The child got the mother's breast, the male received the female's sexual favors, and the family began.

It is difficult to do more than speculate on the exact forms which early families took. There is evidence that these male-female relationships were expressed in polygyny, polyandry, group marriage or monogamy; though some authorities take issue with identifying the first three of these forms of cohabitation as legitimate marriage.[8] But universally the presence of sexual relationships demonstrates the existence and the strength of this biological drive.

In his few brief paragraphs Stokes sets the sexual drive in proper context and indicates his belief that this drive is a basic fact in marriage, a fact which he evaluates elsewhere by saying that it is possibly the best foundation upon which to build a marriage.

II. *Shaped by Social Forces*

Social forces have much to do with the forms which mating and marriage take. When primitive man left off mating and began to marry, he entered into a new and higher stage of interaction. He now became responsible for his actions to others. In essence, he contracted with his partner for an exchange of services. He agreed to be responsible for his mating, his mate, and for his offspring. In a food-hungry culture this was a most important consideration. As Pitts expresses it: "Marriage is the ceremony whereby this maturity [the economic strength to provide for the infant] is certified and whereby a man commits himself to economic and sexual cooperation with a given woman." [9] Biological instincts may have encouraged "flitting from flower to flower to flower," but social instincts (those of a concerned group) demanded that the male be responsible for his woman and his children, indeed, for all of his sexual acts.

It is at this point where the purely biological is recognized, yet controlled, that both the role and the rights of society as related to marriage are clearly seen. Since ultimately the group must deal with the results of all forms of social breakdown, society chooses to get involved in those forms of social action which are apt to bring about trouble. It becomes finally a question of responsibility, or a "moral problem" as Reik terms it. Reik regards the biological drive as dominant, especially in the male nature, and gives an interpretation of how one social force, *i.e.* the female nature, has changed and channeled the expression of the male nature. Within the context of social pressures, the male reluctantly has become at least partially responsible for his sexual urges.

The refined end result of this social pressure as expressed in contemporary Western culture is described by Derrick Sherwin Bailey. The acceptance of mutual responsibility by the two parties joined in the union of marriage is literally demanded by the society. No sexual unions have legal status until the explicit and implicit guarantees of responsible behavior have been given to the body politic through a civil or religious ceremony. Through either one, society, represented by the participating witnesses, is saying, "We recognize, accept, and sanction the responsible vows which you have made today to one another and to the social group." In this way the social group's stake in this new venture is clearly indicated. In essence, a contract has been entered into with legal stipulations and safeguards for all concerned. While the element of commitment is present, the emphasis is on the contractual element and the nature of marriage is delineated by the pressure of the social forces involved.

III. *Modified Because of Personal Concerns*

In recent years marriage has been undergoing a process of modification in the direction of the individual's interests as opposed to society's interests. Personal concerns are becoming the dominant factor. The right to life, liberty, love and the pursuit of happiness, the search for identity, the need to find one's self—all express the typical young American's concern for his own welfare and his own self-fulfillment. The focus is not just on the individual but upon *me* as an individual. Marriage is a means whereby *I* come into my own, *I* experience pleasure, *I* reach maturity, *I* gain identity, *I* fulfill my potential.

Locke and Burgess have described the change in family structure from an institution to a companionship. In their preface they write:

> In the past the important factors unifying the family have been external, formal, and authoritarian, such as the law, the mores, public opinion, tradition, the authority of the family head, rigid discipline, and elaborate ritual. In the new emerging form of the companionship family, its unity inheres less and less in community pressures and more and more in such interpersonal relations as the mutual affection, the sympathetic understanding, and the comradeship of its members.[10]

The emphasis is upon the individual within the marriage. The individual is not particularly constricted nor supported by the social situation. In a very real sense he is on his own and must produce.

In the field of professional research the same stress on the individual can be seen. Professional researchers work with such concepts as interpersonal competence, intrafamily communication, interaction process analysis, role perception, and the like. The emphasis is on the individual's interaction relationships with other individuals and not primarily his relationships with the group.

Marriages which depend so heavily on individual contributions rather than institutional support are subject to their own unique hazards. This is clear in Landis' conclusion that personal happiness is the basic goal of today's marriage. One of these hazards is the difficulty of survival. The figure of over 500,000 divorces in the United States each year validates this point. When Ogburn and Nimkoff [11] published a study of the major changes in American marriage between the years 1850 and 1950, they listed divorce as the most significant change. In fact, all eighteen experts whom they consulted named this as one of the ten most significant factors in the changed marital scene.

This should not come as a surprise. Divorce is not a community or social action. It is an individualistic decision, a self-focused societal act to preserve sanity, health, happiness, specific or general well-being. It may stem from inordinate selfishness. It may, on the other hand, result from the frustration, disappointment and disillusionment experienced in an impoverished and unhappy life. Divorce is one way in which an individual may clearly express an unwillingness to settle for anything less than the best in marriage. As Landis says, "It is doubtful that humanity has ever sought a goal in marriage so difficult to realize and yet so worthy of attainment as 'happiness.' "

Landis is not speaking of happiness in any shallow or hedonistic sense of personal gratification. He believes that the happiness which may be achieved in marriage is a "higher good" than other persons may have thought it to be. The corollary to this is, of course, that when happiness is seen as a reasonable and reachable goal for marriage, then its absence becomes all the more bitter to accept. A person may well conclude that he has been "cheated" and is, therefore, free to seek with another the happiness to which he is entitled.

IV. *Defined by Unconditional Commitment*

Standing across the path of the view given above is one quite opposed which insists that the nature of marriage is best defined by the idea of unconditional commitment. Often this is considered to be exclusively a church-related concept. Actually this is not so.

It is true that the marriage service of the church normally includes the phrase, "until death us do part." Further, this church service seemingly tries to scan all possible futures of the couples concerned by employing such phrases as "for richer, for poorer; for better, for worse; in sickness and in health; forsaking all others," and the like. But what makes marriage a religious experience is not the presence of pastor or priest, incense or candles; it is commitment. As the Truebloods express it: "Commitment is the crucial step in religious experience." [12] All personal commitment has an element of the sacred within it. Those who pledge that they will live together in love "until life's end" are, according to this point of view, among those "whom God hath joined together." And this is true whether or not it be realized or consciously desired, and without any necessary reference to the church.

Unconditional commitment also gives a new depth and strength to the marriage relationship. Through the years health, beauty, passion, fortune, happiness—all may diminish or be lost. In any marriage there may be periods of deep stress and even estrangement. It is when the accoutrements of marriage are stripped away by the storms of life that the significance of a commitment which irrevocably binds two persons together becomes clear. This commitment can be, and often is, the saving element which holds a distressed couple steady on an agreed-upon course until there is time and opportunity to begin to restore the relationship.

Supporting testimony comes from Kinsey. In *Human Male* he reports, "A preliminary examination of the six thousand marital histories in the present study, and of nearly three thousand divorce histories, suggests that there may be nothing more important in a marriage than a determination that it shall persist." [13] In short, the will to be one, the will to remain together, the will "to exclude all others and keep thee only unto her so long as ye both shall live" is at the very heart of the marriage decision. To continue with Kinsey, "With such a determination, individuals force themselves to adjust and to accept situations which would seem sufficient grounds for a break-up, if the continuation of the marriage were not the prime objective." [14]

Commitment, as Thielicke points out, "binds me to the person, not merely to his functions." As a spouse is accepted as a self, in the lived-out relationship of the marriage he or she becomes unique and irreplaceable, "the only one for me." Lacking commitment it is not difficult for people in marital trouble to expend their resources looking for a way out rather than for a workable solution. Energies, concern, interest, memories, and affection which might have healed a breach are shared with others rather than directed towards each other. A relationship lacking this commitment is defective at the core. By contrast, a relationship of commitment entered into freely becomes the most binding of all. Only total freedom allows for total bondage.

V. *Established as a Divine Order of Creation*

Thus far the arguments have dealt with the form of marriage as man has shaped it. However, there are thinkers within the Judeo-Christian tradition who feel that marriage is a part of the divine order of creation and that it must be approached in this way. Barth is one of the chief proponents of this view. He believes that all relationships between the sexes have been established by the will of God and that man will find marital harmony only to the degree that this will is apprehended and obeyed.

In the Old Testament the idea of marital union as something profoundly mysterious and holy is first suggested in the two opening chapters of Genesis. It is the Lord God who says, "It is not good that man should be alone; I will make him a helper fit for him" (Genesis 2:18). And when later, according to the account, woman is created from the rib of man, Adam says, "This at last is bone of my bones and flesh of my flesh" (Genesis 2:23). The creation account closes with this explantory declaration, "Therefore a man leaves his father and his mother and cleaves to his wife, and they become one flesh" (Genesis 2:24). It is indicated that something tremendous and unique has occurred.

Bailey develops the idea, expressed first in the Old Testament and later on in the New Testament, that an essential change is wrought in man by his marital sexual relationship. The word used is *henosis,* or "one flesh." Something profound, mysterious, almost mystical, happens to two persons who enter into marriage. The change in status is so basic that it is no longer proper or accurate to speak of them as two; the better term is "one flesh." For here in this total union of commitment and sexual consummation personal and sexual identity are realized and the absolute base, the *urgrund,* of life is reached.

It does not make any difference that the married couple may not understand the total significance of all that occurs by their entrance into marriage. The heart of marriage will always contain a mystery. Was not the man asleep and unaware when the woman was formed for him? But an openness to this view of marriage, a total commitment to each other, an acceptance of a spouse as in some way a provision of God—all these can add new dimensions to one's understanding of the nature of marriage.

This viewpoint evidences a profound respect for man as an individual person. If man is only a biological creature, an animal, he will mate; little else will be involved. If he is a social being, he will interact within, and perhaps conform to, the wishes of society. If he is an individualist, he will strike out on his own to seek self-fulfillment. But if he is wholly a person and views all men in this light, he will relate himself to another in the most responsible commitment of which he is capable. In and through this relationship he may find his own identity; at least, the opportunity is there.

SUGGESTIONS FOR DISCUSSION

1. Look again at the definition of marriage on page 45. Is it complete enough to serve as the basis for a discussion of the nature of marriage? How might it be improved?
2. Are there differing reactions from the male and female members of the group to Reik's presentation?
3. Bailey rather strongly claims that society has a right to be involved in the personal, private life of two people in love. Is this legitimate? Has the widespread availability of birth control information changed this situation any?
4. Is happiness the single most important value to be found in marriage? Are there others of significance?
5. In one sense the average housewife may find herself in competition with each new movie starlet and with *Playboy*'s monthly playmate. Of what significant value would an unconditional commitment to a marital spouse be in a situation like that?

6. What reactions are there to the statement of Barth: "To enter upon marriage is to renounce the possibility of leaving"? [15]
7. What implications for marriage are there in the Biblical understanding of marriage as creating a union of one flesh?

NOTES

1. Harold T. Christensen, "Development of the Family Field of Study," *Handbook of Marriage and the Family,* ed. Harold T. Christensen (Chicago: Rand McNally & Co., 1964), p. 3.

2. The United Lutheran Church in America, *Minutes of the Twentieth Biennial Convention, 1956* (Philadelphia: The United Lutheran Publication House, 1956), p. 1146.

3. Ernest W. Burgess and Harvey J. Locke, *The Family* (New York: American Book Company, 1960), p. 6.

4. Theodor Reik, *Of Love and Lust* (New York: Grove Press, Inc., 1949), p. 392.

5. *The Occasional Services* (Philadelphia: The United Lutheran Church of America, 1943), p. 65.

6. Th. H. Van de Velde, *Ideal Marriage, Its Physiology and Technique* (New York: Random House, 1965), p. 12.

7. Richard La Piere, *The Freudian Ethic* (New York: Duell, Sloan & Pearce, 1959), p. 124.

8. Bronislaw Malinowski, *Sex, Culture and Myth* (New York: Harcourt, Brace & World, Inc., 1962), p. 33.

9. Jesse R. Pitts, "The Structural-Functional Approach," *Handbook of Marriage and the Family,* ed. Harold T. Christensen (Chicago: Rand McNally & Company, 1964), p. 67.

10. Ernest W. Burgess and Harvey J. Locke, *The Family,* 2nd ed. (New York: American Book Company, 1960), p. vii.

11. W. F. Ogburn and M. F. Nimkoff, *Technology and the Changing Family* (Boston: Houghton-Mifflin Co., 1955), p. 5.

12. Elton and Pauline Trueblood, *The Recovery of Family Life* (New York: Harper & Brothers, 1953), p. 44.

13. Alfred C. Kinsey, Wardell B. Pomeroy and Clyde E. Martin, *Sexual Behavior in the Human Male* (Philadelphia: W. B. Saunders Company, 1948), p. 544.

14. *Ibid.*

15. Karl Barth, *Church Dogmatics,* Vol. III, Part 4: *The Doctrines of Creation,* trans. A. T. Mackay *et al.* (Edinburgh: T. & T. Clark, 1961), p. 203.

CHAPTER **2**

Why Did We Choose Each Other?

The Experts Speak

[ROMANTICISM]

The Romantic Fallacy *

This kind of love [the romantic] has been well labeled: cardiac-respiratory love. It does have certain physiological symptoms that can be observed. One may discover in people who have rounded their corner and found their beloved a certain type of breathlessness as though there was not enough oxygen about,

* Reprinted by permission of Charles Scribner's Sons from *Toward a Successful Marriage*, pages 36–38, by James A. Peterson. Copyright © 1960 by James A. Peterson.

55

palpitation, and deep physical yearning. There is a lightness in the step, a brightness in the eye as though one had a fever, and a general radiance and zest. Most of those who have tried to talk honestly about their condition report that they felt surges of superhuman energy. There is, likewise, a psychological aspect of romantic love. In the first place there are many moments of ecstasy when the whole world seems to lie prostrate at their feet. Discussion between the two is marked by a superlative tenderness. On the other hand, the romantic lover often lapses into a dream state and is easily distracted. Some observers have pointed out the complete loss of perspective of those in love. They plan for a magnificent future before they have met even current daily expenses. Religious or social differences will be resolved automatically. At the same time previous emotional difficulties or neurotic tendencies seem to be repressed so that they do not, at least for the moment, destroy the integrity of the individual. It is this aspect of the situation which is troublesome, the tendency of those who feel this kind of love to escape from the normal demands of life or to fail to bring into focus future problems which might later be terribly upsetting.

Above all, they are positive about their rightness for each other, convinced that nothing can go poorly in their relationship. That one could question the validity of such a marriage is unthinkable, because if one has fallen in love and if one is convinced that destiny is at work for him the result must necessarily be a good one. Any rational investigation of the possibilities of future rapport between such persons is obviously unnecessary. But for the marriage counselor, or any other serious student of marriage, this type of love is not only blind but destructive. These romantically stricken young people never take into consideration their past or their future. They do not ask any questions. They do not even take sufficient time, generally, to test out the relationship. Consequently a large factor in the present high divorce rate is certainly the prevalence of the state of romantic love.

The results can be summarized somewhat as follows: First, romance results in such distortions of personality that after marriage the two people can never fulfill the roles that they expect of each other. Second, romance so idealizes marriage and even sex that when the day-to-day experiences of marriage are encountered there must be disillusionment involved. Third, the romantic complex is so short-sighted that the premarital relationship is conducted almost entirely on the emotional level and consequently such problems as temperamental or value differences, religious or cultural differences, financial, occupational, or health problems are never considered. Fourth, romance develops such a false ecstasy that there is implied in courtship a promise of a kind of happiness which could never be maintained during the realities of married life. Fifth, romance is such an escape from the negative aspects of personality to the extent that their repression obscures the real person. Later in marriage these negative factors to marital adjustment are bound to appear, and they do so in far greater detail and far more importantly simply because they were not evident earlier. Sixth, people engrossed in romance seem to be prohibited from wise planning for the basic needs of the future even to the point of failing to discuss the significant problems of early marriage.

It is difficult to know how pervasive the romantic fallacy really is. I suspect that it creates the greatest havoc with high school seniors or that half of the population who are married before they are twenty years old. Nevertheless, even in a college or young adult population one constantly finds as a final criterion for marriage the question of being in love. This is due to the distortion of the meaning of a true companionship in marriage by the press, by the magazines, and by cultural impact upon the last two or three generations. The result is that more serious and sober aspects of marital choice and marital expectations are not only neglected but sometimes ridiculed.

JAMES A. PETERSON
Social Sciences

Romance and the False Absolutism of Love *

It is in the grandeur of Eros that the seeds of danger are concealed. He has spoken like a god. His total commitment, his reckless disregard of happiness, his transcendence of self-regard, sound like a message from the eternal world.

And yet it cannot, just as it stands, be the voice of God Himself. For Eros, speaking with that very grandeur and displaying that very transcendence of self, may urge to evil as well as to good. Nothing is shallower than the belief that a love which leads to sin is always qualitatively lower—more animal or more trivial—than one which leads to faithful, fruitful and Christian marriage. The love which leads to cruel and perjured unions, even to suicide pacts and murder, is not likely to be wandering lust or idle sentiment. It may well be Eros in all his splendour; heart-breakingly sincere; ready for every sacrifice except renunciation.

There have been schools of thought which accepted the voice of Eros as something actually transcendent and tried to justify the absoluteness of his commands. Plato will have it that "falling in love" is the mutual recognition on earth of souls which have been singled out for one another in a previous and celestial existence. To meet the Beloved is to realise "We loved before we were born." As a myth to express what lovers feel this is admirable. But if one accepted it literally one would be faced by an embarrassassing consequence. We should have to conclude that in that heavenly and forgotten life affairs were no better managed than here. For Eros may unite the most unsuitable yokefellows; many unhappy, and predictably unhappy, marriages were love matches. (pp. 151–152)

Theologians have often feared, in this love, a danger of idolatry. I think they meant by this that the lovers might idolise one another. The does not seem to me to be the real danger; cer-

* From *The Four Loves* by C. S. Lewis, © 1960, by Helen Joy Lewis. Reprinted by permission of Harcourt Brace Jovanovich, Inc.

tainly not in marriage. The deliciously plain prose and business-like intimacy of married life render it absurd. So does the Affection in which Eros is almost invariably clothed. Even in courtship I question whether anyone who has felt the thirst for the Uncreated, or even dreamed of feeling it, ever supposed that the Beloved could satisfy it. As a fellow-pilgrim pierced with the very same desire, that is, as a Friend, the Beloved may be gloriously and helpfully relevant; but as an object for it—well (I would not be rude), ridiculous. The real danger seems to me not that the lovers will idolise each other but that they will idolise Eros himself. (p. 155)

And all the time the grim joke is that this Eros whose voice seems to speak from the eternal realm is not himself necessarily even permanent. He is notoriously the most mortal of our loves. The world rings with complaints of his fickleness. What is baffling is the combination of this fickleness with his protestations of permanency. To be in love is both to intend and to promise life-long fidelity. Love makes vows unasked; can't be deterred from making them. "I will be ever true," are almost the first words he utters. Not hypocritically but sincerely. No experience will cure him of the delusion. We have all heard of people who are in love again every few years; each time sincerely convinced that "*this* time it's the real thing," that their wanderings are over, that they have found their true love and will themselves be true till death.

And yet Eros is in a sense right to make this promise. The event of falling in love is of such a nature that we are right to reject as intolerable the idea that it should be transitory. In one high bound it has overleaped the massive wall of our selfhood; it has made appetite itself altrustic, tossed personal happiness aside as a triviality and planted the interests of another in the centre of our being. Spontaneously and without effort we have fulfilled the law (towards one person) by loving our neighbour as ourselves. It is an image, a foretaste, of what we must become to all if Love Himself rules in us without a rival. It is even (well used) a preparation for that. Simply to relapse from it, merely to "fall out of" love again, is—if I may coin the ugly word—a sort of *disredemption*. Eros is driven to promise what Eros of himself cannot perform.

Can we be in this selfless liberation for a lifetime? Hardly for a week. Between the best possible lovers this high condition is intermittent. The old self soon turns out to be not so dead as he pretended—as after a religious conversion. In either he may be momentarily knocked flat; he will soon be up again; if not on his feet, at least on his elbow, if not roaring, at least back to his surly grumbling or his mendicant whine. And Venus will often slip back into mere sexuality.

But these lapses will not destroy a marriage between two "decent and sensible" people. The couple whose marriage will certainly be endangered by them, and possibly ruined, are those who have idolised Eros. They thought he had the power and truthfulness of a god. They expected that mere feeling would do for them, and permanently, all that was necessary. When this expectation is disappointed they throw the blame on Eros or, more usually, on their partners. In reality, however, Eros, having made his gigantic promise and shown you in glimpses what its performance would be like, has "done his stuff." He, like a godparent, makes the vows; it is we who must keep them. It is we who must labour to bring our daily life into even closer accordance with what the glimpses have revealed. We must do the works of Eros when Eros is not present. This all good lovers know, though those who are not reflective or articulate will be able to express it only in a few conventional phrases about "taking the rough along with the smooth," not "expecting too much," having "a little common sense," and the like. And all good Christian lovers know that this programme, modest as it sounds, will not be carried out except by humility, charity and divine grace; that it is indeed the whole Christian life seen from one particular angle. (pp. 158–160)

C. S. Lewis
Theology

[HOMOGAMY]

Cultural Groupings and Limitations on Choice *

. . . This paper has attempted to throw a light on three questions: *first,* does a biologically mature unattached adult have an equal opportunity to marry an unattached mature adult of the opposite sex? *Second,* what restrictions are placed on his choice by society, and *third,* how effective are certain selected restrictions in limiting his choice? These questions become meaningful only when we relate them to the two propositions outlined in the introduction. There I set up a model with theoretical limits of absolute freedom of individual choice in the selection of a marital partner at one pole, and no choice at the other.

The data presented demonstrate that American culture, as it is reflected in the behavior of newly married couples in New Haven, places very definite restrictions on whom an individual may or may not marry. The racial mores were found to be the most explicit on this point. They divided the community into two pools of marriage mates and an individual fished for a mate only in his own racial pool. Religion divided the white race into three smaller pools. Persons in the Jewish pool in 97.1 per cent of the cases married within their own group; the percentage was 93.8 for Catholics and 74.4 for Protestants. Age further subdivided the potential pool of marriage mates into rather definite age grades, but the limits here were not so precise in the case of a man as of a woman. The ethnic origin of a person's family placed further restrictions on his marital choice. In addition, class position and education stratified the three religious pools into areas where an individual was most likely to find a mate. When all of these factors are combined they place narrow limits on an individual's choice of a marital partner. At the moment we

* From August B. Hollingshead, "Cultural Factors in the Selection of Marriage Mates," *American Sociological Review* XV (October 1950), p. 627.

cannot go beyond this point and assign a proportionate probable weight to each one.

In conclusion, I think the data we have presented strongly support the proposition that one's subculture, and one's race, age, and class position in the society effectively determine the kind of a person one will marry, but not the exact individual. In a highly significant number of cases the person one marries is very similar culturally to one's self. Our data clearly support the theory of homogamy, rather than that of heterogamy, *but* a generalized theory of the precise influence of cultural and individual factors on the selection of marriage mates remains to be formulated. This is an objective for sociologists to work toward.

AUGUST B. HOLLINGSHEAD
Social Science

Homogamy as a Description of Mate Selection *

Engaged couples are seldom able to state why they fell in love with each other. A careful analysis of interview and statistical data however revealed the nature and role of certain factors influencing their choice of a mate.

The first of these, propinquity, was found to be an essential condition, but in only a few cases the precipitating factor. Young people did tend to become engaged with those whom they first met at school or college, in the same recreational and work groups, and so on. Propinquity is therefore mainly a circumscribing factor, providing the spatial limit, social as well as physical, of the contacts that may finally eventuate in marriage.

Like propinquity, the image of the ideal mate in terms of cultural characteristics seems to be a limiting factor, excluding those whom a young man or woman would not consider as prospective wives or husbands. Of all the persons of the opposite sex whom a single person knows only a few qualify as possible mar-

* From Ernest W. Burgess and Paul Wallin, *Engagement and Marriage* (Philadelphia: J. B. Lippincott Company, 1953), pp. 211–213.

riage partners according to the standards, conscious and unconscious, of the ideal mate. Desired physical traits attract initially,
but generally are not binding. The choice of a marriage partner
depends more crucially upon his possession of valued personality characteristics.

Parental image appears to be a positive factor in mate selection. The father image for the daughter and the mother image
for the son seem to influence the choice of a spouse. But the
resemblance is considerably less in physical traits than in personality characteristics. Perhaps also the likeness is not as much
in personality attributes as in the same or similar type of affec-
tional and emotional relationship with the love object and the
parent of the opposite sex. Finally, as indicated earlier, the parental image takes different manifestations. Probably, the person
in the choice of a mate is influenced not by one but by both parents and through those characteristics which were most significant for his emotional development.

Personality need appears to be even more important than
parental image in mate selection. Actually it often includes the
latter. In addition it embraces unsatisfied wants arising from
other experiences. What is necessary in the understanding of
mate selection is to establish the existence of the need and not
its origin. The central question in courtship and engagement
then becomes the determination of the personality needs of the
engaged persons and how completely and satisfactorily they are
being filled.

When parents arranged marriages, social and economic status
was the chief criterion of a successful marriage. In the old-time
rural community economic standards, such as the farming ability of the young man and the housekeeping aptitude of the
prospective wife, were given main attention. With marriage now
in the control of young people, their adjustment to each other in
fulfilling personality needs in a companionship relation becomes
their chief concern in mate selection.

Homogamy is an intriguing aspect of mate selection. It is
probably an interesting outcome rather than a significant factor
in choosing a mate. The study of 1,000 engaged couples con-

firms the findings of previous studies that in many physical, psychological, and social characteristics the tendency of like to
mate with like is greater than that of opposites to be attracted.
So far not a single instance of the reverse has been established.
Interesting as is this fact, it does not imply that people have an
homogamous impulse. The factors already considered—propinquity, image of the ideal mate, parental image, and personality need combined with family and social pressures—are all
that seem to be needed to explain the preponderance over chance
of homogamous unions. This assumed finding should, however,
be demonstrated by research.

ERNEST W. BURGESS
and PAUL WALLIN
Social Sciences

Variant Tastes but Common Values *

What then can we say that will help young people to choose
as wisely as possible? There *are* some established facts, based
on wide experience and supported by research, that can be offered. Let me list them.

1. *Maturity* in those concerned is important. I mean, chiefly,
   emotional maturity. To avoid complications let me define
   this very simply as the stage at which you have grown
   enough to have a reasonably good knowledge of and acceptance of yourself and a capacity to understand and get
   along smoothly with most other people. A few exceptional
   boys and girls reach this point relatively early in life. In
   general, however, I think it is unusual for a girl under
   twenty, or for a boy under twenty-two, to be mature
   enough to marry without taking unwarrantable risks. Most
   people who marry too young do so because they are mal-
   adjusted personalities trying to escape from their conflicts.
2. *Length of acquaintance* comes next. We have all heard of

* From *Success in Marriage* by David R. Mace. Copyright © 1958 by
Abingdon Press. Pp. 17–19.

the couple who met on a summer holiday, fell madly in love, married in a few weeks, and lived happily ever after. We are less likely to hear of the other couples who followed the same course and ended in disaster. Marrying in a hurry is a game of chance. It is gambling with the life happiness not only of the two concerned but also of children yet unborn. In all too many cases, alas, the reason for the haste is that one of these latter is already on the way!

Other things being equal, two people are more likely to see each other in proper perspective during a lengthy acquaintance than during a brief one. The first illusions are gradually shed, the pretenses and deceptions fall away, the realities emerge and are clearly apprehended. American researchers have found that marriages based on a close acquaintance of a couple of years or so proved to be decidedly more stable than those in which the couple knew each other only a few months before they became man and wife.

3. *Values shared in common* seem to matter a good deal in wise choosing. Marriages between people of quite different backgrounds have been known to turn out very happily. But in general the evidence suggests that all wide disparities—of age, of race, of religion, of culture—introduce hazards into the proposed union which must be taken seriously. Where such hazards exist, other factors should be overwhelmingly favorable in order to restore the balance.

These hazards cannot always be clearly perceived before marriage. People who are "different" are often especially attractive to us on that account. Unhappily there is a sharp contrast between this relatively superficial attractiveness and the tensions which may arise when the two people concerned come together in the deeply shared life of marriage.

For successful marriage two people need not, however, be alike in all respects. Variety of tastes, and in some degree even of temperament, offers scope for a marriage which may enlarge the horizons of both partners. What is basic is that both should feel and think alike about the standards, values, and principles upon which their philosophy of life is based, and should have the same fundamental attitudes and outlook.

Much more could be said about the choosing of the marriage partner. Yet I believe that these are the principles that matter most. The couple who have reached reasonably mature judgment, have come to know each other well, and find that increasing knowledge of each other tends to deepen their sense of unity and their respect for each other as persons—this couple may with a reasonable measure of confidence go forward into marriage on the assumption that they have what it takes to build a sound and satisfying relationship.

DAVID R. MACE
Marriage and Family Life

[HETEROGAMY]

Strengths and Weaknesses in Neurotic Relationships *

. . . Some neurotics are nice people, in fact, extraordinarily likeable people, despite their neuroses, or occasionally because of them. Other neurotics are disagreeable persons. People with the same neurosis may be extraordinarily different in their personal values and in the social manifestations of such values. Depending upon their own values, we either like them or find them offensive.

It is often said that one neurotic marries another. But what a neurotic person seeks out is not primarily a partner afflicted with neurosis, but rather an individual who, hopefully, will complement his idiosyncratic emotional needs. The outcome, in mental health terms, of a particular marriage is not contingent exclu-

* From *The Psychodynamics of Family Life* by Nathan W. Ackerman, M.D., © 1958 by Nathan W. Ackerman, Basic Books, Inc., Publishers, New York. Pp. 152–153.

sively on the character of the neurosis of the individual partners. The ultimate effects on mental health are determined rather by the part that neurotic conflict plays in the complex process of integration of the personalities of the partners into the reciprocal roles of husband and wife . . .

In some instances neurotic conflict destroys the marriage; in others it seems to save the marriage. It is common knowledge that the neurotic tendency of one marital partner often complements that of the other. Sometimes the traits of one partner reinforce in the other healthy defenses against neurotic conflict, so that its destructive effects are mitigated. Sometimes this form of complementarity decompensates and the marital relationship disintegrates. The issue is a question not merely of the effect of individual neurotic conflict on the marital functioning but also of the interplay of the two persons sharing one life. The bad marriages that some neurotic individuals make are notorious, but what enables some to make good ones? The wonder is not so much that one neurotic marries another, but rather that some neurotics marry persons who strengthen them against regression and also provide support so that they can function as reasonably good parents.

The potentially hopeful aspect of this whole problem is that some neurotics, despite traumatic childhoods, make fine marriages and fine parents. These are the well-intentioned people who pit a fundamentally sound set of personal values against the destructive expressions of their neurosis. Neurosis in individual personality is not, therefore, the sole factor that predetermines the fate of marriage, family life, and a new crop of children. Were it so there would be little hope for the world. The saving grace is that in certain neurotic marital partnerships the effect each partner exerts upon the other is a favorable one and neutralizes the injurious results of their neuroses. Within this matrix the character of each partner improves.

NATHAN W. ACKERMAN
Behavioral Sciences

Elimination of Neurotic Choices Through Insight Education *

Since human beings are imperfect, since few of us have insight into our conscious purposes when we make our marriage choices, since few of us are emotionally mature when we marry, and since there often are unanticipated changes between the choosing period and the living period, how can we be sure of making a right choice? How can we guide young people or advise them? Are there any ways of testing, any sure indices?

In the present stage of our knowledge we have no sure guides. Our position here is comparable to that of medicine in relation to many illnesses. We can diagnose the existence of an illness, and even know something of its nature, long before we are able either to prevent or cure it. The same thing is true of the problems of marriage. We have no indication that a battery of psychological tests would help us. Furthermore, apart from the fact that it would be impossible practically, we do not even know that universal analysis in the adolescent years would necessarily make for happier marriages.

We can only say that if we strive gradually to modify our whole educational process so as to give every human being from an early age a deeper insight into himself and his own needs; if self-knowledge in depth is no longer the forgotten factor of our whole educational system; if as a result of this we achieve earlier emotional maturity to keep pace with our intellectual and physical maturity; then in choosing our mates our conscious and unconscious goals are likely to coincide much more closely. When we achieve this, as part of many basic cultural changes and developments, then I think we can look forward to sounder choices and therefore to sounder marriages.

In other words, the capacity to choose wisely and soundly and therefore to live in harmony depends upon developmental processes that must start in the early years, affecting the rate of

* From Kubie, "Psychology and Marriage" in *Neurotic Interaction in Marriage,* edited by Victor W. Eisenstein, M.D., Basic Books, Inc., Publishers, New York, 1956. Pp. 39–40.

maturation of the personality as a whole and the ultimate harmony between conscious and unconscious components in that personality. This is of far more importance in marriage than any kind of marriage counseling. The need for marriage counseling is in itself by implication a confession of cultural failure.

Moreover, by implication, a re-examination of the romantic tradition is indicated, and a careful and objective study of the obsessional quality of infatuation must be made. Most obsessions are, of course, quite unpleasant. Infatuations happen to be, in balance, pleasant obsessions, at least while they last. But an obsession is an obsession; and whether pleasant or unpleasant, it is never healthy nor conducive to ultimate happiness.

Granting that most marriage choices are made in the dark, as compromises between obscure conscious and unconscious purposes that are in conflict, what can one do about this? Does partial insight or any degree of retrospective insight help?

The answer is that insight may help in one of two ways: It may, and occasionally does, show that the marriage should never have been made. When this happens, two human beings instead of tearing each other to pieces may agree in all friendliness that each had made an innocent error of judgment in good faith. The tie can then be dissolved with a minimal amount of injury or pain.

In many other situations, however, a recognition of the unconscious as well as the conscious goals makes it possible for the married couple to help each other work out a harmonious compromise between their divergent purposes. Many a marriage has not only been saved, but actually has become deeply significant and constructive and harmonious through insight of this kind.

LAWRENCE S. KUBIE
Behavioral Sciences

[COMPLEMENTARITY]

Marital Choice as Need Gratification *

There is a set of variables upon which homogamy has been shown to function: race, religion, social class, broad occupational grouping, location of residence, income, age, level of education, intelligence, etc. It is my opinion that these variables function to select for each of us the sort of people with whom we shall be most likely to interact, to assure that the people with whom we work and with whom we play and with whom we otherwise associate are more or less like us with respect to that set of variables and also with respect to cultural interests and values. In the sense that these variables determine with whom we shall associate, I suggest that they define for each of us a "field of eligible spouse candidates" within which it is likely that we shall choose our spouses.

It is my judgment that the principle of homogamy does a good job at answering the first question raised a moment ago: What observations can we make about whom one meets or is likely to meet? It is my further opinion that, whereas homogamy can do very little, heterogamy can do a great deal in answering the second question: What do we mean by love, or by falling in love?

. . . .

When a man and a woman are in love, it is evident that there is something about the relationship which causes each to want to be with the other. Since each engages in such goal-directed behavior, it seems reasonable to think that each finds gratification in interaction with the other. If it is reasonable to speak of gratification, then it makes sense to postulate some needs in each which the interaction (and hence the behavior of the other) may gratify. Thus the first step is to postulate for all persons some psychic needs which appear to be relevant to mate selection and

* From Robert F. Winch, *Mate–Selection* (New York: Harper & Brothers, 1958), pp. 14–17.

to the marital relationship. After positing such needs, we might undertake to observe pairs of spouses in interaction for the purpose of determining whether or not the various needs were being gratified. The feasibility of this procedure becomes dubious for a variety of reasons—chiefly the difficulty of getting samples of "natural" interaction between the man and the woman.

Another device is to determine whether husbands adjudged high on one variable (*e.g.,* the need to express hostility) tend to mate with women rated high on some seemingly related variable (*e.g.,* the need to be punished). Here we can use statistical analysis rather than observation to determine whether or not the data support the general hypothesis.

Psychologically this analysis involves the hypothesis that one need in the husbands is complementary to another need in the wives. By "complementary" is meant that as the husbands engage in the behavior which their own needs arouse, this behavior is found to gratify the relevant needs of their wives; and similarly, the wives acting out their, say, masochistic needs are hypothesized to be gratifying the hostile needs of the husbands.

It is reasoned that if the variables function in this fashion, highly hostile husbands and highly masochistic wives will tend to marry, while husbands low in hostility will marry women with relatively little masochism. Such a state of affairs should produce a positive correlation between the hostility of husbands and the masochism of wives. Thus we may think of A's love for B in terms of the needs of A for which B provides either immediate gratification or the promise of future gratification. And we may think of the love relationship between A and B in terms of the idea that, as both A and B act out their own needs, the resulting behavior provides gratification for certain needs of the other. This is what we mean by stating a love relationship in terms of complementary needs of the members of the couple.

ROBERT F. WINCH
Social Sciences

Exploring the Issues

There are a number of thoughtful, descriptive definitions of love. Foote writes, *"Love is that relationship between one person and another which is most conducive to the optimal development of both.* This optimal development is to be measured practically in the growth of competence and interpersonal relations." [1] Bailey describes the experience as "a mutual, though not necessarily simultaneous vision of perfection. . . ." [2] Piper defines love as "a form of sympathy for something or someone based on a sense of belonging together." [3] Tillich thinks of love as "the whole being's movement toward another being to overcome existential separation." [4] To Fromm it is the action which keeps a man sane and which normally results in a mutual expression of the attitudes of care, responsibility, respect and knowledge.[5] Reik says it is essentially the action of one person looking for, and imagining he has found, his own idealized self in the form of the beloved.[6]

Behind these and other descriptions of love there are four basic concepts which are frequently used to explain the question of marital choice. Briefly these are:

I. Romanticism (people marry because they are "in love")
II. Homogamy (people tend to marry persons like themselves)
III. Heterogamy (people are attracted by opposites and marry persons far different from themselves)
IV. Complementarity (people marry those whose psychic needs complement and satisfy their own needs)

I. *Romanticism*

The first of these is an over-idealization of love. It stems from a tradition developed in France in the twelfth and thirteenth centuries which is today an all-pervasive influence in the American youth and young adult culture. Psychologically it can be defined as infatuation, a form of obsessionalism, that "clouds reason and leads to fantasy." [7] It is blatantly encouraged by commercial interests which make immense profits by catering to and encouraging this form of emotionalism. Peterson labels it "cardiac-respiratory love" and regards the entire phenomenon as dangerously and tragically false.

This is not to say that emotion has no place, or only a very limited place, in the man-woman love relationship. On the contrary, there is something almost obsessional in every total commitment, and love normally leads to commitment. But, whereas true love is based on knowledge of another who is appreciated more and more, infatuation is based on a lack of knowledge, on an unreal perception of the other person. The shift from infatuation to love comes only when the partner is seen clearly and realism replaces the false romanticism.

Both true love and romanticism are subject to the heavy, selfish demands of what Lewis defines as Eros. Eros will accept no substitute and brook no interference or rival. To the ones caught up in the emotion, the demands seem perfectly proper and obvious, given the situation and the persons involved. Lewis has a valid warning to offer: Eros cannot produce on all his promises.

II. *Homogamy*

The concept of homogamy is descriptive rather than explanatory. It does not explain why this person marries that person, but it does describe the process by which people are grouped into pools of eligibility. A very simple, clear presentation of the operation of homogamy is provided by Hollingshead. Racial, religious, age, and social stratum factors separate people into categories of alikeness. Literally hundreds of studies have researched these and other grouping factors such as location of residence, degree of education, income, level of intelligence, and the like, and document the operation of homogamous norms in the American marital system.[8]

The operation of homogamy is extremely significant in at least one respect. It establishes standards of eligibility which often may rule out "impossible choices" before they are even considered. Many people who might be attracted to one another for a number of reasons and who, predictably, would establish very weak marriages, do not even have the chance to meet. But this is becoming less and less true as social and geographical mobility increase and racial and religious barriers are lowered.

Less tangible grouping factors are those which deal with values, attitudes, psychological sets, prejudices, ideals, and the like. These are none the less real and bring people together on both the conscious and subconscious levels. Burgess and Wallin speak to this and recognize the effective presence of the subconscious in matters of marital choice. These men verge close to the heterogamous position when they indicate that the central question "becomes the determination of the personality needs of the engaged persons and how completely and satisfactorily they are being filled."

III. *Heterogamy*

The concept of heterogamy which says that opposites are attracted to one another was developed by the psychiatrist and analyst. It was noted in clinical counseling that quite often the neurotic client was married to a neurotic spouse. It was further observed that very often these two neuroses complemented one another in that the neurotic needs of each were being met by the neurotic components in the other's personality. Early reports of this phenomenon were made by Oberndorf [9] and Mittelman.[10] Bergler [11] details histories of a number of such complementary couples. Eisenstein describes the dynamic in many of its ramifications in the book which he edited and published, *Neurotic Interaction in Marriage*.[12] What happens, in brief, is that the sick personality reaches out for someone to support him, to care for him, or to make up his defects. He seeks to achieve and maintain both personal and marital balance by a strong dependency relationship with the spouse.

Sometimes this works remarkably well. Ackerman documents this, pointing out how the interrelationship may be a highly salutary thing for both partners. In fact, this neurotic love between them may quite literally make the partners irreplaceable to each other. At the same time, with the many variables present in each marriage, it is quite impossible to predict whether the neurosis will strengthen or destroy a marital relationship.

The sado-masochistic relationship is a classic illustration in which one spouse receives psychic pleasure (usually subconscious) by inflicting hurt of one kind or another on the married partner. While the victim may outwardly complain and even claim to be grossly mistreated, yet a basic need to suffer is met by these experiences and a strong, highly neurotic bond is evident. The mutuality of this dynamic is so clear that it has become a truism in the counseling profession that you dare not cure a neurotic without curing his spouse. To do so will almost assuredly precipitate an upset of an existing balance in the relationship.

This almost seems to make an individual the prisoner of his subconscious. There are many who feel this to be true. The problem is too large in scope for treatment here. But it should be noted that while subconscious elements of the personality are actively present, the conscious parts cannot be ignored. Conflict between the two forces obviously will produce problems of a serious nature.

There is no easy nor quick answer to such problems. Kubie is helpful. He acknowledges the problem and hopes for an overall improvement of peoples' ability to see themselves in proper perspective (insight) in order that earlier emotional maturation may take place. If then, he suggests, in choosing our mates our conscious and unconscious goals coincide more closely than they now do, there is a good prospect for sounder choices and for sounder marriages.

IV. *Complementarity*

The concept of complementarity or complementary needs is a next logical extension of heterogamy. The basic thesis, as presented by Winch, its chief proponent, is that if neurotics marry in order to satisfy each other's needs (*e.g.,* a "balanced" sado-masochistic relationship), why should this not be true of so-called normals? His research investigation of twenty-five couples which is detailed in *Mate-Selection* convinced him that there were enough complementary patterns evident (*e.g.,* Abasement–Dominance, Achievement–Recognition, Dominance–Submission, Nurturance–Succorance—eighteen in all) to support his theory that *"in mate-selection each individual seeks within his or her field of eligibles for that person who gives the greatest promise of providing him or her with maximum need gratification."* [13]

It must be noted that further testing by Bowerman and Day [14] and Schellenberg and Bee [15] does not support this theory, but neither do they demolish it. A further retest by Kerckhoff and Davis [16] supports both the homogamy and need complementarity theories, but indicates that the latter becomes operative *after* the couple have gone through the idealization phase of their relationship and have come to a more realistic appraisal of each other.

The results of the research leave this somewhat of an open question. But Albert's observation is most *apropos* to this situation. "Because of the *prima facie* logic of his [Winch's] position, however, most authorities still consider it possible that, given enough knowledge of personality, and tools precise enough to measure it accurately, complementarity may yet someday prove a meaningful concept in marriage prediction study." [17]

SUGGESTIONS FOR DISCUSSION

1. Spend some time in an analysis of the contemporary romantic culture. What are some of its obsessional features? How unrealistic are the popular songs of the day? Raise the question of the authority of love (Eros). Does love always make everything right?

2. Is there not a general recognition of homogamy as a social force? Are eligibility pools a good place to start looking for a mate?

3. The fact that heterogamy had its origin in observations of neurotic relationships does not mean it need not be studied

by non-neurotic couples. How significant is the role of the subconscious in mate selection?

4. How plausible, and how sound, does Winch's theory seem? What are the implications of his viewpoint?

5. Assuming that the place of the subconscious in marital choice is accepted, here are some important corollaries to discuss:

   a. Marriage is not for the immature. It is foolhardy to marry before the personality need patterns are set. Time should be allowed for growing up.

   b. There should be sufficient time for both the conscious and the subconscious elements in the personalities of the couple to be thoroughly tested in the premarital period. The engagement period should be long enough in time and broad enough in scope to allow for this significant interaction.

   c. The subconscious bonds may be even more important in marriage than the conscious ones. These hidden ties may add immense, unsuspected strength and meaning to any marriage.

6. Are there couples who might share—

   a. Some of the significant factors which have provided them with assurances that the choice made is sound at both the conscious and subconscious levels?

   b. Some of the essential needs which they feel the partner has met and will continue to meet?

7. What general reactions are there to Mace's point of view?

NOTES

1. Nelson N. Foote, "Love," *Marriage and Family in the Modern World,* ed. Ruth Shonle Cavan (New York: Thomas Y. Crowell Company, 1960), p. 195.

2. Derrick Sherwin Bailey, *The Mystery of Love and Marriage* (New York: Harper & Brothers, 1952), p. 19.

3. Otto A. Piper, *The Biblical View of Sex and Marriage* (New York: Charles Scribner's Sons, 1960), p. 56.

4. Paul Tillich, *Systematic Theology,* III (3 vols.; Chicago: University of Chicago Press, 1963), p. 136.

5. Erich Fromm, *The Art of Loving* (New York: Bantam Books, 1963), p. 22 ff.

6. Theodor Reik, *Of Love and Lust* (New York: Grove Press, Inc., 1941), pp. 100–101.

7. James Bossard and Eleanor Stoker Boll, *Why Marriages Go Wrong* (New York: The Ronald Press Co., 1958), p. 59.

8. Lee G. Burchinal, "The Premarital Dyad and Love Involvement," *Handbook of Marriage and the Family*, ed. Harold T. Christensen (Chicago: Rand McNally & Company, 1964), p. 646.

9. C. P. Oberndorf, "Psychoanalysis of Married Couples," *Psychoanalytical Review* XXV (1938), pp. 453–457.

10. Bela Mittelman, "Complementary Neurotic Reactions in Intimate Relationships," *Psychoanalytic Quarterly*, XIII, No. 4 (1944), pp. 479–491.

11. Edmund Bergler, *Unhappy Marriage and Divorce* (New York: International Universities Press, 1946).

12. *Neurotic Interaction in Marriage*, ed. Victor W. Eisenstein (New York: Basic Books, Inc., 1956).

13. Robert F. Winch, *Mate–Selection* (New York: Harper & Brothers, 1958), pp. 88–89.

14. Charles E. Bowerman and Barbara R. Day, "A Test of the Theory of Complementary Needs as Applied to Couples During Courtship," *American Sociological Review* XXI (October, 1956), pp. 602–604.

15. James A. Schellenberg and Lawrence S. Bee, "A Re-examination of the Theory of Complementary Needs in Mate Selection," *Marriage and Family Living* XXII (August, 1960), pp. 227–232.

16. Alan C. Kerckhoff and Keith E. Davis, "Value Consensus and Need Complementarity in Mate Selection," *American Sociological Review*, XXVII (June, 1962), pp. 295–303.

17. Gerald Albert, "A Handbook to Increase Awareness Among Non-Professionals of Psychological and Related Factors in the Determination of Marital Success and Failure" University Microfilms, Inc. Ann Arbor, Michigan. Copyright 1965 by Gerald Albert. P. 42.

The Place of Sex in Marriage

The Experts Speak

[AS A PHENOMENON OF NATURE AND CULTURE]

Differences Between Sex and Love *

Sex is an instinct, a biological need, originating in the organism, bound to the body. It is one of the great drives, like hunger and thirst, conditioned by chemical changes within the organism. The time is not far distant when we shall think of libido in chemical terms, and in chemical terms only. The sex urge is dependent on inner secretions. It can be localized in the genitals and in other erogenic zones. Its aim is the disappearance of a physical tension. It is originally objectless. Later on the sexual object is simply the means by which the tension is eased.

* Reprinted with the permission of Farrar, Straus & Giroux, Inc. from *Of Love and Lust* by Theodor Reik, copyright © 1941, 1944, 1957 by Theodor Reik, copyright 1949 by Farrar, Straus & Company. Pp. 19–21.

None of these characteristics can be found in love. If we do not accept the opinion of the ordinary man and woman that love lives in the heart we are unable to place it. It certainly is not a biological need, because there are millions of people who do not feel it and many centuries and cultural patterns in which it is unknown. We cannot name any inner secretions or specific glands which are responsible for it. Sex is originally objectless. Love certainly is not. It is a very definite, emotional relationship between a Me and a You.

What is the aim of sex? We have already stated it: the disappearance of a *physical* tension, a discharge and a *release*. What is the aim of the desire we call love? Disappearance of a *psychical* tension, *relief*. In this contrast between release and relief lies one of the most decisive differences. Sex wants satisfaction; love wants happiness.

Sex appears as a phenomenon of nature, common to men and beasts. Love is the result of a cultural development and is not even found among all men. We know that the sex urge is subject to periodic fluctuations of increase and decrease. This is of course quite obvious among the beasts, but survivals of its original nature are easily recognized in men. Nothing of this kind is known about love. Sex can be casual about its object. Love cannot. Love is always a personal relationship. This is not necessarily so with sex.

The object of sex may become of no account, boring or even hateful immediately after satisfaction is reached and the tension reduced. Not so the love-object. Referring to the extreme and crudest cases, the sexual partner can appear as a kind of appendage to the other's sexual parts, as a sexual object only. The object of love is always seen as a person and a personality. The sexual object has to have certain physical qualities which excite or arouse one. If they are lacking one remains indifferent. Not so the love object. It has to have certain psychical qualities which are highly valued, the existence of which is not demanded from a mere sexual object. Even when your object is both loved and sexually desired you can often discriminate between the sex appeal and the appeal of personality, and you know that they are different things. The sex urge hunts for lustful pleasure; love is in search of joy and happiness.

Again considering only extreme types, sex is utterly selfish, using the object only in order to get satisfaction. Love is not unselfish, but it is very difficult to name its selfish aims, other than that of being happy in the happiness of the beloved person. In no case can love be only selfish, or as selfish as sex. Then it would not be love. It is always concerned with the welfare or happiness of the other person, regrets the other's absence, wants to be together with the object, feels lonely without it, fears calamity or danger for it. There is nothing of this kind in crude sex. If the individual is not aroused by sexual wishes the presence of the sex object is not desired and its absence not regretted. The same is true after sexual satisfaction is reached. I have heard men say that the only wish they felt after a satisfactory intercourse was to be left alone—alone meaning that the sexual object should leave them. One man said, "Women should be like stars—rise late in the evening and disappear early in the morning." No such wish is imaginable toward a loved object.

Sex (always considering the crudest types) is undiscriminating. It wants "a woman." It is modest in its demands. But love always makes a choice. It is highly discriminating. It insists on "this woman" and no other. There is no such thing as an impersonal love. The sensually desired person and the adored one, the sex object and the love object, can be two different persons. The sex object can become the center of all one's wishes under the pressure of sexual needs. It can, for moments, be idolized. It cannot be idealized. Only love can work that. . . .

The sex aim is not identical with the love aim. Recently a patient said of her partner, "He is not the person I love, but the person who gives me sexual gratification." Sex is a passionate interest in another body; love a passionate interest in another personality, or in his life. Sex does not feel pain if its object is injured, nor joy when it is happy. It is possible to possess another person in sex, but not in love. In love you cannot possess another person, you can only belong to another person. You can force another person to sexual activity, but not to love.

THEODOR REIK
Behavioral Sciences

Sex in Other Cultures *

The relationship between father and mother in the nuclear family is solidified by the sexual privilege which all societies accord to married spouses. As a powerful impulse, often pressing individuals to behavior disruptive of the co-operative relationships upon which human social life rests, sex cannot safely be left without restraints. All known societies, consequently, have sought to bring its expression under control by surrounding it with restrictions of various kinds. On the other hand, regulation must not be carried to excess or the society will suffer through resultant personality maladjustments or through insufficient reproduction to maintain its population. All peoples have faced the problem of reconciling the need of control with the opposing need of expression, and all have solved it by culturally defining a series of sexual taboos and permissions. These checks and balances differ widely from culture to culture, but without exception a large measure of sexual liberty is everywhere granted to the married parents in the nuclear family. Husband and wife must adhere to sexual etiquette and must, as a rule, observe certain periodic restrictions such as taboos upon intercourse during menstruation, pregnancy, and lactation, but normal sex gratification is never permanently denied to them. . . .

As a means of expressing and reducing a powerful basic drive, as well as of gratifying various acquired or cultural appe-

* From George Peter Murdock, "Structures and Functions of the Family," in *Selected Studies in Marriage and the Family,* ed. Robert F. Winch, Robert McGinnis, and Herbert R. Barringer (New York: Holt, Rinehart and Winston, 1962), pp. 21–22. Adapted from *Social Structure* by George P. Murdock, copyright 1949 by The Macmillan Company, New York.

tites, sexual intercourse strongly reinforces the responses which precede it. These by their very nature are largely social, and include co-operative acts which must, like courtship, be regarded as instrumental responses. Sex thus tends to strengthen all the reciprocal habits which characterize the interaction of married parents, and indirectly to bind each into the mesh of family relationship in which the other is involved.

To regard sex as the sole factor, or even as the most important one, that brings a man and a woman together in marriage and binds them into the family structure would, however, be a serious error. If all cultures, like our own, prohibited and penalized sexual intercourse except in the marital relationship, such an assumption might seem reasonable. But this is emphatically not the case. Among those of our 250 societies for which information is available, 65 allow unmarried and unrelated persons complete freedom in sexual matters, and 20 others give qualified consent, while only 54 forbid or disapprove premarital liaisons between non-relatives such as cross-cousins. Where premarital license prevails, sex certainly cannot be alleged as the primary force driving people into matrimony.

Nor can it be maintained that, even after marriage, sex operates exclusively to reinforce the matrimonial relationship. To be sure, sexual intercourse between a married man and an unrelated woman married to another is forbidden in 126 of our sample societies, and is freely or conditionally allowed in only 24. These figures, however, given an exaggerated impression of the prevalence of cultural restraints against extramarital sexuality, for affairs are often permitted between particular relatives though forbidden with non-relatives. Thus in a majority of the societies in our sample for which information is available a married man may legitimately carry on an affair with one or more of his female relatives, including a sister-in-law in 41 instances. Such evidence demonstrates conclusively that sexual gratification is by no means always confined to the marital relationship, even in theory. If it can reinforce other relationships as well, as it commonly does, it cannot be regarded as peculiarly conducive to marriage or as alone accountable for the stability of the most crucial relationship in the omnipresent family institution. . . .

In view of the frequency with which sexual relations are permitted outside of marriage, it would seem the part of scientific caution to assume merely that sex is an important but not the exclusive factor in maintaining the marital relationship within the nuclear family, and to look elsewhere for auxiliary support. . . .

GEORGE PETER MURDOCK
Social Sciences

[AS A SOURCE OF PLEASURE]

Gratification of Sexual Wants *

3. *Guilt and anxiety.* Since premarital sex relations are no longer viewed as morally reprehensible or sinful by most educated and informed individuals, there need be no intrinsic guilt attached to them.

People who are anxious and guilty because of their premarital affairs are usually emotionally disturbed individuals who are also anxious and guilty about many of their non-sexual participations. On the other hand, many people today are becoming anxious and disturbed because they are *not* copulating before marriage. . . .

. . . .

7. *Exploitation of one's sex partner.* Exploitation of one's sex partner generally takes place when one individual (usually the male) has sex relations with another under false pretenses—pretending that he loves her, will marry her, or something on that order. Such exploitation doubtless often occurs in premarital affairs: not because of the affairs themselves, but because of the dishonesty of the people engaging in them.

* From Albert Ellis, *Sex Without Guilt* (New York: Lyle Stuart, 1958 and 1966).

Where both partners, moreover, frankly have sex relations for the sexual (as well as other) satisfactions they thereby derive, such exploitation is reduced to a minimum. Consequently, the more open, honest, and frequent premarital intercourse tends to become, the less does it remain potentially exploitative.

. . . .

9. *Sex without love*. Premarital copulation, it is alleged, leads to sex without love. This is sheer nonsense: since most of the great love affairs of human history, such as that of Heloise and Abelard, appear to have consisted of fornicative ones. Sex, no matter how it is indulged, normally creates and enhances love.

Virginity, especially when it is prolonged and taken to extremes, seems to be the true enemy of love (and often engenders deep-seated hostility to others). Sex without love, moreover, is hardly a heinous crime, and appears to be quite delightful and to add immeasurably to the lives of literally millions of individuals.

. . . .

13. *Subsequent adultery*. It is said that those who have premarital affairs are more likely to engage in adultery after marriage. Granted that this may be so (for there is at least a little factual evidence that would seem to point in this direction), it has never been shown that those who copulate premaritally engage in considerable adultery after marriage, nor that they were adulterous because of their premarital affairs, nor that their adultery is particularly inimical to their marriages.

On the contrary, there is some evidence that adultery may aid, save, and stabilize a marriage rather than disrupt it and lead to its dissolution. (pp. 39–43)

Let us admit, at the outset, that many of the old grounds for opposing adultery are just as senseless, in today's world, as many similar grounds for combatting premarital sex affairs. For example:

Intelligent and informed modern men and women do not consider adultery intrinsically wicked and sinful and therefore often commit it with little or no guilt or anxiety.

. . . .

Thus, it may be said with little fear of scientific contradiction, that literally millions of men and women who engage in adulterous affairs thereby gain considerable adventure and experience, become more competent at sexual pursuits and practices, are enabled to partake of a high degree of varietism, and have substantial amounts of sexual and nonsexual fun that they otherwise would doubtlessly be denied. These, in a world that tends to be as dull and drab for the average man as our own, are no small advantages.

Should, then, the informed and intelligent husband and wife in our society blithely go about committing adultery? The answer, paradoxically enough, seems to be, in most cases, no. Why so? For several reasons:

1. Although, in some ideal society, it is quite probable that husbands and wives could be adulterous with impunity, and might well gain more than lose thereby, ours is definitely not such an ideal society. For better or worse, we raise individuals to *feel* that their marriages are in jeopardy and that they are unloved if their mates have extramarital affairs.

Whether, under these circumstances, adultery actually *does* destroy marriages or *does* prove lack of love, is beside the point. Once one is raised to *feel* that these things are true, they tend to *become* true; and, under adulterous circumstances, damage often *is* therefore done to marriage. . . .

2. Because people in our culture *believe* adultery to be inimical to marriage, husbands and wives who engage in extramarital relations generally have to do so secretly and furtively. This means that they must be dishonest with their mates; and, although their adultery, in itself, might not harm their marriages, their *dishonesty* about this adultery (as about any other major issue) may well prove to be harmful. (pp. 54–56)

. . . It does not appear to be very difficult for intelligent and informed men and women in our civilization to accept fully the fact that premarital sex relations are a good thing and to become entirely guilt-free in this connection. But, as yet, it does appear to be most difficult for them to accept the fact that they and their mates may be adulterous without sabotaging their marriages. Several past and present societies other than our own have condoned adultery; and it is possible that we, too, may do so sometime in the future. For the present, however, adultery, except under certain limited circumstances (such as individual's being away from home for a long time), would appear to be impractical rather than sinful for most people.

Today's adulterer need not feel evil or wicked. But, from the standpoint of impairing his own marriage, he may well be acting irrationally and neurotically. If he thinks of adultery not in terms of sin but in terms of the possible *adulteration* of his own marital happiness, he should be able to make wiser choices in this connection. (pp. 58–59)

ALBERT ELLIS
Behavioral Sciences

The Playboy Philosophy *

Since one of the things *Playboy* is especially concerned about is the depersonalizing influence of our entire society, and considerable editorial attention is given to the problem of establishing individual identity, through sex and as many other avenues of expression as may be available in a more permissive society, it is wrong to suggest that we favor depersonalized sex. Not unless, by depersonalized sex, we are referring to any and all sexual activity that does not include extensive involvement, commitments and obligations. In this sense, it is true, to the extent that the magazine emphasizes the pleasures rather than the problems of sex, and focuses on that period of life in which real personal involvement is not yet desirable—a time of transition into maturity, prior to accepting the responsibilities of marriage and family.

I certainly think that personal sex is preferable to impersonal sex, because it includes the greatest emotional rewards; but I can

* From "The Playboy Philosophy," Hugh M. Hefner, from *Playboy* Magazine, December 1964.

see no logical justification for opposing the latter, unless it is irresponsible, exploitive, coercive or in some way hurts one of the individuals involved. I stated before that *Playboy* doesn't purport to present more than a part of life in its pages; but I would also add that there are certainly a plentitude of publications, and numerous other sources of opinion in our society, that are forever stressing togetherness, and the trials and tribulations of total commitment.

As for the Playboy Club, I think there is every justification for keeping its sex depersonalized, uninvolved and untouchable; nor is there anything inconsistent in this. Far from being anti-sexual, it is simply a policy that separates business from pleasure.

. . . .

The fact that there is still extensive sexual sickness in society —and I would be the first to agree that there is—doesn't mean that we're not involved in a sexual revolution; it only indicates the extent to which a radical readjustment of our sexual values is needed. And far from pandering to the negative sexual concepts of the past, we are among the most outspoken advocates of a more healthy, open and positive outlook on sex. We treat it with humor, which helps to take the onus off it; we place our emphasis on approval rather than negation; and we attempt to treat sex in as attractive and appealing a light as possible.

HUGH M. HEFNER
Publisher

[AS A MEANS OF DISCOVERY]

Discovery of One's Own Sexual Identity *

What then is the secret that is revealed to us in sexual intercourse? All sexual desire is basically intent upon solving the

* Reprinted by permission of Charles Scribner's Sons from *The Biblical View of Sex and Marriage* by Otto A. Piper. Copyright © 1960 Otto A. Piper. Pp. 40–42.

question: Why is it that I am not simply a person but rather a human being either of the male or female sex, and therefore one who is sexually attracted to persons of the other sex? This is not the scientific question concerning the nature of sexual differentiation but rather the existential problem of the purpose of my own life as a man or a woman. The enigmatic character of our masculinity or femininity is disturbing until the solution is found. Therefore, the potent development of the sexual instinct adds an impatient urgency to young people's restlessness and makes them desirous to discover the meaning of their lives. How absurd that modern naturalistic ethics should contend that sex as such has no problem in the face of the intimate connection between the sexual instinct and the quest for the meaning of personal existence! In vain do people hope to get rid of the vexing enigma of sex by denying its problematic character and by focusing all attention on the pleasure it provides. How much more realistic is the recognition that beyond the pleasure derived from sex the meaning of my sexually conditioned nature is revealed to me in sexual intercourse.

What is the experience sustained by the partners in sexual union? Generally speaking, it is an experience of happiness caused by the fact that the original antagonism implied in sexual differentiation is resolved when at the peak of the union all consciousness of difference vanishes. This experience moves through a number of stages each of which makes its own contribution to sexual knowledge. First of all, the man concentrates all his desire on the possession of the beloved woman which is met by her willingness to surrender herself. Even when she deliberately sets out to win a man the roles of the sexes are reversed as soon as he accepts her challenge because then he becomes the active one who demands. This creates a conflict of wills. The woman, though characterized by Goethe, as the "one easily seduced," does not surrender her individuality without resistance, and only during the progress of love-play and the erotic contest will she submit to his urging and desire. She offers opposition yet hopes that he will break her resistance so that she may experience his superiority. Although the female sex seems to be defenseless against the man's wooing the part the woman plays in sexual relations is not entirely passive. Yes, he takes eventual possession of her body but not until she has surrendered it to him. She is as active in receiving as he is in giving.

A distinctive feeling of well-being suffuses both persons at the completion of the sexual act. The man experiences release from tension and a sense of satisfaction because finally the restless striving of his will and desire has found its respite through this person. The woman too feels enriched by the assurance that she has encountered the person who gives meaning to her womanhood. Both partners are happy in the joyful certainty of mutual blessedness and of belonging together. This sense of belonging together implies on the part of the man the jealous wish to possess his partner for himself alone; while on the part of the woman there is the desire to bind him to herself in permanent union. Furthermore both take pride in their procreative ability. Although the desire to propagate is not the motive of sexual union mature persons know that sexual intercourse implies the possibility to create new life. Thus they realize not only their distinctive qualities of manhood and womanhood but become, in their sexual intercourse, also aware of their fatherhood and motherhood.

Thus the unity of the flesh is experienced as a fusion of the two individuals into a mutuality of existence, a common destination for reciprocity of life and experience. In sexual intercourse both partners come to understand what it means that their Self is a masculine or a feminine one, namely that to be a man means to be destined for a woman and vice versa. While the biologist, who studies sex from the outside as an objective observer, may be inclined to deny that there is such a thing as masculinity or femininity, and that the term sex merely denotes a differentiation of physical organs and functions, sexual experience teaches that both partners need each other.

. . . .

Sexual intercourse supplies knowledge of our selves as sexually determined bodies. However, this is not simply an objective knowledge of our corporeality but rather it tells us why our existence in this world is tied up with a physical body. We also comprehend why no person is able to solve this mystery for himself since sexual partnership is the prerequisite of its solution.

OTTO A. PIPER
Theology

Growing Knowledge of Another Self *

The Old Testament uses the verb "to·know" (*yada*) frequently to indicate sexual relations. This usage was by no means confined to marital coitus, though it is clear that such "knowledge" belonged ideally in marriage. The Hebrew was not being delicate about sexuality, substituting the phrase "he knew her" for some expression more direct or coarse. The choice of words was deliberate, as Otto Piper has pointed out in his book *The Christian Interpretation of Sex*. What is, in fact, conveyed in sexual intercourse is a knowledge both of one's self and of another. No man really knows what it means to be a man until he has experienced sex with a woman; and every woman is similarly innocent until she has had relations with a man. This is the knowledge about which youth expresses insatiable curiosity. Not simply "the facts of life," the familiar and agonizing parental lecture on the birds and the bees and the flowers. That is merely words, an abstraction from life. What the young seek is firsthand knowledge, the experience itself. So Professor Piper places great emphasis upon the first act of coitus, for it is there that the secret is unlocked, the knowledge attained. Now at last one knows the essence of masculinity and femininity. Here the two become "one flesh." But the Old Testament does not confine the use of "knowing" to first coitus, and this again deliberately, with the unconscious profundity so often displayed. For there are always deeper levels of knowledge to be plumbed, knowledge of one's self and of another.

If . . . sex is in some sense central to and symbolic of the

*From William Graham Cole, *Sex and Love in the Bible* (New York: Association Press, 1959), pp. 276–278.

marriage relationship, then as a man and his wife grow in mutual understanding and ability to communicate themselves to one another, this growth is expressed in and deepened by their sexual intercourse. The word *intercourse* itself means "communication." Carried to its highest level, this reaches the point when the man and his wife are naked and unashamed. They know one another fully and accept each other completely. This is the essence of the marital union, symbolized in the perfection of Eden before the Fall. It is this knowledge which is sought through all of the existential distortions of marriage as it is experienced in the world of sin and estrangement. Hosea traced the sins of Israel, who had been a faithless wife to Yahweh, to her lack of knowledge of God. She had never known him properly and had therefore gone astray in her national life. This viewpoint is amazingly Freudian. The good Doctor Sigmund believed that neurosis was caused by a disturbance in the sex life. Hosea declared Israel's iniquities traceable to her failure to know God aright. Freud asserted that no neurosis is possible with a normal *vita sexualis*. Hosea promised Israel forgiveness and restoration if only she would truly know her God. Sex symbolizes selfhood. As goes a man's interpersonal relations in general, so goes his sexual orientation. Insofar as a marriage is sound, its sexual aspect will also prove sound and satisfying to both partners. Any disturbance in the marriage will quickly reflect itself in a disturbed sexual relationship. Not that marital harmony can be attained through the direct pursuit of sexual harmony, through consulting books on technique. That is to place the horse behind the cart. Sexual happiness follows marital happiness, not vice versa, though certainly a basically good relationship between husband and wife is deepened and reinforced by their sexual sharing.

But even on a superficial level, in a shaky marriage, or outside of marriage, sex does communicate knowledge. One always learns something about another in shared sexuality. Where the knowledge is without guilt or shame, as in marriage, it leads to trust and the willingness to explore and to communicate further. Where the knowledge is acquired clandestinely or illicitly, it leads to putting on "aprons," to hiding even levels of the personality which have been revealed before. A man and woman who have been close friends frequently find that an adulterous episode raises barriers between them that did not previously exist, though they have known each other more intimately than ever.

WILLIAM GRAHAM COLE
Theology

[AS A BOND BETWEEN PERSONS]

Establishment of the Union *

Not *every* sexual act, however, sets up a valid *henosis,* but only that which is done under conditions implying consent as it has usually been understood—consent, not merely to an act of intercourse, but to everything that follows from it. Mutual consent, therefore, is in fact fundamental, as Christian tradition has always insisted—but it is fundamental, not because by itself it effects an ontological change in the relation between a man and a woman by uniting them in the unique, mysterious *henosis* of "one flesh," but because it is essentially prerequisite to the sexual intercourse by which that *henosis* is established. This important distinction has not been appreciated simply because marriage has always been viewed institutionally rather than ontologically.

At this point a difficulty must be faced. If sexual intercourse is so significant an act, and is attended by such momentous consequences, what are we to make of St. Paul's assertion:

Know ye not that he that is joined to a harlot is one body?
For, the twain, saith he, shall become one flesh. [I Cor. 6:16]

Is there not a radical contradiction in the statement that even the most irresponsible and ephemeral connexion between a man

* From pp. 50–54 in *The Mystery of Love and Marriage* by Derrick Sherwin Bailey. (Harper & Row, 1952.) Reprinted by permission of the publisher.

and a woman (whether in ignorance or defiance of the consequences) makes them, like husband and wife, "one flesh"? In fornication every condition necessary for the establishment of a true *henosis* is absent; there is consent, perhaps, but it is directed to a wrong end; there is certainly no love, apart from a perverted *eros;* there is no intention of fidelity, no making and sharing of a common life, no recognition of any responsibility to the community—yet "he that is joined to a harlot is one body [with her]." The fact that St. Paul's assertion has received little attention from commentators in the past suggests that it has generally been found a hard saying, though it is clearly integral to his argument at that point, and cannot be dismissed as a reckless *obiter dictum.* . . .

. . . .

. . . Intercourse . . . is much more than a mere physical act which takes place on the periphery, as it were, of personal experience; it involves and affects the whole man and the whole woman in the very centre and depth of their being, so that afterwards neither can ever be as if they had never come together. This is true even of fornication, which cannot be excused or dismissed as something insignificant, done in complete detachment, and from which no consequences follow. Thus the verbal substitution serves both to reveal the true character of sexual union, and to expose the fallacy, as common now as it was among the Corinthians, that casual and promiscuous intercourse is "natural," means nothing.

But while we allow, with St. Paul, that sexual intercourse always establishes a "one flesh" union, it is clear that in every case the character of the union will be determined by the character of its constitutive act. Thus a distinction may be drawn between two sharply contrasted states of "one flesh":

1. The true, authentic *henosis* is effected by intercourse following consent between a man and a woman who love one another and who act freely, deliberately, responsibly, and with the knowledge and approval of the community, and in so doing (whether they know it or not) conform to the

Divine law. In this class must also be included unions of the kind described by Augustine in *de bono conjugali 5* (v), which lack nothing but public recognition.

2. The false, invalid "one flesh" union is effected by casual or mercenary acts of fornication, or by adultery.

It would seem desirable to add to these a third category:

3. There are very many unions which appear to be valid, but which must properly be termed defective. These are the marriages which have no foundation in love, as it has been described in this study, or which, because of sexual or psychical maladjustment, represent a level of personal relation which falls considerably below the ideal implied by "one flesh."

There are cases, however, such as rape and the seduction of the young or the feeble-minded, where it would be absurd to press the application of St. Paul's principle; it was clearly never intended to apply to them, and it is certain that the mere occurrence of the sexual act without consent, desire or understanding cannot be held to make two persons "one body." But whenever a man and a woman enter freely into sexual relation, the principle holds good; their intercourse always makes them in some sense "one flesh", and where the union is false and invalid its redemption in marriage is possible through the growth of love and responsibility.

Sexual intercourse is an act of the whole self which affects the whole self; it is a personal encounter between man and woman in which each does something to the other, for good or for ill, which can never be obliterated. This remains true even when they are ignorant of the radical character of their act. It cannot, therefore, be treated simply as sensual indulgence. Fornication is more than an isolated, pleasurable exercise of the sexual organs; it is the expression of an attitude of mind in which God, other persons, and the self are all involved. But sexual intercourse, although an act in which the whole man and the whole woman engage, is nevertheless without meaning unless it consummates a true love and expresses their acceptance and affirmation of the consequent ontological change in themselves and their relation. That is to say, their intention and the context of their intercourse determine the character both of the act itself and of the resultant state of "one flesh." In their coming together they either affirm or deny all that sexual intercourse means. In the one case they become knit together in a mysterious and significant *henosis* and fulfil their love as husband and wife; in the other they merely enact a hollow, ephemeral, diabolical parody of marriage which works disintegration in the personality and leaves behind a deeply-seated sense of frustration and dissatisfaction—though this may never be brought to the surface of consciousness and realized. So profound, however, are the consequences of sexual intercourse that they can only be adequately expressed by saying that every act initiates or maintains a state of "one flesh" which either affirms or negates its own inner meaning. In this sense sexual union is more significant for marriage than consent, and is the criterion with reference to which the character of all sexual relation must be estimated.

Derrick Sherwin Bailey
Theology

Communication of the Everyday *

Conjugal love . . . grows as the marriage progresses, thrives on companionship, common experiences, and the number of happy episodes which are scattered through a rich marriage. Conjugal love builds on the familiar, the mementos, the souvenirs, and waxes stronger with each additional year of marriage. Unlike romantic love, conjugal love is impossible for newly acquainted young people, since it requires time to form and grows from continuous association. Romantic love is greatest where each party knows least about the other—reality gets in the way of romance. This is the love that is blind.

* Reprinted by permission of the publisher, from Evelyn M. Duvall and Reuben Hill, *Being Married* (Lexington, Mass.: D. C. Heath and Company, 1960), pp. 340–342.

As conjugal love comes to the fore in marriage, the relationship is strengthened. Few marriages in America persist over any length of time without developing conjugal love sentiments, because they are based on companionship and common interests which intertwine the experiences of established marriages. In contrast, romantic love gradually disappears in the partnership marriage except for the lip service paid it in the exaggerated moments of bliss which occasionally occur throughout married life. Romantic love as a solidifying factor in marriage gives way to conjugal love, which is more mature and more compatible with the companionable features of contemporary marriages.

. . . .

Married love, which we have called conjugal love, finds expression in many day-by-day experiences. None of these is more effective as a unifying force than regular, satisfying sexual intercourse. Sex is potentially solidifying because it requires a complement of two in order to function. The regular release of tension in coitus is extremely satisfying in the purely physical sense, and in addition it serves as an expression of fulfillment for the entire relationship.

. . . .

Take a really satisfying day from the life of Fred and Mabel, who have been married long enough to have achieved a satisfactory sex adjustment. Fred comes home from a busy day at the plant full of the doings of his day. He tells Mabel about how grouchy the boss is, how green his new assistant is, how much progress he is making on his new machine, what he had for lunch, and what a funny duck he got to talking to on the way home on the bus. This conversation takes up most of the dinner hour; it leaves Fred relaxed at having spilled his day's experiences and gives Mabel the feeling that she has been a part of Fred's day.

Mabel too has things to relate. She wants to share excerpts of the letter she has just received from her folks. She is eager to discuss with Fred what they will do with her mother when her father goes (this last letter tells of another heart attack, and both

Fred and Mabel know that some day soon there will be one too
many of them). Although they don't reach a final decision,
Mabel senses that Fred is back of her, whatever happens, and
she feels a sudden burst of affection for her good old dependable
Fred right there while they are finishing dessert. She gets confidence to confess that she has been running over her budget for
the month, which they talk over with some heat. They end up
with an understanding of the financial situation, and the atmosphere is cleared, leaving them both relieved.

After supper they do the dishes together. Fred drops and
breaks the jelly dish. Mabel starts to fuss and then admits that
she hated the thing anyway. They got it last Christmas from
Aunt Harriet, whom she always has disliked. Fred grins and
says he can't stand her either, as he kisses the back of Mabel's
neck. She leans against him for a moment and observes that this
is one thing she likes about him: they both dislike the same
people.

Aunt Harriet gets a going over by both of them as they move
into the living room. Fred puts on some records that they both
enjoy and goes over his paper once more, and Mabel sews in
front of the fire. The clock strikes ten as the symphony hour
comes on. They are both tired but agree to stay up until the program is over. Mabel puts up her sewing and stretches out on the
sofa. Fred drops his paper and comes over to sit beside her. As
a favorite passage of music flows into the room, Fred squeezes
Mabel's hand and smiles into her eyes.

By bedtime there has developed a strong sense of belonging
to each other, a feeling of true unity. Sex intercourse then becomes not just a physical release, but a symbol of the whole
relationship. Into it flow the meanings and the feeling tones of
the broken jelly dish and the music and Fred's boss and Mabel's
mother and all the security that has come from working it all
through together.

Next morning Fred gets up feeling like a million, and leaves
for work with the conviction that it would take a dozen bosses to
get him down today. Mabel goes out to shop with a tune on her
lips, and in her mind a resolution to economize. Both face the

new day with more poise, more peace, more strength and courage, because the two are more than ever one.

The accompanying diagram shows roughly what the sex relationship has meant to Fred and Mabel in symbolizing their sense of unity.

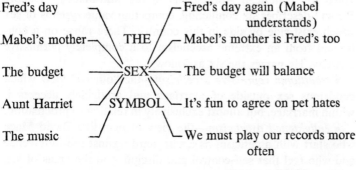

Fred's day ——— Fred's day again (Mabel understands)

Mabel's mother——— THE — Mabel's mother is Fred's too

The budget ——SEX—— The budget will balance

Aunt Harriet — SYMBOL — It's fun to agree on pet hates

The music —— We must play our records more often

EVELYN M. DUVALL
and REUBEN HILL
Marriage and Family Life

Exploring the Issues

Men and women are drawn together and engage in intercourse because of the unrelenting pressure of the sexual impulse. As a result, reproduction takes place, the race is preserved, and other values such as pleasure, permanent association, the responsibilities and joys of family life may also ensue.

But because there is no single social pattern of expression which these sexual instincts *must* take, each participant, or potential participant, must conclude for himself just what the experience of sexual intercourse means. This evaluation should include a judgment as to what this may mean both for any one individual and for the life of the social group. Despite contemporary protestations that "what we do is our own business," studies show that all human communities have found it necessary to regulate sexual expression in one way or another. And the ways in which individuals and societies express themselves sexually most often reflect the values which are ascribed to the act of intercourse.

In an issue of the *Journal of Marriage and the Family,* devoted to "American Adolescents in the Mid-Sixties," Isadore Rubin [1] describes six conflicting, competing value systems of sex which exist side by side in this country. These range on a continuum from an extreme asceticism to a completely permissive anarchy. He names the six as follows:

• *traditional repressive asceticism*—the "official" view which condemns sex outside of marriage and grudgingly accepts it within marriage, but almost exclusively in relation to procreation.

• *enlightened asceticism*—the view of men like David Mace who start with asceticism as a safeguard against self-indulgence and who feel that self-control and discipline in the areas of sex are absolutely essential.

• *humanistic liberalism*—the concept that values inhere not in sex *per se* but in the quality of the interpersonal relationship which exists or is brought into being. The chief exponent is Lester Kirkendall who is striving to supply internal controls to replace discarded external ones.

• *humanistic radicalism*—the philosophical position of Walter Stokes that society needs to be modified to the point where it will accept a code permitting almost complete sexual freedom to the young.

• *fun morality*—the proposition of Albert Ellis that sex is fun, and that the more sexual fun well-adjusted and well-informed people have, the better off they will be. Therefore, premarital sex and extramarital sex are to be permitted and at times even encouraged.

• *sexual anarchy*—within the basic restriction that no one may injure or do violence to his fellows, Rene Guyon denounces all anti-sexual taboos and calls for the elimination of all notions of sexual immorality or shame. He openly attacks chastity, virginity and monogamy.

Somewhere within this spectrum each adult must arrive at a judgment as to the way sexual intercourse should be understood and valued. To begin with, no thinking person can ignore the fact that it was through such an act that he himself was conceived. It logically follows that an act which can produce something as uniquely valuable as a human personality is itself of significant value. Thus, it may be true that the value a person ascribes to intercourse will reflect the value which he places upon man. More specifically and quite unconsciously, it may well reflect his own self-image.

The functions which intercourse performs are many and varied. For many centuries the church, which was both the giver and arbiter of morals, determined that reproduction was its only proper function.[2] While the Apostle Paul's sexual prejudices show through rather plainly, yet he is not quite as ascetic as some of his interpreters have made him out to be. Paul sees sex as a legitimate function of the marital relationship. Each of the partners has a "right" to be sexually satisfied. This he makes clear.

The husband should give to his wife her conjugal rights, and likewise the wife to her husband. For the wife does not rule over her own body, but the husband does; likewise the husband does not rule over his own body, but the wife does. Do not refuse one another except perhaps by agreement for a season. (I Cor. 7:3–5a)

The church taught Augustine's views, not Biblical views, and marriages suffered accordingly. Today the church widely recognizes the supportive, nurturative role of sex.

Intercourse is a life-authenticating experience. It relates man who lives in a brick and asphalt, neon and plastic world to something which renews his ties with nature. Further, sexual intercourse is one of the last great frontiers in which individual competition and conquest can be had. And finally, it is both a new and a renewing experience; it need not become "old hat." There can be something fresh and unique about each encounter.

The church has not produced any single, widely accepted interpretation of intercourse. However, Seward Hiltner, a theologian-counselor, presents one viewpoint which commends itself for the purposes of this manual. He writes:

CARL A. RUDISILL LIBRARY
LENOIR RHYNE COLLEGE

The essence of the Christian view is that sex is inevitably radical and serious, that it is a function of the whole human person including biology but also more than biology, that it looks toward deeper self-discovery and to the awareness of greater depth in the other, that it is a mystery in that total spiritual meanings are conveyed through biological means.[3]

In essence this is a very concise summary of the four views of sexual intercourse which follow:

    I. A Phenomenon of Nature and Culture
    II. A Source of Pleasure
    III. A Means of Discovery
    IV. A Bond Between Persons

I. *A Phenomenon of Nature and Culture*

It is a physiological fact that very few human bodies are of such shape and dimension that intercourse is an impossibility. There are relatively few physical barriers to sexual activity between almost any man and any woman. The argument often follows that since the sex organs exist as parts of the body they may be, and should be, used as indiscriminately as the individual desires.

If sexual intercourse were merely a pleasurable exercise of the genital organs, this would be permissible and perhaps even desirable behavior. But, as Reik points out, there is a profound difference between sex which is a function of nature and love which is a function of culture. Sex is focused on the self; it is essentially selfish and may be both crude and cruel. It is non-selective; any body will do for the moment. The other party is perceived as an object, rather than as a person. According to Reik, none of these things is true of love. "The object of love is always seen as a person and a personality." Love is selfless. Love is tender and concerned. It wants to help and to protect. Love is highly selective. In fact, this is one of its chief and unique characteristics. It looks outward towards another. It is discerning.

It is in the context of this definition that one should examine the study by Murdock which indicates that sexual exclusiveness is not a universal practice. The statistical truth of this can be accepted without in any way committing a person to accept it as a way of living. Murdock has been studying and reporting on a large number of cultures, some of them quite isolated from the mainstream of civilized life. It does not follow that sexual promiscuity or, at the very least, multiple liaisons are so desirable that this should be the goal of social planners. There may well be serious problems in sexually free cultures. In Melanesia, for example, it has been observed that there are very few in-depth relationships evident between men and women. American culture, on the other hand, has shaped marriage into the most intense, close relationship that history records. It is at least possible, therefore, that "the love of the islanders" just may not be very workable in the United States. And it should be reiterated that this is where most of the marriages now under discussion will be lived out.

II. *A Source of Pleasure*

There are four physical pleasures which are universal: the cessation of pain, the elimination of bodily wastes, the satisfaction of hunger and thirst, and the meeting of sexual needs. From the fourth century the church's attitude has been that intercourse is exclusively for procreation and that any pleasure received is, at worst, the result of sinful concupiscence and, at best, something that is not to be deliberately sought. One of the first recorded breaks in this tradition is found in the writings of Jeremy Taylor, a seventeenth-century English divine, who wrote that sex serves to "lighten and ease the cares and sadnesses of household affairs." [4] It is quite probable that intercourse was understood as a pleasurable experience whether or not the church approved. "Sex is the poor man's leg of mutton," is the sense of an old English proverb.

Partly because it is pleasurable, and partly because such pleasure has been so often specifically forbidden, sexual intercourse is now valued by some solely for its pleasurable aspects. Reik observes, "The expression 'to have fun' is becoming in America more and more synonymous with having sexual intercourse." [5]

The search for this "fun" has reached obsessional levels in many areas of society.

The particular view that sex is for pleasure is a natural corollary of the current American preoccupation with the rights and concerns of the individual. Sexual intercourse becomes another area in which the cause of individualism can be furthered even though the act, by definition, cannot be an individual thing. Intercourse always involves two people, each with his or her own body, personality, and needs. Since the pursuit of pleasure is usually a self-directed activity, the securing of it in the sex act, even if both partners feel fully compensated and satisfied, may still be exploitative in nature.

There are those who accept a basically hedonistic view of sex. The most verbal and consistent spokesman for this point of view is Albert Ellis, a New York psychologist, author, and editor. Ellis proposes one simple formula: *Have fun.* His single operational standard is: *Don't exploit.* In his mind there is pleasure in sex and sex is for pleasure. After describing the amount and variety of sexual and nonsexual adventure and fun which he feels men and women receive by engaging in adulterous affairs, he concludes, "These, in a world that tends to be as dull and drab for the average man as our own, are no small advantages." This is a good summary of his outlook on sex.

Ellis speaks of being scientific and yet is hardly that. He states that "sex, no matter how it is indulged, normally creates and enhances love." The researching of premarital sex liaisons by Kirkendall [6] is sufficient grounds upon which to disagree with Ellis. Kirkendall analyzes what he terms six levels of sexual liaisons— those with prostitutes and pickups, casual acquaintances, dating partners with no affection, partners with affection, and engaged couples. The overwhelming evidence is that there is very little progression from sex to love.

Another current exponent of the sex for fun concept is Hugh Hefner with his male-oriented "Playboy Philosophy." To Hefner a woman is essentially a sex object, at best an ornament and at times merely a trophy. Hefner's philosophy must ultimately be labeled as anti-feminine, anti-personal, and anti-sexual. It is clear that in his thinking the feminine gender is not to be valued as highly as the masculine; rather she is to be used primarily to enhance the male's ego, pleasure or status. He does not suggest communicating with a woman as a person, a possible mate, but as an object, only a playmate. And he does not look upon sexual intercourse as expressive of any definitive kind of personal relationship, but merely a way to secure pleasure for the male. This same pleasure, experienced apart from any personal involvement with another, is akin to the enjoyment of masturbation: sex when there is no partner.

There is here no intent to downgrade the pleasure received in intercourse. C. S. Lewis writes that this is probably the strongest element in holding a newly-married pair together long enough for them to discover they enjoy being married, in addition to enjoying the sexual pleasure involved.

III. *A Means of Discovery*

Both Greek and Hebrew mythology regard man as a male-female entity. According to the Greeks the two originally were one, became divided, and are now seeking to be reconstituted as one. This is accomplished through sexual union in which they discover one another as counterparts. In the Hebrew myth of creation in Genesis, God casts the original human entity "Adam" (man) into a deep sleep and then resolves "Adam" into its component sexual elements, viz., man and woman. The man, not understanding *how* this has happened, nevertheless perceives that the two inexplicably belong to each other and pronounces, "She at last is bone of my bones and flesh of my flesh." The truth in the myth is that there is a mystery in sex which man does not intuitively understand. But understanding does come in the experience of intercourse which the Hebrew tongue speaks of as "knowing" another. This usage is not an example of circumlocution or the employment of a delicate euphemism. It is a clear statement that in Hebrew thought sex was regarded as a means of discovery.

The unknowns to be discovered are twofold: first, a knowledge of one's self and, concurrently, a knowledge of another. The first is part of the adolescent identity crisis. The adolescent asks,

"Who am I? What am I? What does it mean to belong to one-half of the human race and not the other half? What does it mean to be a male rather than a female, and vice versa? How can I find answers to these questions?" Piper calls this "the existential problem of the purpose of my own life as a man or a woman." An empirical solution can only be gained in the experience itself. Therefore, it can be said that the first act of intercourse in maturity is profoundly significant. A man owes a tremendous debt of gratitude to the woman who first shares her sexuality with him. The same debt is owed by the woman to the man who first shares his maleness with her. Through this act, shared with another person, self-knowledge is gained which can be secured in no other way.

Hence, the first act of sexual intercourse holds an absolutely unique place in the life experience of that individual. The significance of the partner as participant and revealer cannot be over-estimated. This role will never be played by another person; this scene can never be re-enacted. Sensing this, the Biblical writers have sought to both dramatize and make concrete what has happened by declaring that this male and this female, by this mutual act of self-discovery, must henceforth be regarded as one flesh—as "Adam" reconstituted.

The generation of each person through the sexual intercourse of his parents is the first element of deep significance which must be attributed to sexual intercourse. The second is the resolution of part of the identity problem. A third lies in the way in which sexual intercourse opens up and keeps open the channels of communication. Cole indicates that the gaining of knowledge about another through intercourse can be a continual thing. The discovery of a person's own sexual identity is essentially a one-time experience; it is not repeated but only reinforced by subsequent acts. But the discovery through intercourse of the psychical depths of another person need never end.

IV. *A Bond Between Persons*

The dictionary provides two definitions of the verb *to prostitute:* viz., "to offer indiscriminately for sexual intercourse, especially for money," and "to devote to corrupt or unworthy purposes." The first is actually a concrete example of the second. Whenever sexual intercourse becomes anything significantly less than a full-orbed personal relationship, then a "corrupt or unworthy purpose" is being served. This is true because intercourse normally has within it, as a live possibility, the development of binding unions between men and women.

It has already been said that sexual intercourse is the *sine qua non* of the marriage relationship. But Bailey indicates that an act of intercourse creates a bond between persons even though the sex act was experienced outside marriage. It may be a responsible act between two persons committed to one another. This produces an authentic, valid one-flesh union. On the other hand it may be an act best described as casual, emotionally detached, noninvolving. This creates something which is a parody of the real union because it denies its very essence. The result is an unauthentic, invalid caricature.

To state the above is to say that sexual intercourse involves the whole person. Impersonal or casual sex is both a denial that there is any significance in sex and a denial of the specifically human or personal qualities of the partner. Instead of producing the integration of which sex is capable, it brings about disintegration. For something, good or ill, occurs in the life of each participant in the act of intercourse. This act can contribute to the humanness of a partner; it can also rob the partner of any sense of being human or of being treated as a person.

In any partnership there are appropriate ways of expressing the meaning of the relationship. This is especially true in marital love. The uniqueness of the "one-flesh" entity should find expression in some action that is particularly unique to it. This is provided in the act of intercourse. The exclusive form of sharing provided in the act of intercourse conveys between the two principals many facets of their life together.

Sex continues to be a specific means of "communication." It is a pathway of forgiveness and acceptance. Many feelings which cannot always be verbally expressed are communicated in sexual love. Many emotional hurts and abrasions need not be brought up for accusatory review if the sex relationship is viable enough. The process of "knowing" is a continual experience for the married couple. Marital love need not become less and less inviting or less and less meaningful. The basic feeling of love may well change in character from romantic love to conjugal love as Duvall suggests, but the heart of the whole process is still the giving and sharing of the body and of the total marital life in sexual embrace.

The potential for communicating some of the most delicate nuances of personal life through intercourse is so great that no third person can be included if the sanctity, the authenticity, and the effectiveness of the relationship are to be preserved. The involvement of a third party would, at the very best, divert some of the essential elements away from the relationship and, at worst, would threaten it with destruction.

SUGGESTIONS FOR DISCUSSION

1. How basic are Reik's distinctions between sex and love?
2. What weight should be given to statistics or to reports from various subcultures about their practices relating to sexual intercourse?
3. What basic concepts come to mind when an examination is made of the root meanings of the word *intercourse;* namely, "to run between, to exchange, to communicate"?
4. Quite often after a sexual episode the explanation or excuse is given, "But it didn't really mean anything." Is this not the heart of the problem? Can an act which potentially is so full of meaning be regarded as meaningless without some serious harm resulting?
5. Is it reasonable to expect that sexual intercourse be given the same valuation by the unmarried as it is by the married or soon-to-be married? What difference might be expected?
6. In light of the crisis of self-identity and sexual identity, discuss the significance of the first mature act of sexual intercourse.

7. Discuss the meaning of conjugal love as over against romantic
   love.

NOTES

1. Isadore Rubin, "Transition in Sex Values—Implications for the Education of Adolescents," *Journal of Marriage and the Family* XXVII (May, 1965), pp. 186–187.

2. For a concise account of the development through the centuries of religious thought dealing with sex, see Derrick Sherwin Bailey, *Sexual Relations in Christian Thought* (New York: Harper & Brothers, 1959).

3. Seward Hiltner, *Sex Ethics and the Kinsey Report* (New York: Association Press, 1953), pp. 21–22.

4. Quoted by Derrick Sherwin Bailey, *Sexual Ethics: A Christian View* (New York: The Macmillan Company, 1963), p. 90.

5. Theodor Reik, *Sex in Man and Woman* (New York: Noonday Press, 1960), p. 206.

6. Lester A. Kirkendall, *Premarital Intercourse and Interpersonal Relationships* (New York: The Julian Press, Inc., 1961).

CHAPTER **4**

Sex Before Marriage: *Yes* or *No?*

The Experts Speak

[PREMARITAL INTERCOURSE EVALUATED]

Nature and Effects of Premarital Intercourse *

It does not suffice to show that the persons who have had or who have not had premarital experience are the ones who make the best or do not make the best adjustments after marriage. For premarital intercourse is always a complexity of things. It is, in part, a question of the sort of individual who has the intercourse and the degree to which the premarital activity is acceptable or unacceptable in the individual's whole pattern of behavior. It de-

* From Alfred C. Kinsey, Wardell B. Pomeroy and Clyde E. Martin, *Sexual Behavior in the Human Male* (Philadelphia: W. B. Saunders Company, 1948), pp. 561–562.

pends upon the extent of the psychic conflict which may be evoked for an individual who transgresses the ideals and philosophies by which he has been raised, and to which he may still subconsciously adhere. For a person who believes that premarital intercourse is morally wrong there may be, as the specific histories show, conflicts which can do damage not only to marital adjustments, but to the entire personality of the individual. For a person who really accepts premarital intercourse, and who in actuality is not in conflict with himself when he engages in such behavior, the outcome may be totally different.

Again, the effects of premarital intercourse depend upon the nature of the partners with whom it is had, and the degree to which the activity becomes promiscuous. It is a question of the nature of the female partners, whether it is had with girls of the same social level or with girls of lower social levels, whether it is had as a social relationship or as a commercial relation, whether or not it is had with the fiancée before marriage. The effect of premarital intercourse upon the marital adjustment may depend upon the extent to which the female partner accepts the intercourse, and the extent to which the male accepts the idea of his wife's having had intercourse before he married her. Even in those cases where both the spouses believe that they accept the idea, situations of stress after marriage may bring the issue up for recriminations.

The significance of premarital intercourse depends upon the situation under which it is had. If it is had under conditions which are physically uncomfortable and not conducive to a mutually satisfactory relationship, if it is had under conditions which leave the individuals disturbed for fear that they have been or will be detected, the outcome is one thing. If it is had under satisfying circumstances and without fear, the outcome may be very different.

. . . .

The significance of premarital intercourse depends upon the success or failure with which the couple avoids an unwanted pregnancy. It is much affected even by the fear of such a pregnancy. . . .

. . . It is, of course, equally inadequate to treat marital happiness as a unit character. There are many factors which may affect marital adjustment, and the identification of the part which the sexual factor plays must depend on an exceedingly acute understanding of the effects of all these other factors.

ALFRED C. KINSEY
Social Sciences

Benefits of Premarital Intercourse *

There are, nonetheless, many obvious benefits to be derived from antenuptial sex relations. Here are some of them:

1. *Sexual Release.* Most human beings require some form of steady sexual release for their maximum healthfulness, happiness, and efficient functioning. If these individuals are not married—which many millions of them, of course, are not —perhaps the best form of release from sexual tension they may obtain is through having heterosexual premarital relations.

2. *Psychological Release.* In many, though by no means all, instances individuals who do not have premarital affairs are beset with serious psychosexual strain and conflict and tend to be obsessed with sexual thoughts and feelings. Most of these individuals can be considerably relieved of their psychosexual hypertension if they have satisfactory nonmarital affairs.

3. *Sexual Competence.* In sexual areas, as in most other fields of human endeavor, practice makes perfect and familiarity breeds contempt for fear. In the cases of millions of unmarried males and females who are relatively impotent or frigid, there is little doubt that if they engaged in steady heterosexual relations they would become enormously more sexually competent.

4. *Ego Enhancement.* Although . . . engaging in premarital

* From Albert Ellis, *Sex Without Guilt* (New York: Lyle Stuart, 1958 and 1966), pp. 46–48.

affairs involves distinct risks, especially the risks of being rejected or emotionally hurt, there is almost no other way that a human being can enhance his self-esteem and desensitize himself to emotional vulnerability except by deliberately taking such risks.

Confirmed male and female virgins in our culture usually dislike themselves immensely, knowing that they do not have the guts to live.

5. *Adventure and Experience.* A rigorous restraint from premarital affairs leads to neutrality or nothingness: to a lack of adventure and experience. Particularly in this day and age, when there are few remaining frontiers to explore and unscaled mountains to climb, nonmarital affairs furnish a prime source of sensory-esthetic-emotional experimentation and learning.

6. *Improved Marital Selection.* Because marriage, in our society, is usually infrequent and long-lasting for any given individual, the person who marries should have the kind of knowledge and training that will best fit him to make a good marital choice. There is little doubt that the very best experience he can acquire in this connection is to have one or more premarital affairs and, through these affairs, be able to discover much relevant information about himself and members of the other sex.

Moreover: the individual who has such affairs is well able to wait patiently until he is in a good psychological and socioeconomic condition to marry; while he who has no such affairs is often impelled to make a rash and poorly selected marriage out of (conscious or unconscious) sexual deprivation.

ALBERT ELLIS
Behavioral Sciences

A Redefinition of Virginity *

Just what does premarital chastity entail? Technically, it means that a person has not engaged in behavior involving the penetration of the vagina by the penis. In the case of the female, it also means that the woman is expected to possess a hymen, *i.e.*, the fold which partially blocks the opening to the vagina. These physical conditions of virginity can and are met by persons who have engaged in genital apposition, mutual masturbation, and mutual oral-genital stimulation, to mention but a few of the heavy petting practices fairly common among our virginal groups. Moreover, one could have indulged in these practices with scores of partners and still be considered virginal. Now, does such a definition of virginity delineate those who are likely to be faithful?

. . . .

The "promiscuous virgins" of petting without affection do not seem especially likely to be faithful in marriage. Such females have not built up a standard of discrimination; they have not controlled their sexual activity according to the affection they felt, nor have they discriminated on any other basis besides physical attraction. It is true that such a female has avoided sexual intercourse, but in a technical sense only. Orgasm experienced by bare genital contact is quite close to orgasm experienced by actual coitus. How much difference in her character would it have made if such a female had actually copulated? This sort of promiscuous virginity brings to mind the story of the man who, while ill for an entire month, was being fed by intravenous injections instead of by mouth. The man later claimed he had not really eaten for that month because no food entered his mouth. In a technical sense, he was right. But in a more meaningful sense, this man and a promiscuous virgin are both more accurately classified as "experienced."

. . . .

* Reprinted with permission of The Macmillan Company from *Premarital Sexual Standards in America* by Ira L. Reiss. © 1960 by The Free Press, a Corporation.

Such a physical definition might not be so faulty if our interest were only in a physical state, but most people are interested in what they believe such a physical state symbolizes—the presence of a "pure" female or male; one who will be faithful in marriage. In order to see if this connection necessarily exists, compare a promiscuous virgin female with a non-virginal female who accepts permissiveness with affection. Who is more likely to be faithful in marriage—everything else being equal—a woman who has experienced a few affairs involving coitus with men she loved, or a woman who has experienced scores of relationships involving heavy petting with men for whom she did not care. It seems probable that the non-virginal woman will have built up habits of associating sex with affection, of monogamous affairs, of emotional maturity, which all may tend toward faithfulness in marriage. The petting without affection adherent does not seem so likely to have developed such attitudes and habits. I think we can all agree that, in this case, the virgin, from a theoretical point of view, certainly seems to be more likely to be unfaithful than the non-virgin.

It seems more reasonable to determine faithfulness by an examination of a person's attitudes and beliefs rather than by an examination of physical characteristics. As shown previously, a female who is non-virginal physically may be virginal mentally, *i.e.,* her attitudes may be discriminatory and likely to lead to faithfulness in marriage.

IRA L. REISS
Social Sciences

[NEW SEXUAL STANDARDS PROPOSED]

Sanctioning of Experimental Love *

Often, however, love does not choose right the first time. I should rather say, first love often does not choose permanently right. Many teen-age "pashes" and "crushes," however violent at the time, and many cases of adolescent calf-love, though often valuable and indeed "right" in the sense of providing necessary experience to the callow personality, are soon outgrown.

Even when it comes to marriage, many first choices are wrong, and later ones may be much more right. The relation between love and marriage urgently needs reconsideration. For one thing, in our Western societies, we have become too credulous about romantic love, just as earlier ages were too credulous about religious faith. Both can often be blind, and then both can mislead us. For another, we have become obsessed with the rigid moralists' stern insistence on the inviolability and indissolubility of marriage—a religious doctrine imposed on a social bond.

The emotional certitude of being in love with someone does not guarantee either its rightness, or its uniqueness, or its permanence, any more than it insures that the love shall be reciprocated. And the undoubted general desirability, both social and personal, of long-enduring monogamous marriage does not preclude the occasional desirability of divorce and change of marriage partner, nor justify the branding of any extramarital love as a grave social immorality or personal sin.

. . . .

Love presents, in intensive form, man's central and perennial problem—how to reconcile the claims of the individual and of society, personal desires with social aims. The problem is perhaps most acute in adolescence, for this involves a disharmony of

* From Julian Huxley, *New Bottles for New Wine* (New York: Harper & Brothers, 1957), pp. 226–229. Reprinted by permission of A. D. Peters & Company.

timing: our sexual desires arise, and in males arise in fullest
force, several years before marriage is desirable or possible.
Different cultures have met this problem in very different ways.
Thus in eighteenth-century England and in nineteenth-century
France it was the acknowledged thing for upper-class young men
to take a mistress, while this was frowned on in Geneva and New
England. In twentieth-century America, dating and petting have
superseded "bundling" as the recognized formula.

. . . .

In modern civilization the problem is very real and very
serious. On the one hand, clearly both undisciplined indulgence
and complete promiscuity in love are individually damaging, or
anti-social, or both; but on the other hand, complete repression
of this most powerful of impulses is equally damaging, and so is
the self-reproach that the indulgence or even the mere manifesta-
tion of the impulse arouses in sensitive adolescents who have had
an exaggerated sense of sin imposed on them. From another
angle, it is tragic to think of millions of human beings denied
the full beauty and exaltation of love precisely while their impulses are strongest and their sensibilities at their highest pitch.

. . . .

Love between the sexes can provide some of the highest fulfilments of life. It also provides an important means for the development of personality: through it we learn many necessary
things about ourselves, about others, about society, and about
human ideals. We must, I think, aim at a moral and religious
climate of society in which the adolescent experiments of love,
instead of being branded as wicked or relegated to furtive and
illicit gropings, or repressed until they collapse in neurosis or
explode in lust, or merely tolerated as an unpleasing necessity,
are socially sanctioned and religiously sanctified, in the same sort
of way as marriage is now. Adolescent affairs of the heart could
be regarded as reverent experiments in love, or as trial marriages,
desirable preparations for the more enduring adventure of adult
marriage. Young people would assuredly continue to make mistakes, to be selfish or lustful or otherwise immoral; but matters

would I am sure be better than they are now, and could not well be much worse.

JULIAN HUXLEY
Philosophy

Permissiveness with Affection *

... As one looks at our past, particularly at the double standard, one finds that sexual activity was usually a divisive force— a force which kept men and women from really knowing and loving each other. . . .

By forbidding premarital coitus to the female, the double standard makes premarital relations a forbidden fruit and sets up a barrier between men and women. Girls use sex as the bait, and men use lines to obtain the lure. Sex becomes a weapon between men and women.

Permissiveness with affection, together with petting with affection and the transitional double standard, are changing this situation. For the first time in thousands of years, we have sexual standards which tend to unify rather than divide men and women. Especially in permissiveness with affection, coitus is no longer forbidden, and the motivation to deceive the opposite sex in order to obtain pleasure is greatly reduced. For the first time in many millenniums, Western society is evolving sexual standards which will tend to make men and women better able to understand and live with each other.

Past sexual standards were developed by parents—by those in authority. These standards were devised, consciously and unconsciously, so as to make the "best" match for offspring. As has been shown, about the end of the nineteenth century, the balance of power in mating choice shifted to the young people themselves. Things changed quite rapidly. Love became the crucial basis for marriage. Still, the young people kept the older, adult-devised

* Reprinted with permission of The Macmillan Company from *Premarital Sexual Standards in America* by Ira L. Reiss. © 1960 by The Free Press, a Corporation.

sexual code and tried to adjust to it. Now a new code is being fashioned and, for the first time, by young people themselves. Since they are the ones to choose their mates, they must also decide how to act in courtship. Because this new code is being devised by young people, it is concerned with their problems and desires. The situation today is most sharply distinguished from the past in that sexual behavior is now almost fully separated from pregnancy and marriage, if one so desires. That is, the chances of pregnancy occurring can now be controlled, and since marriages are arranged by young people themselves, they need not marry the person they have sexual relations with, and parents cannot force them to do so. In the past, the only time sexual behavior could be separated from pregnancy and marriage was when it occurred in a house of prostitution. This exclusive franchise no longer exists.

Our newer affectionate standards merely say "not all sex is bad," they do not say "all sex is equally good" or "all sex is good but some better." They have thus not fully lost their Puritanism. Many of the believers in these newer sex codes think they are holding "individual" beliefs. In reality, their beliefs are social and are well rooted in our emerging society. Permissiveness with affection, for example, is based on our cultural blending of sex and affection and on our custom of allowing free choice of one's mate. Such a new code is no more an individual matter than was our older double standard or abstinence code which was rooted in parental choice of mate customs and the separation of sex and affection.

The transition to a newer code has occurred along with the change in marriage from a union of two families to a union of individuals. As this change took place, economic reasons for controlling one's children's sexual behavior lessened, and the balance of power moved from the parents to the young people themselves. This, of course, is not an all-or-none matter—parents still have some say in mate choice. But, as parental controls diminished, new sexual codes were devised by the young people themselves—more liberal codes, to be sure, but codes which nonetheless were still rooted in our past. Permissiveness without affection and the strong-affection subtype of permissiveness with affection are, to a great extent, free of our older sexual taboos, but these are minority positions. Nevertheless, the newer affectionate codes are new in that unlike the orthodox double standard, they have linked sex and love, and they are capable of generating understanding between men and women. This is indeed something new in Western society.

IRA L. REISS
Social Sciences

Building on Interpersonal Relationships *

. . . What can adults working with young people do to help them think through the issues involved in premarital intercourse so as to achieve better personal interrelationships?

First, I return to my earlier suggestion that the central concern must be for improved personal interrelationships rather than with sex *per se*. This means a reorientation in thinking for many, but it is an approach which "makes sense" to young people in a way no other approach does. At the same time, it is in harmony with religious concepts. It is spelling out so far as sex behavior is concerned, the meaning of the injunction, "Love thy neighbor as thyself," and of the Golden Rule. It answers positively the question, "Am I my brother's keeper?" It puts sexual morality on a meaningful basis.

. . . .

Second, the . . . counselor and teacher needs to remember that young persons cannot and ought not to be forced into any pattern of sexual behavior. No one, minister, parent, counselor, or teacher, can supervise young people so closely, or teach with such authority, that they can insure no "stepping out of bounds" sexually. Their very success would result in inhibitions so severe as to destroy the whole spontaneity of life, and make the individ-

---

* From Lester A. Kirkendall, "Premarital Sex Relations: The Problem and Its Implications," *Pastoral Psychology* VII (April, 1956), pp. 46–53.

ual an emotional invalid. They can only give young people help in thinking through their problems, and hope that when they do have to make actual decisions they will be able to make them wisely. The problem is that young people today are called upon to make many decisions without guidance, adequate information, or insight.

. . . .

By the freedom which has been extended an engaged couple in our society we seem to have implied that, if after weighing the evidence conscientiously and sincerely they decide to enter intercourse, it is their own business. Having thus relaxed our sanctions, logically we should re-examine the basis of our judgments. They should be made in terms of the demonstrated effects which intercourse has upon the quality of interrelationships between the partners and the larger society, now and later.

We will be able to accept this view only as we are able to be less shocked and fearful of sex. Many young people have premarital intercourse and go on living successful and happy lives. Others, of course, meet with unhappy and even disastrous experiences. Our failure to discuss sex matters and issues freely as we do other issues of consequence has, however, left us unaware of the possibilities, outcomes, and problems involved in this area of conduct.

Third, we need to be realistic about the existing situation as it is related to sex standards. Young people themselves are fully aware of conditions. Data from the Kinsey research have been printed in most of the widely circulated publications. Newspapers and magazines carry numerous articles on almost every aspect of sexual functioning. Sexual intercourse is a common topic of conversation at the high school level. . . . Contraceptive information of a kind is available to most high school youth, and about as frequently the contraceptives themselves.

Fourth, we need to build a different concept of the nature of sex and sex education. Young people ask for help on interrelationships. What they are given is either reproductive or physiological information or strictures against certain kinds of behavior without accompanying insight or understanding. They want help in understanding the emotional aspects of their sexual nature and that of the other sex, together with outcomes which can result from the various possible uses of sex in relationships with other persons.

. . . .

Sexual feelings will always be a part of the normal individual. A knowledge of his own motivations and needs, however, helps a great deal in living easily with sex. Individuals can order and direct their sexual impulses in much the same manner that they manage their other impulses. This capacity for direction is again influenced by psychological factors. The person who is more mature emotionally, is achieving normally in his educational and occupational pursuits, and who feels himself loved and appreciated has a greater capacity for self-direction of his sexual impulses. So, in a very real sense, the greatest assistance we can give a person in achieving sexual morality is to help him toward maturity, give him a sense of individual worth and acceptance, and help him attain satisfying personal interrelationships.

LESTER A. KIRKENDALL
Marriage and Family Life

[NEW THEOLOGICAL VIEWPOINTS PRESENTED]

Chastity Defined as Sexual Honesty *

. . . The inductive point of view starts from the primacy of persons and personal relationships. It insists, to quote Howard Root's eminently sane and, I should have thought, unexceptionable lecture on "Ethical Problems of Sex" in *God, Sex and War,* that "marriage, like the Sabbath, was made for man, not man for marriage." But one has only to say this to be suspected of advocating laxity and immorality. In fact, it is to plead for a

---

* From *Christian Morals Today,* by John A. T. Robinson. Published in the U.S.A. by The Westminster Press. Copyright © 1964 SCM Press. Limited. Used by permission.

much more searching and demanding criterion of ethical judgment, both inside and outside marriage, than the simple application of an external rule. The ground on which the decision must be based is what deep Christian love for the other person as a whole person (as opposed to exploitation and enjoyment, even if mutual) really demands—and that within the total social context. Now one of the factors, indeed a major factor, in this decision is the unity I referred to before between bed and board. Outside marriage sex is bound to be the expression of less than an unreserved sharing and commitment of one person to another. It certainly cannot be guaranteed as such within marriage, but in both cases this is the moral criterion. The decisive thing in the moral judgment is not the line itself, but the presence or absence of love at the deepest level. The inductive approach rests upon the fact that at this ultimate level, in the sight of God (and here is where the Christian finds himself constrained by the distinctive revelation of *agape* in the face of Jesus Christ), persons matter more, imponderably more, than any principles. And therefore principles can never *dictate* to persons, however, much they may help them (and often, indeed, save them) in their moral choices.

. . . .

But in sex ethics in general, Christians seem to *fear* changes in fact, as weakening the moral foundations. This in turn provokes non-Christians into embracing them as *providing* moral foundations, which of course, they can never do: for no "is" can of itself supply an "ought." Thus, we have the familiar sterile antithesis. On the one hand there are those who say that no social or physical changes can make any essential difference to moral judgments: the principles remain the same and unaffected. On the other hand, we have those (often indiscriminately identified with "the new morality") who say that trends in our society, or the strength of sex impulses, or the widening gap between physical maturity and educational independence, are themselves reasons for changing our morals. The effect of both attitudes is to restrict the area of personal responsibility for decision. In the former case, the moral judgment is already settled beforehand: the individual has simply to choose whether to accept it.

In the latter case, the issue has ceased to be debated at the moral level: the individual has merely to decide with which impulses, trends or conventions to go along.

My concern is that Christians, in love as in war, should *have* the terrible freedom with which God has endowed us, and should exercise it responsibly. They must decide *for themselves*—though this certainly does not mean that they must decide on their own. They should not be loaded with the burden of decision alone. Nevertheless, the Church cannot take it *from* them. . . .

I am concerned that the young, like others, should genuinely be free—to decide responsibly for themselves what love at its deepest really requires of them. But there could hardly be anything further from that than "free love"—which is usually neither "love" nor "free".

Consider, for instance, this conversation from the film, *Room at the Top:* "I *do* love you," she protests; "I would do anything for you." "Sure," he retorts, "you would do anything—except the one thing any girl would do for the man she loves." So she succumbs—the victim of emotional blackmail.

That is not love. It is much more fear than love—fear of losing him if she doesn't. Under that sort of fear, persons are not free. And thousands of young people today are simply being played upon in this matter of sex. They cannot afford not to go along with the rest. "Dread of being a social outcast is the main reason why teenagers have sexual intercourse before marriage," writes a girl student in *Sixth Form Opinion*.

I want a morality which frees people from that. But I know we shall not get it by simply saying "Thou shalt not!" a bit louder. Young people today ask "Why?" They want a basis for morality that makes sense in terms of personal relationships. They want *honesty* in sex, as in everything else. And that is what chastity is —inside marriage or out of it. It is not just abstinence. It is honesty in sex: having physical relationships that *truthfully express* the degree of personal commitment that is there underneath.

JOHN A. T. ROBINSON
Theology

Biblical Concept of Responsible Freedom *

One cannot, however, have it both ways. To set up a series of "Thou shalt nots," clearly labeled as sins, either mortal or venial, is plainly to rob men of their freedom. And such a series, while it may control behavior, cannot control inner attitudes and desires. To emphasize spontaneity and freedom in an individual motivated by love of God and neighbor, on the other hand, is to invite the possibility of misdemeanors and misdeeds, no matter how pure the spirit involved. The issue squarely before the world of Dr. Kinsey is a crucial question of policy. Given the gross violations of society's legal codes, what shall be done? Should the laws be strengthened, the sanctions increased, an even sterner morality enjoined? Or, is a radically new direction indicated, an entirely different method called for? To the present writer, the indications point inescapably to the latter. . . .

What seems required is a new approach, based squarely upon a biblical understanding of Christian freedom. . . .

The emphasis must be exactly where the New Testament places it, on the inner motivation and not the outer act. It is never enough to concentrate narrowly on what people do. That is the method of Kinsey and company: to deal with sexual relations as contacts. We must always ask the deeper questions: "What does the act mean?" "Why are they acting as they do?" Holding hands or a good-night kiss may, from this perspective, be harmful and evil if persons are being treated as things, as mere bodies to be exploited for personal pleasure. The central importance must be given to love—not romantic, erotic love, as the modern world understands it, an ephemeral, highly unstable motion of the feelings, but *agape,* which means respect, reverence, and concern for persons as channels through whom Christ confronts us, saying, "Inasmuch as ye have done it unto one of the least of these my brethren, ye have done it unto me." To abuse another human being is to do violence to God and to self.

* From William Graham Cole, *Sex and Love in the Bible* (New York: Association Press, 1959), pp. 428–434.

The law of love means that we cannot allow our personal whims to dictate our treatment of others. Every man lays claim to our compassion and our concern. This is the measuring rod which must be set beside our sexual acts and attitudes, rather than a law outside of ourselves declaring arbitrarily what we may or may not do. It is not this or that act which is right or wrong, but the inner meaning of the act, the motivation it represents and the attitude it carries. Those who are fearful of reliance on love and therefore retreat to law are thinking of romantic love, rather than of love as the New Testament understands it. *Agape* is responsible love, not selfish, unstable emotion.

Given, then, the centrality of the law of love, the Christian man can say with Paul, "All things are lawful for me." The question so frequently asked by young people, "How far is it all right to go?" becomes meaningless because it focuses entirely on external behavior. It may not be "all right" to go anywhere at all if selfish sensuality is being expressed. On the other hand, it may be "all right" to go quite a way if one is operating in a context of mutual love, respect, and reverence. But no one outside can determine the limits. This is a decision each couple must make in fear and trembling, recognizing that there are risks involved at every step and that the risks increase, the more steps are taken. But life itself is filled with risks, and no one can avoid them. The moralistic law seeks to deliver us from responsibility for our acts, guaranteeing us objective certainty from outside ourselves. But no law can deliver us from responsibility or risk, for we must take the responsibility for accepting its claim upon us and run the risk that it may be wrong. . . . We cannot evade the necessity of answering for our acts; we cannot shift the burden to an infallible Book, to an infallible Church, or to an infallible Law. For we are the ones who agree to the infallibility, and we may be wrong!

. . . .

The biblical conception of responsible freedom seems the only viable alternative in the present parlous situation of sexual anarchy. Some express fear that the young under such guidance might go astray, misunderstanding or rationalizing. That such a possibility exists clearly cannot be denied. But it is painfully apparent that the young are certainly "going astray" anyhow, despite the specific prohibitions and dire warnings from moralistic legalism. Perhaps a new approach might prove more effective. If young people are going to misbehave, all of the external restrictions in the world cannot keep them from it. The only practical barriers to misbehavior are internal ones, built into the self and therefore willingly affirmed and accepted.

WILLIAM GRAHAM COLE
Theology

[TRADITIONAL POSITIONS RESTATED]

Reserving of Sex for Marriage *

Two people of opposite sexes can create more enduring happiness in a permanent relationship than in any temporary affair. Their mutual pleasure in each other is more than instinct in action. Their satisfaction comes from learning to respond fully and completely to one another. Their response depends upon adjusting to each other mentally and emotionally as well as physically. Their full enjoyment as a couple therefore normally grows as they grow, and develops as they develop more and more experiences and interests in common.

Sexual intercourse reserved for marriage enjoys a maximum of security and privacy. The married couple are expected to live together as husband and wife. They enjoy their intimate moments with one another with a feeling that what they are doing is right, has the blessing of their family and friends, and the approval of society. They come together secure in each other and in their relationship. As a married couple they have privacy and per-

* From Evelyn Millis Duvall, *Why Wait Till Marriage?* (New York: Association Press, 1965), pp. 89–90.

manence—two precious factors usually lacking in love affairs not blessed by marriage.

Married lovers come together free of guilt and shame. They have fewer qualms of conscience than do those who are haunted by the ghostly reminders of previous affairs. Jealousies born of comparisons with former partners are avoided by husband and wife who wait for marriage before being active sexually. It is a rare husband who is completely happy in the knowledge that his wife has slept with some other man before she married him. Even the most sophisticated lover is proud to marry a virgin whom he alone possesses. The predominant reaction of wives discovering their husbands' premarital experience with previous girl friends is unfavorable, according to Professors Burgess and Wallin. Sex reserved for marriage starts out with a clean slate upon which the married partners write their own love story in their own way from the beginning.

When sexual gratification is available only in marriage, it becomes unique. This special quality of the husband-wife relationship strengthens their union and stabilizes their marriage. Emotionally the two associate their sex life with marriage, and so are continually rewarded as they build their home together. Their thoughts are of each other as they develop a common past, and as they plan for a mutual future as wedded lovers. Such sex partners become partners in parenthood secure upon the strong foundation of marriage and family life.

. . . .

Numerous studies over the past thirty years find premarital chastity associated with both engagement success and marital adjustment. There are some with previous sex experience who make successful marriages. There is some evidence that physical sexual adjustment in marriage is somewhat related to sex experience. But there is more to a good marriage relationship than an immediately satisfactory sexual adjustment. In general, premarital chastity is a favorable beginning for a marriage, for one's own marriage adjustment, and for the happiness of one's marriage partner.

. . . .

The simple conclusion is that intercourse is most meaningful when you are living together as husband and wife. Sex in marriage celebrates the simplest joy and symbolizes the most profound faith two people can know. As a unique thread through marriage, sex weaves significance into the warp and woof of everyday living in a way that is impossible otherwise. Sex belongs in marriage for the sake of continuing, complete fulfillment of man and wife, and for the sake of the marriage and family that it secures.

EVELYN MILLIS DUVALL
Marriage and Family Life

Value of Premarital Continence *

An integral (but sometimes overlooked) part of the problem of social change is the fact that many people, both young and old, have now arrived at a point where they have accepted change—change in any form—as a value in itself. For them, that which is traditional has become suspect. This has led to value conflict and even more difficulty for parents who would like to preserve something of our cultural heritage of sexual morality, yet at the same time don't want to appear old-fashioned or, if you will, "square" by sternly denouncing all premarital sexual activity.

Moreover, some of the same social changes which have conditioned our society continually to upgrade the value of change itself, have increasingly caused many people to downgrade the value of premarital chastity. Increased cross-class associations, theoretically better contraceptive devices, supposedly improved venereal disease control, the all-pervasive commercial glorification of sex, and the general "eat, drink, and be merry" philosophy of these times of boom and crisis, have all contributed to the demotion of premarital continence from its former status as a

* From *The Family and Sexual Revolution,* edited by Edwin M. Schur. Copyright © 1964 by Indiana University Press. Reprinted by permission of the publisher. Pp. 83–85.

first-class cultural value. One need look no further than some of our marriage relations books which include sections on "positive values of premarital intercourse" to see how far the quasi-official downgrading of chastity has gone. By contrast, it is still almost unthinkable that any American book would have a section on the positive values of blasphemy, trampling the flag, or eating human flesh.

But in place of chastity, no widely acceptable "modern" standard of sexual behavior has been offered from any source. "Permissiveness with affection," identified by Ira Reiss as a contemporary observed "standard," actually has very little that is standard about it. There is no standard for the degree of permissiveness to be offered and no standard for the degree of affection to be required. Moreover, the distinction between permissiveness with affection and outright sexual exploitation is dependent upon a knowledge and perception of adult motivation and emotional reaction that is almost unteachable to inexperienced children. . . .

And most of the suggestions from professional counselors and educators—both moralist and anti-moralist—in recent years have done little to help parents with their practical problems in moral education, regardless of the theoretical merits of those suggestions. Robert Harper, along with Albert Ellis, has been insistent that parents, in dealing with children, should "stop teaching them that premarital sexual intercourse is bad" and instead ". . . teach them how to exercise their own critical faculties about deciding under what sorts of circumstances and with what sorts of partners it is likely to be functionally desirable for all parties concerned." But even the parent who is emotionally able to adjust to the unconventionality of these directions and who is able to accept their implications both for child and for society, soon finds that the proponents have few practical suggestions to offer as to how such teaching may be effectively accomplished with normal, sexually curious but emotionally immature, children. Moreover, Ellis himself concedes that parents who try to carry out such directions ". . . not only have to explain their view to their own children (which is difficult to do when the children are quite young), but they also have to explain that other people think differently, and that there might be difficulties in presenting their views to these others. Raising children in a nonconformist manner, therefore, is much harder than raising them to conform to the sexual prejudices of their community."

Ultimately, however, perhaps the most insidious of all the confusions impeding more effective moral guidance is the widely believed allegation that premarital sexual intercourse has become so general that we can no longer hope for *any* real premarital sexual morality on the part of young people. The implication of this is that no fair-minded parent or educator should expect his child to buck the trend and stand up against the alleged majority in defiance of the supposedly steady march toward complete sexual freedom. No one actually knows for sure how far this trend has gone in the main stream of our society. But many people, fearing the worst, seem to feel that about all they can do now is to help children protect themselves from unwanted pregnancies by handing out contraceptive advice.

While there may be wide regional and subcultural differences, this complete defeatism concerning young people's current sexual morality seems unwarranted for our society as a whole. After some years of counseling and teaching and after examining the complete returns from the Alabama survey which is the main subject of this paper, it seems clear to the writer that individual young people (especially young women) can still be taught to believe in the personal importance of premarital continence to the point where these beliefs are not negative inhibitions, but positive values from which they can gain self-esteem. One 22-year-old woman student told how she thought it should be done in the survey. She said:

Parents must teach their children in such a way that they will not want to go counter to what they believe to be right and just and good. Done this way, taboos become wilful self-restraints. They are not set out as things that under the prevailing circumstances the child himself wishes not to become part of him. This has worked for me; I would not want it otherwise.

RICHARD H. KLEMER
Marriage and Family Life

Exploring the Issues

The church's traditional view of the place of sexual intercourse in male-female relationships has been expressed succinctly:

Sexual intercourse finds its proper fulfillment only in marriage. It is indissolubly related to marriage, to the fulfillment of a man's or a woman's life in terms of the most intimate union and companionship known on earth, and to the establishment of a home and the rearing of children.[1]

Too often in the past the church has merely stated its conclusions on this subject without bothering to document its position, or to take seriously those who might disagree. The assumption has been that these are self-evident truths. Consequently, when this position has been seriously challenged, the reaction has ranged from righteous indignation to panic to paralysis. Dietrich Bonhoeffer, whose theological insights have radically affected the last thirty years of Protestant thinking, wrote in his *Ethics:*

The Church confesses that she has found no word of advice and assistance in the face of the dissolution of all order in the relation between the sexes. She has found no strong and effective answer to the contempt for chastity and to the proclamation of sexual libertinism. All she has achieved has been an occasional expression of moral indignation.[2]

Since the church has been one of the chief proponents of premarital continence of an absolute kind, this is an admission of serious failure.

But today this statement of Bonhoeffer is no longer applicable. In recent years there has been a serious re-searching by the church of the relationship between the sexes. This chapter contains some insights, both old and new, from the church and from without the church, that apply to the specific question of premarital intercourse.

It it not necessary to document at any length the widespread divergence between preaching and practice, between sense and nonsense, in the area of sexual behavior in America. Within a sensual atmosphere almost completely devoid of restraining influence, the young are handed the sexual codes of bygone days and told to live by them. Meanwhile, the automobile, the contraceptive pill, the penicillin shot, and mass media have revolutionized sexual life. Appeals to shame and to fear have lost their force even though the numbers of out-of-wedlock pregnancies and the incidence of venereal disease are both on the increase.

In the United States there are around 1,000,000 premarital pregnancies each year; some 300,000 result in marriage. About 300,000 babies are born out of wedlock, most of whom are placed for adoption, and a minimum of 300,000 abortions are performed. This latter is considered a very low estimate. These statistics all indicate the same thing; namely, that there is in operation a social, cultural code which declares that marriage and childbearing go exclusively together. Whether marriage and sexual intercourse are also exclusively joined together is *the* sexual question of the day.

This subject of premarital intercourse is examined under four headings:

    I. Premarital Intercourse Evaluated
   II. New Sexual Standards Proposed
  III. New Theological Viewpoints Presented
  IV. Traditional Positions Restated

I. *Premarital Intercourse Evaluated*

If the question of the rightness, wrongness or appropriateness of premarital intercourse were to be decided on the basis of common practice, the issue would be resolved without much argument. In 1948, Kinsey reported that, except for the 15 per cent of the population going to college, "most males actually accept premarital intercourse, and believe it to be a desirable part of a normal human development." [3] His associates now believe that even this exception no longer prevails. In the companion volume dealing with female sexual behavior, Kinsey reports that by the age of twenty-five about 35 per cent of the unmarried females in his total sample had experienced intercourse. [4]

Kinsey makes far fewer claims than many of his readers. His sense of scientific objectivity prompts him to observe: "Premarital intercourse is always a complexity of things." He points out that the effects of premarital intercourse on the individuals involved are dependent upon a host of factors, some of which cannot be determined in advance. Questions like the following come to the fore: "Who is involved? What is the situation? Have any codes been violated? If so, how much guilt can be tolerated?" Reiss concurs in Kinsey's judgment that people cannot go beyond their own standards without risk of severe psychic conflict.[5] And Kirkendall writes: "Participation in premarital intercourse is like driving a speeding car on a crowded roadway; the consequences of the experience can be known for certain only after the course had been run." [6]

Ellis is not as restrained nor as scientifically objective as Kinsey. Many of his statements will be recognized as unsupported assertions. It is doubtful, for instance, if Ellis can document his claim that "confirmed . . . virgins in our culture usually dislike themselves immensely, knowing they do not have the guts to live." He is probably correct, however, in indicating that sexual adventure can lead to ego enhancement, and his observation that some people rush into poor marriages because they are sexually deprived has substance.

Too often the basic issues of sexual relationships have been obscured by what Cox refers to as "dead-end arguments about virginity and chastity." [7] It may be of far greater importance to discuss the meaning virginity has for the individual rather than merely to ascertain that it exists. Even to accomplish the latter is extremely difficult in the midst of some of the heavy petting practices of the day.

Reiss points up a real issue when he expresses doubt that a woman—a "promiscuous virgin," to use his term—who pets to orgasm with many different men whom she does not love and yet never really engages in intercourse is developing attitudes that will lead to "fidelity to persons." He contends that a woman who has had only a few affairs involving intercourse with men she loved is a person "whose attitudes may be discriminatory and likely to lead to faithfulness in marriage." For attitudinally she is a person with a virgin mentality.

Reiss' examples are too broadly drawn. There are many other options open between these two extremes. It is almost as if he were to claim that one bullet in the head is much better than two. Actually, either experience is detrimental to well-being and may well prove fatal. No bullets at all would be far preferable.

II. *New Sexual Standards Proposed*

There is little question but that social trends are oftentimes nonreversible. But the direction in which they go is not beyond some control. This is one of the presuppositions of education. The three men whose proposals for new sexual codes are here examined are of one mind in believing that the trend in sexual relationships has gone so far, and the problems with the old views have become so overwhelming, that, instead of seeking to reinforce or rebuild the old, new ways of relating sexually must be found. They offer three separate but similar approaches to the problem of regulating sexual intercourse before marriage.

In America, as in many other places, the height of the physical sexual drive normally comes several years before the adolescent is ready for marriage as society defines it. Huxley suggests that this cannot be overlooked any longer and that society must recognize it not by dangerous suppression, but by finding a place for adolescent experiments in love. He wants marriage restructured in such a way that adolescent sex activities become socially and religiously acceptable and are regarded as "reverent experiments in love, or as trial marriages."

Reiss reports on a new movement in which young people are developing their own codes—codes which will unite rather than divide. He calls it "permissiveness with affection." This is quite different from other codes current in American society. *Abstinence* declares that premarital intercourse is wrong under any circumstances. The *double standard* allows intercourse for the man and forbids it for the woman. *Permissiveness without affection* describes intercourse which results primarily from physical attraction. The new code, *permissiveness with affection,* says

Reiss, puts the focus on the other as a loved person. Intercourse then is permissible if there is a strong, stable love between the two parties concerned. According to this code, the essential question is not where this relationship will lead—to the altar or to a separation—but what it means right now. The test is one of subjective feelings. Reiss believes that since coitus is not forbidden where love exists, then the need to deceive has been eliminated. This is too big an assumption. It contains no recognition of the possibility of deceptive exploitation. A male need only convince the female that she is "loved" in order to secure her sexual favors—which has a familiar ring.

The third proposal is also person centered. Kirkendall lays his stress on the quality of the interpersonal relationship. Intercourse is given a value on the basis of the significance of that relationship. Reference has already been made to the six levels of liaison which his studies described. Coition with a prostitute with no interpersonal relationship involved is apt to mean far less than coition between persons who are engaged. The emotional content of the relationship becomes definitive. The crux of Kirkendall's position may be summed up as follows: If persons are able to communicate fully, handle unexpected emergencies, be concerned about each other, and let the personal relationship have priority over the sexual relationship, then intercourse before marriage may well be a positive factor. He paints the opposite picture in this sentence: "Immaturity, with its accompanying lack of judgment and incapacity to deal with potential outcomes, would appear to be one of the most serious hazards in relationships involving premarital intercourse." [8]

Two observations on these three proposals come immediately to mind. The first is that it may not be so easy to separate *psyche* and *soma* in terms of non-personal sex. The Biblical insights as to what occurs negatively when a man experiences intercourse with a prostitute (he becomes one-flesh with her) are not so far removed from the insights of contemporary psychosomatic medicine. The actions of mind and body are intertwined and deeply affect one another.

The second observation is that these three positions are idealistic in the extreme, each demanding a very high level of maturity. To expect maturity in some of these relationships is unrealistic since a great many of the relationships can and do form at the high school level. Sex play may begin even earlier than this. The questions must be answered: What percentage of adolescent sexual relationships meet these high standards? What happens to those persons who are not mature and who discover they cannot cope with the situation? Who picks up the pieces of broken lives? At what point does society begin to view these forms of sexual activity as "reverent experiments in love" or as "desirable preparations for . . . adult marriage"? One thinks of the copulating children in *Brave New World* with a slight feeling of nausea.

III. *New Theological Viewpoints Presented*

Today the theological world is looking for new answers to continuing questions, or at least for new ways of applying old answers. There is a general repudiation of rigid interpretations and a much deeper concern for the individual. The traditional rule of thumb that sex inside marriage is good and sex outside of marriage is bad is no longer viable. The evidence of sexual exploitation within marriage has exploded this.

But the proposals of Reiss that affection (level undetermined) makes premarital sex right, or of Kirkendall that a good relationship does the same are not acceptable as they stand to the theologian. Robinson seems to echo Kirkendall by speaking of "the primacy of persons and personal relationships" and saying that persons matter more than principles. He is concerned that "Christians . . . should have the terrible freedom with which God has endowed us and should exercise it responsibly." He wants sexual value judgments to be moved away from *what* occurs to *why* it occurs. The degree of honesty in the latter will ultimately determine the former. But then he adds a new dimension by employing the old phrase "bed and board." Intercourse without continuous cohabitation which only marriage affords is, in his view, going to be less than "an unreserved sharing and commitment of one person to another."

A concept widely used in theological discussions of human

relationships is *agape,* that form of love which is total, unde-
served, reverent, and of divine quality. Cole designates this as
the basis for sexual morality. "Every man lays claim to our compassion and concern," and sexual acts and attitudes are to be
measured accordingly. This replaces any reliance upon external
codes. To say "Thou shalt not," to label any action as sin "is
plainly to rob men of their freedom."

Cole feels that with America in a stage of sexual anarchy sexual rules are no longer relevant or effective nor will they be in
the future. The alternative that he proposes is to go the Biblical
route of responsible freedom in which "an individual motivated
by love of God and neighbor" makes his own sexual decisions.
As this individual does so, he accepts the risks which freedom
may bring, including the inevitability of some mistakes. Man
cannot have both law and freedom at the same time. But this is
true only in the absolute sense. There is freedom within law and
oftentimes freedom is fostered by law. Entire cultures governed
either by primitive taboos or sophisticated legal systems provide
a great deal of individual freedom. It is hard to picture any of
them functioning without these supporting boundaries. Man is
rarely able to secure all that his individual desires may prompt.
He lives with others, and codes, legal or moral, furnish guidelines for group living, dealing with everything from zoning restrictions to premarital intercourse. Individual rights must often
give way to group rights.

Many actions are unacceptable in any specific society, *e.g.,*
incest, murder, and the like. To prohibit murder is hardly rob-
bing men of their freedom. It rather reminds them who they are.
Since sexual activity, marriage, birth, and family matters all
involve more than one person, some codification is not only
proper but is demanded.

Again, an impossible idealism is noted. It is assumed that
people are going to be very mature and unselfish at the time when
these decisions are faced. This simply does not take seriously
enough man's capacity to deceive others, and himself, in order
to get what he wants. *Time* magazine reports on a conference at

which Joseph Fletcher, spokesman for this subjectivistic approach, was present.

In the situational approach of the new morality, he [Fletcher] said, "one enters into every decision-making moment armed with all the wisdom of the culture, but prepared in one's freedom to suspend and violate any rule except that one must as responsibly as possible seek the good of one's neighbor." Which is quite a long thought for an 18-year-old during a passionate moment in the back seat of a car.[9]

IV. *Traditional Positions Restated*

A serious restatement of a position must be accorded the same significance as a completely new one. It is actually a proposal addressed to the situation of the moment. So Duvall's conclusions cannot be dismissed merely because they have been said before. Behind her matter-of-fact observations lies a question which she addresses to those who are seeking "enduring happiness." Why unnecessarily risk something wonderful by insisting upon having it before the proper conditions have been established for safeguarding it?

Duvall is trying to "make sense" just as earlier proponents tried. She is concerned about such real and practical matters as emotional stress, guilt, maturity, economic security, babies, legal responsibility, social approval, family accord, and marital happiness. In her mind the proper development or resolution of these issues can most easily be worked out within the permanent partnership of marriage.

The value of continence before marriage has been raised for debate. There is little doubt that many have decided against it, and for a number of reasons either practice or advocate premarital intercourse. Klemer believes that the size and extent of this trend has been overrated. He does not see premarital intercourse being practiced so generally as to be almost universal. He takes sharp issue with Reiss, Ellis and Harper, who, he believes, have little of value to offer in place of the principle of chastity which they have discarded. His own experience leads him to believe that young people "can still be taught to believe in the personal importance of premarital continence."

This helps to identify another problem. Kinsey reminds his readers that there is no provision in this society for legal sexual activity on the part of unmarried persons. There are some who see this as a justification for sexual activity outside of marriage. This, however, clearly implies that to be deprived of intercourse is detrimental, if not damaging, to the individual concerned. If man were only a sexual animal, this might have validity. But man is a person. It is on this premise that Phenix writes:

There is no evidence, scientific or otherwise, that personal and social well-being is proportionate to the degree of sexual gratification enjoyed. In fact, it may be closer to the truth to say that the refinement and ennoblement of personality and the advancement of civilization are in proportion to the degree of discipline and control of sexual appetite.[10]

Should it be said, then, that intercourse belongs exclusively within the marriage relationship? If marriage is thought of primarily as a ceremony, the thoughtful answer may be "No, not always." But if the heart of the marriage is "a relationship of commitment between two persons, male and female, who live together in a sexual union, in a mutually sustaining state intended to be permament," then the answer might well be "Yes," whether or not there has been a ceremony. There are couples who move from love to intercourse to ceremony to a stable, happy marriage—in that order. What was the relationship in its early stages? What did the intercourse mean? As examined in Chapter 1 perhaps the conclusion is that the intercourse was the consummation of a commitment, resulting in marriage. Even the church cannot label the action as "fornication" since a marriage came into being when the two met in sexual embrace. Perhaps intercourse, limited to two persons planning an early wedding, should be designated as pre-ceremony sex instead of premarital sex, it being understood that in actuality a marriage has come into existence.

But what about the missing factor, the involvement of society through the ceremony? Of what significance is this? Is it really possible to leave out the public aspect of the marriage—namely, the ceremony—without serious loss? Is commitment truly complete until it has been publicly stated and the socio-legal bonds and responsibilities have been clearly and specifically accepted? Will there not be something defective, or at least incomplete, in a sexual relationship which the participants have failed to declare? May not the deceit involved even flaw the wholeness and the sanctity of the relationship?

These questions will be resolved only by those who are willing to seek for the essence of sexuality and seriously inquire as to what intercourse truly means. It is clear that in sexual matters, as in many other significant areas of life, the external control is law and the internal control is purpose. Only as there is an understanding and acceptance of sexuality as uniquely purposive will there be rational reasons for respecting and disciplining its expression.

SUGGESTIONS FOR DISCUSSION

1. Oftentimes engaged couples seem to look upon themselves as "already married" and readily move into sexual intercourse. How realistic is this when statistics show that 50 per cent of engagements are broken?
2. Petting in marriage and without is a natural physiological prelude to intercourse. It has been said, "Morally, petting is the equivalent of intercourse. It also contains an inherent psychological contradiction, in being at once an invitation to pleasure and a frustration of desire." [11] What sexual insights are found here?
3. Is there any validity or helpfulness in making a distinction between pre-ceremony sex and premarital sex?
4. Might there be any significant differences in the future man-woman relationships of an engaged couple who had had intercourse and a young married couple if
   —the man returned from combat blinded or emasculated?
   —the woman became seriously ill and faced extended hospitalization and convalescent care?

5. What reactions are there to this statement: "The first sexual experience is so overwhelming and so different from any other experience that it is better reserved as a means of symbolizing and giving meaning to marriage"? [12]
6. What does the concept of God's total forgiveness and acceptance mean in the area of sex?

NOTES

1. Commission on Research and Social Action, *The Church and Human Sexuality* (Minneapolis: The American Lutheran Church, 1966), p. 1.

2. Dietrich Bonhoeffer, *Ethics* (New York: The Macmillan Company, 1962), p. 50.

3. Alfred C. Kinsey, Wardell B. Pomeroy and Clyde E. Martin, *Sexual Behavior in the Human Male* (Philadelphia: W. B. Saunders Company, 1948), p. 559.

4. Alfred C. Kinsey, Wardell B. Pomeroy, Clyde E. Martin, and Paul H. Gebhard, *Sexual Behavior in the Human Female* (Philadelphia: W. B. Saunders Company, 1953), p. 288.

5. Reiss warns, "If one tries to alter his beliefs too rapidly, he may indeed suffer strong qualms. Strong abstinence believers are likely to suffer from very disturbing guilt feelings." Ira L. Reiss, *Premarital Sexual Standards in America* (Illinois: The Free Press of Glencoe, 1960), p. 168.

6. Lester A. Kirkendall, *Premarital Intercourse and Interpersonal Relations* (New York: The Julian Press, Inc., 1961), p. 182.

7. Harvey Cox, *The Secular City* (New York: The Macmillan Co., 1965), p. 215.

8. Lester A. Kirkendall, *op. cit.*, pp. 158–159.

9. "Morality," *Time*, March 5, 1965, p. 44.

10. Philip H. Phenix, *Education and the Common Good* (New York: Harper & Brothers, 1961), p. 153.

11. *Ibid.*, p. 155.

12. William Hamilton, *The Christian Man* (Philadelphia: Westminster Press, 1956), p. 61.

CHAPTER **5**

Changing Role Patterns for Husband/Wife

The Experts Speak

[AUTHORITARIAN INSTITUTIONAL PATTERN]

The Dominant Spouse *

The story is told of a strapping big lieutenant who married a young woman of small stature who was inclined to be bossy. After carrying her across the threshold, he took off his pants, handed them to her and commanded her to put them on. She put them on, and then protested, "Why, Bill, they're three times too big for me."

His reply was, "Don't ever forget that."

That is one way to work out a problem of who is to wear the pants in the family. It is not the best way for most marriages, yet throughout history, in the relationships of husbands and wives,

*From Paul H. Landis, *For Husbands and Wives* (New York: Apple-ton-Century-Crofts, Inc., 1956), pp. 55–57.

143

dominance and submission have been the most characteristic relationships, with the male more often assuming the dominant role. If the wife, by custom or inclination, surrenders most of her prerogative as an individual at marriage, the male need surrender few of his. This solution of the problems of adjustment is a simple, clear-cut arrangement which is remarkably effective if each member of the pair can accept the assigned role. There is little quibbling over issues and little time squandered in family councils.

Many of the peaceful marriages of an earlier day, in which there were never any real quarrels, are explained by this clear distinction in authority in roles of man and wife. The male decided; the female acquiesced. It is little credit to such grandparent couples that they never quarreled. If grandpa was the patriarch that most men were in his time, he blew off steam and the wife humbly took it, slipping off into the bedroom to cry rather than fighting back.

A survey covering 2,596 well-educated famliies attempted to learn not only who was boss, but also whether or not the couple was happy with the arrangement. Students in three colleges— the University of California, Oklahoma Agriculture and Mechanical College, and Columbia University—were asked by Paul Popenoe of the American Institute of Family Relations to rate couples with whom they were well acquainted and who had been married at least five years, as to (1) who was boss in the family and (2) happiness of the marriage. It was found that men were dominant in 35 per cent of the cases; women in 28 per cent; and in 37 per cent of the cases there was a democratic partnership. Of the democratic partnerships, almost nine out of ten were found to be happy; of the male-dominated couples almost two-thirds were happy; of the wife-dominated marriages, less than half.

There are a number of factors that contribute to the survival of this age-old marital pattern in our society. Our literature, our traditions, even many of our popularly held values are outgrowths of the old pattern. The idea of the powerful overbearing man, the subservient, even fearful wife still carries a romantic appeal, despite our allegiance to equality and comradeship. Novels and moving pictures featuring such a pattern are perennial hits. A love story of equals seems unromantic in comparison.

Our continuing traditions, too, foster the survival of dominance-submission patterns. Even the young women who want most to cultivate a democratic marriage feel bound to seek in a man "greater strength, courage, ability and drive" than they themselves possess. To expect less, according to American tradition, is to settle for inferiority. "She married a charming fellow, but she'll make him toe the mark." "He loves her, yes, but he doesn't have enough sense to put her in her place now before it's too late." These, and similar, statements remind young people—men and women alike—that in the eyes of the world, the husband who isn't clearly the "boss" has lost status and prestige.

Finally, we know that many marriages, beginning democratically enough, have become autocratic over a period of time. If one mate is by nature the stronger, if arguments and questions are not met democratically, it is easy enough to turn to dominance-submission as a way out.

Counselor David Mace emphasizes the point that there are, even today, many patterns of marriage which can succeed. He believes that the marriage in which dominance and submission are the characteristic pattern often has a place, concluding that "there are people who want to be dominated—and not all of them are women."

The democratic ideal, while it is a norm for the urban-industrial marriage, certainly need not be attained by all persons in order for them to be happy. Many couples can and do live together very successfully in a relationship of dominance and submission. It is when one insists on this kind of relationship and the other finds it incompatible, that trouble begins.

PAUL H. LANDIS
Social Sciences

The Competitive Spouse *

We hear also of the "battle of the sexes," the rivalry of male and female for a position of dominance. We hear of "Momism," the overweening aggressiveness of women, and the weak, submissive spinelessness of many men. What has happened to the complementarity, the natural union and completion of male and female in one another? There is a great change, to be sure, but it is not in the position of women in society alone. If the behavior of women is now different, it is in relation to the changed behavior of men. A shift in the one sex entails a shift in the other.

It is true that women enjoy greater freedom. But have they learned what to do with it? Have they really matured? Have they used their increased sexual freedom to come into their own as women? Are they really more feminine? The relations of male and female are in a state of flux. Perhaps the potential for a better quality of sexual complementarity exists in the present fluid instability of male-female relations. But at present the pattern of balance between the sexes too often gets derailed. If women were actually becoming more feminine, then men should be becoming more masculine. What do we actually see? In many parts of society, men seem to be turning less masculine. If so, we can only assume that women are not becoming more feminine but less so.

The issue is not one of orgastic capacity in women. The test of femininity is not merely their ability to experience orgasm. This is much too narrow a view. Some women can be orgastic without being truly feminine; they become conditioned to orgastic response in a setting in which they experience sexual relations as a hectic, violent, competitive battle with the male. Orgasm comes to mean triumph. To judge femininity by the presence or absence of orgastic response is to mechanize the woman, to view her female body only as a sexual machine. This is a twisted, obses-

* From *The Psychodynamics of Family Life* by Nathan W. Ackerman, M.D., © 1958 by Nathan W. Ackerman, Basic Books, Inc., Publishers, New York. Pp. 77–78.

sive, and critically inadequate criterion for femininity. The standard of femininity must be one that reflects the total quality of the woman's adaptation to the man and to her child, not just her sexual performance.

Today's women are freer, often more assertive, but they compete like men and in so doing move away from femininity. If they compete, it is better that they compete as women, not as men. Men and women both are oriented to the struggle for competitive dominance. The effect of this, in the long view, is to obscure the essential difference and the essential mutuality of male and female, to alienate the two sexes. Men become less masculine, women less feminine. Both suffer a distortion and loss of psychosexual identity. A further complication results when the disturbed psychosexual identity of a pair of parents confuses the emotional development of their child.

Yet there need be no clash, no sacrifice of the one to the other with resultant damage to the child. Increased freedom for both sexes should mean the realization of a better complementarity and "homeostatic" balance between them. Ideally, there is an interweaving of the balance of equilibratory forces all along the line. "Homeostasis" of mother and child and man and wife are linked to the homeostasis of the entire family group. The balance of relations of mother and child are affected by the balance between mother and father, father and child, child and sibling, etc. Moving a step further, the internal organization of the family is influenced by the family's position in the larger community.

NATHAN W. ACKERMAN
Behavioral Sciences

[EQUALITARIAN COMPANIONSHIP PATTERN]

Tensions of Equality *

Marriage . . . is an institution of close complementary co-operation. Its success or failure depends upon the couple's ability to work together as a team and to get along. Young people today who have gone to college and competed both there and later at work find that the competitive habit can often bring great difficulty to marriage, for it is hard not to carry over the competitive attitude.

If both continue to work, they may feel they are competing with each other in the amount of income they earn, in the type of expenditures they are able to afford, and in many other aspects of their personal relationship. This is one of the great difficulties faced by the emancipated couple today. . . .

. . . Rather than being a co-operative sharing, the marriage is subjected to the same strain as business and social life outside the family, where rivalry for position and influence replaces a genial spirit of working together. This is one of the important reasons why every marriage for the well-informed modern couple is a marriage of constant adjustment.

. . . .

Paul Popenoe, Director of the American Institute of Family Relations, says that the American male wants a woman who will bolster his ego—give him sympathy, warmth and security, not outdo him. In writing to college-trained women, he has warned that men, even in our sophisticated age, are not interested primarily in college degrees. They want a woman in marriage to satisfy emotional needs that cannot be met in the competitive activities of work life.

Women, too, in marriage are, in the final analysis, looking for

* From Paul H. Landis, *For Husbands and Wives* (New York: Appleton-Century-Crofts, Inc., 1956), pp. 63–66.

the emotional security that comes from being wanted, loved, and cared for. They crave a sense of belonging. They want this without paying the price of sacrificing their right to be individuals.

The American marriage today sets before men and women the highest ideal of which man has ever dreamed—that of sharing on the basis of complete equality, or recognizing each other as full, complete, and self-sufficient individuals, with rights, privileges, and aspirations to be satisfied both within and outside the marriage. This type of marriage is a much finer relationship than one based on dominance and submission, and yet it is one which is increasingly difficult to attain. This is not because men and women do not realize its merits, but because they are built for competitive relationship and cannot meet the demands of such a marriage. Consequently, most marriages are a compromise.

The secret of a happy marriage, like a happy romance, is cooperative, self-sacrificing sharing. It is the part of each spouse to bolster, support, and build up the ego of the other. Both men and women seek to satisfy their wish for emotional security in marriage. Both must also find success and recognition to be happy.

PAUL H. LANDIS
Social Sciences

Companionship of Equals Who Are Different *

When we speak of marriage partners as equals, we speak only half of the truth. As persons who have entered into a partnership, husband and wife should divide the duties and share the privileges. Marriage, however, is not one relationship, but two. It is a relationship between partners; and it is a relationship between lovers. To succeed in marriage it is necessary to succeed in both relationships. To be good partners is not enough. To be good lovers is not enough. It is necessary to be both good partners and good lovers.

* From *Whom God Hath Joined,* by David R. Mace, Ph.D. The Westminster Press. Copyright 1953, by W. L. Jenkins. Used by permission.

In the relationship between two lovers, the idea of equality is foreign and irrelevant. The last thing lovers want is to be equal and alike. What gives them joy in each other is precisely the difference between them, the fact that each is able to contribute what the other lacks. They do not, as lovers, think of themselves as individuals asserting their rights over against each other. They think of themselves as merged in a stimulating and satisfying unity in which they complete and fulfill each other. They are not equal but reciprocal; not alike, but complementary.

So much emphasis has been placed, in recent years, on the idea of the equality of men and women that the difference between their masculine and feminine natures is often underestimated. Men and women, as persons in society, work together and play together as never before. Because of their continual cultural, social and vocational contacts they come to feel that they have a very good understanding of one another. When they go into marriage, however, they are faced with a new kind of man-woman relationship, in which each is playing a very different role. Often they are startled and bewildered to discover how little real understanding they have of one another. Sometimes they refuse to admit the reality of the difference between them. The man treats his wife as he would another man, and is disconcerted when she fails to respond. The woman expects her husband to understand her, and is annoyed and hurt by his obtuseness and lack of sensitivity. The result can be the worst kind of deadlock, in which each disillusioned partner blames the other in bitterness of spirit. The number of marriages that fail for this reason must be legion.

It is tragic when husband and wife thus lose communication with each other. It means that the very differences that should have united them have in fact divided them. The man was made for the woman and the woman for the man; and when a couple turn this natural attraction into repulsion, they are punishing themselves as much as each other. They are quarreling about the very thing which to the happily married couple is the chief source of their delight.

Nothing brings a greater reward to married people than the

determined effort to understand their masculine and feminine differences and the needs that arise out of those differences. When the husband can be to his wife all that she expects a man to be, and when the wife can respond to her husband in the way he desires a woman to respond, both are abundantly fulfilling one another. Such a couple will be bound to one another by a mutual dependence which fills their hearts with affection and gratitude. (pp. 63–64)

Apart from the sexual attraction which they feel for one another, two people marry because a deep friendship has grown up between them which they find very satisfying. The element of comradeship is a most important one in the marriage relationship. All marriages are not blessed with children. Even if they were, children come and go, leaving the couple alone together again. Parenthood, therefore, may enrich marriage; but it will not sustain marriage. Neither will sex. There is much more in marriage than physical love-making. In the daily living together of husband and wife, amid all the changes and accidents of human life, what will matter most of all is that they are true and trusty friends.

We all need friends. Of all the experiences that men and women can encounter, loneliness is one of the most dreaded. As the Bible says, it is not good that a man, or a woman, should be alone. One of our deepest human needs is the need to love and be loved.

Of course that need can be satisfied apart from marriage. But the close and intimate life together of husband and wife has always provided the ideal solution for most people. Sharing their resources, their plans, their hopes, the married couple grow into a fellowship of warm affection and mutual trust which becomes more and more precious to them as the years go by. At least, that is what marriage ought to be. (pp. 24–25)

DAVID R. MACE
Marriage and Family Life

[BIBLICAL PATTERN]

Sequential Order of the Sexes *

The disjunction and the conjunction of man and woman, of their sexual independence and sexual interrelationship, is controlled by a definite order. As the attitude and function of the man and those of the woman must not be confused and interchanged but faithfully maintained, and as on the other hand they must not be divorced and played off against each other but grasped and realized in their mutual relatedness, so they are not to be equated, nor their relationship reversed. They stand in a sequence. It is in this that man has his allotted place and woman hers. It is in this that they are orientated to each other. It is in this that they are individually and together the human creature as created by God. Man and woman are not an A and a second A whose being and relationship can be described like the two halves of an hourglass, which are obviously two, but absolutely equal and therefore interchangeable. Man and woman are an A and a B, and cannot, therefore, be equated. In inner dignity and right, and therefore in human dignity and right, A has not the slightest advantage over B, nor does it suffer the slightest disadvantage. What is more, when we say A we must with equal emphasis say B also. . . . Man and woman are fully equal before God and therefore as men and therefore in respect of the meaning and determination, the imperilling, but also the promise, of their human existence. They are also equal in regard to the necessity of their mutual relationship and orientation. They stand or fall together. They become and are free or unfree together. They are claimed and sanctified by the command of God together, at the same time, with equal seriousness, by the same free grace, to the same obedience and the reception of the same

* From Karl Barth, *Church Dogmatics,* Vol. III, Part 4: *The Doctrine of Creation,* trans. A. T. Mackay *et al.* (Edinburgh; T. & T. Clark, 1961), pp. 168–171.

benefits. Yet the fact remains—and in this respect there is no simple equality—that they are claimed and sanctified as man and woman, each for himself, each in relation to the other in his own particular place, and therefore in such a way that A is not B but A, and B is not another A but B. It is here that we see the order outside which man cannot be man nor woman be woman, either in themselves or in their mutual orientation and relationship.

Every word is dangerous and liable to be misunderstood when we try to characterize this order. But it exists. And everything else is null and void if its existence is ignored, if we refuse to recognize it as an element in the divine command, if it is left to chance. If order does not prevail in the being and fellowship of man and woman—we refer to man and woman as such and in general, to the rule which is valid both in and outside love and marriage—the only alternative is disorder. All the misuse and misunderstanding to which the conception of order is liable must not prevent us from considering and asserting the aspect of reality to which it points. A precedes B, and B follows A. Order means succession. It means preceding and following. It means super- and sub-ordination. But when we say this we utter the very dangerous words which are unavoidable if we are to describe what is at issue in the being and fellowship of man and woman. Let us proceed at once to the very necessary explanation. When it is a question of the true order which God the Creator has established, succession, and therefore precedence and following, super- and sub-ordination, does not mean any inner inequality between those who stand in this succession and are subject to this order. It does indeed reveal their inequality. But it does not do so without immediately confirming their equality. In so far as it demands subjection and obedience, it affects equally all whom it concerns. It does not confer any privilege or do any injustice. It lays a duty on all, but it also gives to all their right. It does not deny honor to any, but gives to each his own honor . . .

Only as he accepts her as fellow man, only together with her, can he be the first in his relationship to her—the first in a sequence which would have no meaning if she did not follow and occupy her own place in it. If it is understood in any other way, and not as a primacy of service, the pre-eminence of man is not the divine order but a particular form of human disorder. The exploitation of this order by man, in consequence of which he exalts himself over woman, making himself her lord and master and humiliating and offending her so that she inevitably finds herself oppressed and injured, has nothing whatever to do with divine order . . .

For woman does not come short of man in any way, nor renounce her right, dignity and honor, nor make any surrender, when theoretically and practically she recognizes that in order she is woman, and therefore B, and therefore behind and subordinate to man. This order gives her her proper place, and in pride that it is hers, she may and should assume it as freely as man assumes his. She, too, has to realize that she is ordered, related and directed to man and has thus to follow the initiative which he must take. Nor is this a trifling matter. Properly speaking, the business of woman, her task and function, is to actualize the fellowship in which man can only precede her, stimulating, leading and inspiring. How could she do this alone, without the precedence of man? How could she do it for herself and against him? How could she reject or envy his precedence, his task and function, as the one who stimulates, leads and inspires? To wish to replace him in this, or to do it with him, would be to wish not to be a woman. She does not admit any false superiority on his part when she not merely grants him this primacy of service, for it can be nothing more, but is glad that man has and exercises this function in the common service of the common cause of humanity, he himself being also subject to order in his own place. Why should not woman be the second in sequence, but only in sequence? What other choice has she, seeing she can be nothing at all apart from this sequence and her place within it? And why should she desire anything else, seeing this function and her share in the common service has its own special honor

and greatness, an honor and greatness which man in his place
and within the limits of his function cannot have? . . .

KARL BARTH
Theology

Exploring the Issues

In the French Chamber of Deputies a bill dealing with wom-
en's rights was being hotly debated. In the midst of the discussion
one deputy remonstrated loudly, "But, gentlemen, there is a difference." "Vive la différence!" shouted another in reply and the
debate concluded in a storm of approving applause.

On the basis of "la différence" various types of male-female
relationships have developed in human society. The historian
can trace the past of some of these relationships; the anthropologist can describe the traits of others. This chapter is concerned
with an examination of the chief patterns of husband-wife role
patterns as seen in the main stream of American culture; it does
not deal with such interesting phenomena as Amish marriages
or New England celibate communities.

It has already been stated that the patterns of American marriage are in flux. Many of the more significant changes that have
been taking place have come about within the last 100 to 150
years. In a study published in 1955, Ogburn and Nimkoff [1] describe how they contacted eighteen acknowledged experts in the
field of marriage and family life and asked them what, in their
opinion, were the most significant changes in the American family since the year 1850. There was unanimity at only one point:
the increased amount of divorce and the change in the societal
attitude towards divorce as a way out of marital difficulties. In
all, some twenty-one different changes were identified, seven of
which are listed in the tabulation which follows. It should be
noted that six out of the top seven have to do specifically with
the husband-wife relationship. The results were as follows:

The Change	*Mentioned by:*
Increasing divorce and changing attitudes toward divorce	18
Decline in the authority of husbands and fathers	12
Increase in number of wives in the working force	11
Increase in amount of premarital and extra-marital sex	11
Increase in individualism and freedom of family members	10
Decline in size of the family	10
Transfer of protective functions to outside authority	10
(There were fourteen others with no more than eight supporting votes each.)	

The first five of these are specifically related to the single most important change—the movement from a male-dominated culture toward one in which women have an equal value and play an equal role. One major factor in bringing this change about has been the greatly improved economic position of women. In a capitalistic society money is power and as women, primarily through employment outside the home, have gained control of an increasing amount of income, they have used this power to free themselves from economic and other forms of bondage. A woman who can work if she chooses to has options other than marriage and subservience. Furthermore, her relationships with a husband are on a different footing when she too becomes a breadwinner. And, finally, with an open labor market she no longer needs to put up with an oppressive marriage if she chooses not to. She can function as an independent individual rather than as a dependent with few personal rights of her own. The balance of marital power is radically affected by this change in the balance of economic power.

The movement of women from the home to the outside labor market has also greatly affected the labor roles within marriage.

When there was no place for a woman except in the home, there was a rather clearly defined division of labor. This is no longer as true and the options provided the wife have confronted her husband with other options much less pleasing to him. As a result, there is now a "blurred division of labor" with consequent possibilities for misunderstanding, or even serious conflict.

Closely related to this is the influence which education has had on marital role patterns. Betty Friedan in *The Feminine Mystique,*[2] the book which gave the current women's liberation movement its initial impulse, identifies what she perceives as a widely felt basic dissatisfaction with their roles on the part of many women. They have been told for years that to be truly feminine is to desire love, marriage, and children and the chance to nurture these children within the confines of home and community. But education has prepared them for any number of demanding, exciting, and significant activities outside these narrow limits. She feels that women are basically frustrated and are only going to lose this frustration when they recognize that many of the repetitious tasks of motherhood are not intrinsically related to being a mother. She states that a woman's desire to contribute in other ways to the culture is not some kind of sinful desire that needs to be suppressed but is rather a natural concomitant of educational experiences. As Mead says of the American housewife, "She chose wifehood and motherhood, but she did not necessarily choose to 'keep house'." [3] She just might want "to do something" after she gets married.

Another factor is the new sexual psychology as it relates to women. Women are now coming to appreciate their sexuality and are as desirous as their husbands are to experience and to express it. Instead of being a passive partner in the sexual embrace of her husband, a woman is now an equal initiator and participant in sexual activity and intends to retain her new status. She wants equal opportunity to develop and to enjoy her sexual powers.

The dissatisfaction of women with traditionally defined marital roles coincides with an uncertainty which has developed within the male ego. With the disappearance of the frontier and the wild, brash openness of the free enterprise system the average man can no longer test himself against either men or projects which are in scale with his resources. In times past a man could shoulder his gun and axe and lay claim to, and eventually conquer, a section of wilderness land. Both the struggle and the conquest contributed to his sense of masculine well-being. But today he is not allowed to make his way with a physical test of strength against his competing peers. He is up against the big job, the big machine, the big company, the big union, the big computer, the big government. Decisions made by men halfway around the world can make him unemployed. He cannot guarantee his wife the stability and security she wants for herself and her children. Hence, there are insecure, weak men and there are "strong women" who, almost in moves of desperation (often at the subconscious level), take over leadership in the home, filling a security vacuum, as they seek to make secure the future for themselves and their children.

Since cultural transition normally moves along a very broad front, not all groups and subgroups are moving at the same rate. So the readings must be considered under the heading of generalizations which are not universally applicable but do represent clearly discernible trends. The husband-wife role patterns to be discussed are:

I. Authoritarian-Institutional Pattern
II. Equalitarian-Companionship Pattern
III. Biblical Pattern

I. Authoritarian-Institutional Pattern

In the middle of the nineteenth century male and female marital roles were rather clearly prescribed. The husband was the head of the family, the provider and the defender of the same, the representative to the community, and a father to his children. His authority was unquestioned. It rested, not in the fact that he fulfilled any of his roles in a fashion superior to what his wife might have done, but simply in that he was a male. There were certain masculine rights, privileges, and duties which pertained to marriage, and these were part of a widely accepted tradition, were carried in the community mores, and written into the law of the land. The doctrine upon which his position ultimately rested was that of male superiority. Marriage was a male-dominated institution.

His wife, for the most part, accepted her subservient role. In the home she prepared and preserved the food, produced or purchased the clothing, and fulfilled her responsibilities as mother and teacher of children. She was married for better or for worse and only death could break the marriage. She made the best of it and often made of it one of the best of marriages.

Today, as has already been indicated, basic changes have occurred which have radically altered this status. The trend in marriage roles for several decades has been to move *from institution to companionship*.[4] In the process the husband lost many of his "rights," not in any absolute sense, but through the process of allowing his wife to enjoy them as well.

Marriage has changed so much that it is virtually impossible in the 1970's to find any large section of society still under the influence of the authoritative pattern of the nineteenth century. The change in the legal structure alone has produced far-reaching modifications of the social scene though much still remains to be achieved. But this does not mean that in various subcultures, in particular families, and in the make-up of individuals there are not strong leanings in this direction and an acceptance of the dominant male role as proper and preferable in marriage. Landis very thoughtfully demonstrates how this pattern may be what many people want and need. Therefore, it is not to be condemned outright as inferior or defective. It remains a part of that freedom to develop its own relationship which each couple should enjoy.

Landis speaks of the "democratic ideal" as "a norm for the urban-industrial marriage," but between this ideal and the reality there is an interesting and widespread phenomenon. It is the arena of competition and conflict generated by transition. The husband may logically realize—and even intellectually acquiesce in the idea—that his wife is his equal in the marriage, but the momentum of tradition, the emotional stakes involved, and the lack of guidelines have coalesced in bringing about a state of conflict and confusion. His wife is no better off. In seeking equality with the male, she may move away from femininity and compete like a man. The net result is simply to replace male dominance with female dominance. Thus, Popenoe's study (see Landis) speaks of men being dominant in 35 per cent of the marriages studied; women, in 28 per cent.

The study by Winch referred to in Chapter 2 provides insights as to how this can occur quite legitimately and with salutary consequences. But oftentimes this is not the case. In this highly competitive, hopefully transitional, phase of marital patterns the authority can be exercised by either husband or wife, according to the issue under dispute, and it can shift as the power factors change. The result is at best instability; at worst, open conflict. After providing a succinct analysis of this competitive process, Ackerman expresses his hope that men and women will move toward the ideal of the full complementarity of equals with each making his or her natural contribution to a balanced, happy relationship.

II. *Equalitarian-Companionship Pattern*

The following sentence very aptly sums up the husband-wife role pattern which the majority of young couples in America seem to have chosen for themselves:

> The companionship concept of marriage emphasizes the equality of husband and wife, their consensus in arriving at decisions, the emotional and intellectual interstimulation of the couple, the personal happiness to be achieved in the union, and the wholesome development of personality.[5]

This type of marriage is a natural climax to the individualistically oriented peer group activities in which a great many young people participate. As Blitsen writes,

> A capacity for cooperation and friendly competition, pleasure in working with others for collective goals, ability to exercise authority among equals and to submit to it, talent for improvisation, and

willingness to learn are in the United States excellent traits to bring to marriage, and many Americans have them.[6]

The result is that "companionship has emerged as the most valued aspect of American marriage today." [7]

But the description of an ideal does not mean that it has been reached or is even reachable. The very fact that so many human values are associated with marriage makes it extremely vulnerable. The finding of happiness in marriage does not depend, as it once did, on carrying out one's marital role as a dutiful, faithful and loyal spouse; now it depends upon the subtle balance between personalities, the mutual expression of affection, and the resolving of differences by consensus. The emotional demands placed upon marriage participants in the equalitarian marriage far exceed anything previously expected of married couples. This realization has caused Landis to first warn of the pitfalls of continuous competition and then to speak of American marriage as "the highest ideal of which man has ever dreamed."

It has also been identified as the most difficult role ever assigned to man in his 10,000 years of recorded history. For example, a man who has voluntarily assumed the intricacies of the relationship described above must also advance himself in his profession, be a sober, reliable and efficient worker, a good provider, a pleasant companion and satisfactory lover for his wife, a wise and patient parent, and possess enough social graces to be acceptable. His wife may or may not be a wage earner. But in either case she is to be a satisfactory companion and sexual mate to her husband, to bear and rear children, to manage the household, to drive the car and chauffeur the family, to keep the family social contacts alive, to be able to render first-aid, to nurse the sick, to decorate the house, to shop and expend money wisely and, if possible, to maintain her school-girl complexion and pin-up girl proportions.[8] Perhaps most important of all, she is to use her mind and other endowments in ways which bring her deep satisfaction in her life as an individual and in the life she shares with her husband.

The equalitarian role pattern in its prime form is not institutionalized; its very nature makes this impossible. Hence, there are no clearly defined, stable role patterns. Roles are always in the process of being culturally redefined because they are always in the process of being personally redefined by the couples who live them. The criteria are that the marriage must be satisfying to both, flexible as regards changes, and creative in relation to the future.

Mace prescribes some salutary ingredients: the recognition and use of differences; the need to marry someone who is a rich and true friend and who will continue to be such throughout married life, and the need to be lovers as well as partners. Some of the material presented thus far has been alarming and almost discouraging; Mace is reassuring and helpful. He sees in the personal appreciation of "la différence" the addition of the balance of perspective that will cause the partnership to result "in a stimulating and satisfying unity."

III. *Biblical Pattern*

The equalitarian pattern is seemingly so vulnerable and fragile that one is tempted to question its chances of survival. The three strongest factors in its favor are the strength with which the ideal is held, the needs of people which are met in this kind of a marriage relationship, and the tremendous coping power of the human psyche. There is a fourth element, found specifially in the Pauline understanding of marital roles, which could give a new dimension of stability to the equalitarian-companionship pattern; namely, the assignment of final responsibility to the husband.

Such a statement needs some careful examination lest it be quickly dismissed as male chauvinism. This is not a return to the male-dominated authoritarian pattern of the past; it is an attempt to build into marriage a dynamic that will safeguard the continuity of a relationship already described as extremely vulnerable. It is best outlined in Paul's letter to the Ephesians where the apostle writes:

Be subject to one another out of reverence for Christ. Wives, be subject to your husbands, as to the Lord. For the husband is the head of the wife as Christ is the head of the church, his body, and is himself its Savior. As the church is subject to Christ, so let wives also be subject in everything to their husbands. Husbands, love your wives, as Christ loved the church and gave himself up for her. (Ephesians 5:21–25)

Even so husbands should love their wives as their own bodies. He who loves his wife loves himself. For no man ever hates his own flesh, but nourishes and cherishes it, as Christ does the church. (Ephesians 5:28–29)

The Bible says simply that man is the leader. But no one can lead if he has no follower. Nor can a person be a follower if he has no leader. Barth uses the letters A and B to illustrate his point. A (man) comes before B (woman) only in sequence, not in value. There is an absolute equality of value between the two. The difference lies only in the roles defined by God. Each sex has a place in that ordered definition from which he or she cannot be displaced without total disruption of the order. One sex cannot replace the other any more than one letter in a word can replace another. Nor are they competitive; they are correlative equals, and both man and woman have a responsibility to carry out their assigned roles.

This is not an arbitrary, anti-feminine pronouncement. It is more descriptive than prescriptive, for an examination of male and female make-up suggests that in many ways leadership initiative belongs with the male. This is, of course, a position that will be debated widely and sharply as the women's liberation movement grows in scope. It is clear, however, that in the physical structure of the bodies of men and women there is obvious evidence of differences which have a genetic origin. Furthermore, there is other evidence of differences which invade the emotional-psychical areas of life as well. This is why Piper writes that "man's superiority consists in his obligation to take the initiative and to assume the responsibility for their common life." [9] Here, too, the emphasis is on precedence, on initiative, and not on value. Theodor Reik once wrote that the differences between men and women are so comprehensive that one could almost regard them as two different species rather than as masculine and feminine genders of the same species.

But what of the question of authority? By the specification of an order of precedence, a final authority is established. Paul is quite clear at this point. "As the church is subject to Christ, so let wives also be subject in everything to their husbands." (Eph. 5:24) The prime responsibility for the relationship is lodged, not with the one whose role is follower, but with the one who is designated as leader.

The significant thing is that final responsibility has been established. The lack of this is the fatal flaw in the totally equalitarian pattern. Somewhere, precedence and authority must be lodged. Not to have it so is to invite conflict without final resolution, impasse, and ultimate disintegration.

Where this authority is acknowledged it is possible in a crisis of marital survival to get a decision that may prevent a breakup of the marriage. The question as to whether it is the best decision or the wisest, or the most unbiased, is for the moment irrelevant. The important thing is that a definitive, authoritative word can be heard.

The areas in which such authority is exercised are not in the choice of a new car or a decision on a vacation spot. These can normally be compromised by reason, rage, tears or trickery. It is when the issue has taken on the menacing appearance of an ultimatum, a showdown, or an impending collapse, that the need for a final authority becomes very clear.

It should be evident, however, that a decision will not resolve a problem unless the authority involved is recognized as legitimate. If the decision is accepted only because more power is used, or more deceit practiced, by one partner than by the other, then it is simply a matter of living by wits and might, and the battle of the sexes is joined in earnest. But if this Biblical insight is accepted, then there is a new safeguard added to marriage which can at least buy time until equitable and mutually acceptable solutions are developed.

Still another implication of the Biblical concept of order is revealed when Barth speaks of the husband's primacy as "a primacy of service." It is possible to read Ephesians 5 and see only that line where the husband is pictured as the "head of his wife." This headship has been expressed in marriages in all kinds of cruel and exploitative ways. The qualifications, however, are that "the husband is the head of the wife *as Christ is the head of the church*," and "Christ loved the church and gave himself up for her." The husband, the "head," is to love and give himself on behalf of his wife after the example of Christ. The context is important here. There is really only a superficial similarity between the authoritarian pattern and this Biblical pattern. Actually, the Biblical pattern incorporates into itself in the ramifications of that single phrase, "As Christ loved the church and gave himself up for her," many of those basic qualities which are natural to the equalitarian pattern, such as intimate communication, sympathetic understanding, common interests, mutual respect for the equality of each other, and shared and individual patterns of behavior.[10] The Biblical pattern provides the widest range possible for the nurturing and development of the individual personality, and provides for a definition of roles based on the premise that men and women are *equal but different.*

Many varieties of cultural, community, and family expectations in regard to roles exist. Bowman [11] makes it clear that the final appraisal of a man's success or failure as a husband is going to be made by his wife (and vice versa). This means that while society may help determine what the marital role pattern should be, a large influence will be exercised by the tastes, attitudes, hopes, expectations, assumptions, and biases of the marital partner. This suggests further that creative marital roles can probably best be forged *after* the marriage has begun, as the relationship grows and develops, and with a realistic recognition that these two persons, as they now stand, constitute the raw material from which this marriage is to be constructed.

SUGGESTIONS FOR DISCUSSION

1. How many authoritarian-institutional pattern marriages are the group members acquainted with? Are they male- or fe-

male-dominated? What about the apparent degree of happiness?

2. To what extent are any equalitarian marriages with which the group is acquainted still in the competitive, transitional period?

3. Discuss Mace's sentence: "They [the couple] are not equal but reciprocal; not alike but complementary."

4. Does Barth's concept of "primacy of service" produce any new insights?

5. Has the presentation of the Biblical pattern modified any one's preconceptions about what the New Testament teaches concerning husband-wife relationships? What is done with Ephesians 5:21 ff.?

6. Which pattern are these couples anticipating as they move into marriage? How realistic are these expectations?

NOTES

1. W. F. Ogburn and Meyer F. Nimkoff, *Technology and the Changing Family* (Boston: Houghton Mifflin Co., 1955), p. 5.

2. Betty Friedan, *The Feminine Mystique* (New York: Dell Publishing Co., 1963).

3. Margaret Mead, *Male and Female* (New York: New American Library of World Literature, Inc., 1949), p. 247.

4. Ernest W. Burgess and Harvey J. Locke, *The Family: From Institution to Companionship* (New York: American Book Co., 1950), p. 22.

5. Ernest W. Burgess and Paul Wallin, *Engagement and Marriage* (Chicago: J. B. Lippincott Company, 1953), p. 26.

6. Dorothy R. Blitsen, *The World of the Family* (New York: Random House, 1963), p. 48.

7. Robert O. Blood, Jr. and Donald M. Wolfe, *Husbands & Wives* (New York: The Free Press of Glencoe, 1960), p. 172.

8. Largely drawn from James Bossard and Eleanor Stoker Boll, *Why Marriages Go Wrong* (New York: The Ronald Press Co., 1958), pp. 4–5.

9. Otto A. Piper, *The Biblical View of Sex and Marriage* (New York: Charles Scribner's Sons, 1960), p. 96.

10. Harvey J. Locke, reported by Eleanor Luckey and Gerhard Neubeck, "What Are We Doing in Marriage Education?" *Marriage and Family Living* XVIII (November, 1956), pp. 349–354.

11. Henry A. Bowman, *Marriage for Moderns* (New York: McGraw-Hill Book Company, Inc., 1960), pp. 32–33.

CHAPTER 6

Being a Responsible Parent

The Experts Speak

[TO PLAN CONCEPTION]

Blight of Irresponsible Conceiving *

Children properly conceived are the blessings of a shared love. When a man and woman deeply love each other, they desire to realize the sharing of this love in the birth of a child to their union. A baby has been called God's greatest reach humanward and the human creature's greatest reach Godward. It is not only shared love between man and woman, but shared love with God, the Creator. Conception is a mystery beyond our understanding; a force greater than ourselves, not to be dealt with lightly, but reverently, hopefully, and in the fear of God.

* From Russell L. Dicks, *Premarital Guidance* (Englewood Cliffs: Prentice-Hall, Inc., 1963), pp. 58–59.

All too often it is not. We see awkward, arrogant, undisciplined boys impregnating lazy, rebellious, vulgar, irresponsible girls. We see ignorant, profane, crude, abusive men impregnating shrewish, cross, ill-tempered, unresponsible women. We see the emotionally handicapped, the uncontrolled, the vengeful, the haters and the destroyers who are often incapable of a single positive good or commendable act reproducing their kind with complete abandon; with no thought of either how they will support children nor whether they are capable of loving them. These persons are mothers and fathers. The parenthood is neither planned nor desired. The child is neither welcomed nor sought. Certainly the picture is overdrawn, but how much? How different is the hovel and the mansion, the poor and the privileged? Both seem to be able to reproduce their own self-centered kind and when their kind is measured in terms of creativity or destructiveness, of maturity or irresponsibility, of usefulness or parasitism the difference is not great.

The indiscriminate breeding that takes place among persons filled with anxiety and insecurity, the bringing forth of children into cesspools of fear and hate as now happens in great numbers threatens the very future of the nation. There is a serious question in the minds of some whether we can generate the healing stuff of love fast enough to offset the destructiveness of anxiety that propagates illness and despair. Already, known suicide is the tenth highest cause of death in the United States. This does not include those countless deaths upon the highway listed as accidental which are actually caused by anger and despair. Alcoholism is now considered by authorities to be the third greatest health problem of the nation; self-destruction the hard way.

God is not blind to our feelings and our needs, but he must find it hard to tolerate some of the things we do to children, not the least of which is conceiving them.

RUSSELL L. DICKS
Theology

Medical Prescription of Birth Control *

Many developments have contributed in recent years to instill the concept of family planning deeply in the American way of life. In the sixties, even more than in earlier decades, physicians recognized that child spacing is good medical practice, and that medical indications for contraception include factors other than serious illness. . . . As a result, birth conrtol is prescribed by doctors and practiced in the United States today mainly to achieve these four goals: better maternal health, improved child care, financial stability, and family happiness.

A couple may practice birth control for one reason during one phase of life, and for quite different reasons later on . . .

About half of the contraceptive users in the United States begin the use of birth control before their first pregnancy. Undoubtedly this is the result of the trend toward earlier marriages. . . . These young couples use birth control during their early years together to help them make the psychological and financial adjustments which are so important in marriage . . .

During their period of mutual adjustment, a young man and wife should not have to worry about an immediate pregnancy before they learn each other's needs and moods and habits in a way that only living together can teach them. The thrilling anticipation of their firstborn should not be blunted by forced competition with this process of sexual and domestic adjustment. Before the bride and groom share themselves with a new family member, they should have ample opportunity to share themselves solely with each other. Then, when a child is planned to arrive some time later, they will be secure with each other and ready to extend their love unstintingly toward the baby.

Many newlyweds also face problems of money, employment, continuation of schooling, or temporary family disruption because of military service. Any of these or other good reasons

* From Alan F. Guttmacher, Winfield Best, Frederick S. Jaffe, *Planning Your Family* (New York: The Macmillan Company, 1964), pp. 15–18.

may cause them to postpone having babies. In order to set up housekeeping in the way they want it for themselves, and frequently to provide income so that they need not live with parents or in-laws, many newlyweds agree that the wife as well as the husband should be employed outside the home during the first phase of marriage. Several decades ago, the typical American marriage started with the bride withdrawing from any paying job or "career" she might have had and demurely hanging curtains—and shortly thereafter, diapers. Today, the popular pattern is for the new husband and wife to hang the curtains together—after they get home from work—and to aim toward a more secure financial situation before the diaper phase is launched.

Newly-married couples also use this "teammates" approach to give the husband a better opportunity for job advancement. I know numerous young wives who are the principal breadwinners while their husbands are engaged in some special training or schooling which temporarily prevents them from holding remunerative jobs. . . . The wife as the willing breadwinner, or both members of the couple being fully occupied in full-time study, is becoming ever more common with the increasing number of skilled occupations and professions which require years of advanced training or education.

As an obstetrician, I feel I must inject at this point a strong warning: If childbearing is postponed for too long a period, the delay may hide a physical obstacle to having children which should be treated as early as possible. Some years ago, I prescribed contraception as a routine matter for a young woman at the time of her marriage. I had known her and her family personally for years and was aware of her desire to have "lots of babies—when we are settled and ready." I told her, "Don't wait too long—no woman knows for sure that she can produce babies until she's had one." But evidently she did not take this seriously, and she and her husband found one reason after another why they weren't "quite ready" to start a family. First they quite responsibly sought to achieve a certain level of financial security before having children. Then they wanted to buy a

house, "so we'll have a good place for a family"—again a worthy
objective. Then there were other things. At last, when she was
more than 30, they were "ready." After attempting for many
months to conceive without success, the young lady came to me
in panic. Examination disclosed that in the years since her marriage she had developed a tumor. To remove this growth we also
had to remove her womb which, of course, made her permanently sterile.

Aside from such specific infertility problems, a woman's ability to have children normally wanes with age—at first very
slightly. Many studies have shown that the decrease occurs ap-
preciably in women after the age of 30.

ALAN F. GUTTMACHER
Medical Science

Theological Basis for Contraception *

In birth control the theological issue is not whether things
work out any better because of conception limitation, but
whether conception control is not man's responsibility under
God as a part of his elevated status above all other creatures.
Birth control requires a level of maturity. This is why it is often
referred to as responsible parenthood. What of those who have
not attained to this maturity? Are they mature enough for the
greater responsibility of *being* parents? Here is the irony of the
argument.

. . . .

The reasoning of those who espouse the rhythm method for
religious reasons is based upon a respect for nature that identifies the natural processes with the moral law. In other words, in-
tercepting the semen in intercourse would be contrary to what
would happen in intercourse without this interception. Since the
interception is a device of man's mind to prevent some of the

* From *The Pastoral Care of Families* by William E. Hulme. Copyright
© 1962 by Abingdon Press. Pp. 38–44.

consequences of this action of his body, it is morally wrong. From the biblical point of view this is simply bad theology. Christianity is no nature cult. We are to subdue nature, not to worship it. Instead of submitting helplessly to the processes of nature, the Christian as a worker together with the Creator channels and subdues these processes to serve the purposes for which God has created and redeemed us. The birth control controversy cannot be dismissed as simply a difference over method. Behind this difference is a theological conflict over whether there is not a higher source for the revelation of God's will than the processes of nature.

. . . .

Even on the basis of its own claim to virtue—that it is in harmony with nature—the rhythm method has some serious shortcomings. Actually it runs counter to *human* nature as God created it. Eros by its very nature cannot be arbitrarily scheduled. By attempting to do so the rhythm method disregards the role of desire in the marital relationship. Sexual desire is fluctuating. It is difficult to know all of the factors that may be involved in the stimulation of desire. Physical factors are involved. Certainly mental ones are. The things that take place in a couple's day— their life together, their vocational and relaxational vicissitudes, their social and recreational experience, casual moments of affection and consideration, the natural reaction to sensory appeal, emotional ups and downs—all these and more play their role. There is reason to believe also that many women experience an increase of desire during their fertile period. This is only what we would expect in a nature intelligently designed. Yet at precisely the time when husband and wife may mutually desire each other, the wife may be in her fertile period. Even affection must be curtailed, lest in fanning the flame of desire, it lead only to frustration.

. . . .

Although contraceptives are about as old as civilization, they have been improved and made more generally available in our modern times. May this fact have something to do with our potential today for developing more fully the total meaning and experience of marriage? The answer to this question depends upon one's theological conception of marriage. We see again that the controversy over birth control is not simply a question over method but a question of differing conceptions of marriage and the role of sex in marriage.

There is good reasons for identifying birth control with responsible parenthood. When a person takes the responsibility for conceiving a child, he is likely also to take the responsibility for preparing himself for parenthood. On the other hand when a couple take no responsibility for controlling conception, they may feel equally as irresponsible about preparing for parenthood. There is a sense of fatalism about the "act of God" that can as readily justify irresponsibility for one as for the other. Parenthood is a big undertaking and preparation for it is important even though there is much that can neither be learned nor understood until one is actually in the parenthood role.

· ·

In these matters of responsible parenthood, birth controls help the couple to carry out these decisions made under God and so serve a useful purpose not in creating small families, but in creating wholesome families. The two purposes of marriage fit together. When through intelligent means the obstructive anxieties over pregnancy and guilt over its prevention are removed, the natural desire of those who share their love and life together, is to have a child together. And in having a child together they are drawn by this common concern and experience to a greater intimacy and devotion to each other.

WILLIAM E. HULME
Theology

[TO PROVIDE LOVE]

Need for Security *

If an infant is held and then suddenly deprived of support, he becomes terrified. This is one of man's few "instinctive" reactions. It suggests that the need for security is present in human beings from the very beginning of life. "Insecurity" is used as a catchall explanation of numerous personality traits and types of behavior, especially when not all of the factors in a given situation can readily be diagnosed. The concept has considerable usefulness and validity, nonetheless. Throughout his life the individual does those things which, according to his particular frame of reference, will produce security or avoid insecurity.

A child is not born with a feeling of security; he acquires such a feeling through experience. He learns it first from his parents through their manner of treatment of him. A young child's world is almost completely filled with the processes of functioning physiologically, growing, and learning. Because his experiences are limited and the cumulative total is small, each separate experience constitutes a relatively larger part of the whole, so to speak, than is true with an adult. For example, eating is an insignificant part of an adult's total life activity, whereas it is a very significant part of a young child's. Similar experiences are not in the same proportion in child life as in adult life. Furthermore, both needs of behavior are more elemental in a child than in an adult. As a result, some things which adults take for granted are more fascinating, more poignant, more meaningful to a young child and are, therefore, more likely to be a source of learning for the child than for the adult. In the light of this it may readily be seen that such things as feeding, cuddling, fondling, holding a child, which an adult often mistakenly assumes are more or less incidental, may lay the groundwork for the child's feeling of

* From Henry A. Bowman, *Marriage for Moderns* (New York: McGraw-Hill Book Company, Inc., 1960), p. 453.

security. Such experiences leave an indelible, though usually not recalled, impression on the child. Such a simple procedure as a mother's holding her baby snugly in her arms, or a father's holding the baby in his even stronger arms, is one of the roots of a child's feeling of security. It is no accident that hymns and other religious utterances sometimes refer to the "arms of God' in an attempt to describe figuratively the type of security which an individual may derive from religious faith.

HENRY A. BOWMAN
Marriage and Family Life

Unconditional Quality of Parental Love *

The family is the fundamental social unit, and for its establishment sexual life exists. The importance of the family is in proportion to the dignity and worth accorded the individual person, for in the family new persons come into being and are cared for with unbounded concern for their well-being. In this activity of procreation and care for children the self-regarding and self-serving ways of the parents are to a large degree transformed into acts of self-giving and self-sacrifice. Thus, the family may be a source not only of human generation but also of regeneration, in which the usual gain-seeking attitudes are replaced by ones of self-forgetful dedication and joyful responsibility.

The family is the source and bulwark of democracy. The very idea of the boundless worth of the individual person can be truly and inwardly understood largely through the experience of the parent-child relationship. In the larger social community, in the affairs of business, and in civic life the notion of the infinite value of personality is a noble abstraction more than a living reality. Yet in the ordinary family the assurance of unconditional concern is an everyday actuality. . . .

. . . .

* From Philip H. Phenix, *Education and the Common Good* (New York: Harper & Row 1961), pp. 147–149.

The fundamental source of family degeneration is the insinuation of the way of desire into the pattern of family relationships. The parents may regard the child as a means to fulfill their own ends. Through their progeny they may seek to overcome a feeling of loneliness, emptiness, or uselessness. In return, they may try as far as possible to supply the child with what he desires. This reciprocity is in effect a commercial one: the parties to the transaction exchange benefits with one another on a *quid pro quo* basis.

Ideally, the parents' devotion to their child should be unconditional in character. All traces of bargaining should be excluded. The child is not to be welcomed, accepted, and appropriately rewarded when he yields satisfaction to his parents, and rejected when he fails to produce as desired. He is to be accepted and cared for as a person, without regard to how well or how poorly he may live up to his parents' expectations and hopes for him. He is not a marketable commodity, to be bought up or written off, and measured by price. He is a unique person to be loved for himself, without measure or calculation of benefits.

In its unconditional quality the love of parents for the child is to be like their love for one another. But the parent-child relationship differs from the parents' relation to each other in this respect: while the parents entered into a joint covenant of mutual dedication, the parent-child relationship was established by the parents' intention and action without any possibility of the child's knowledge or consent. From this basic inequality in the establishment of the relationship stems the demand for a unilaterally unconditioned love of the parents for the child.

From this statement of the ideal of family love it should by no means be inferred that wants and satisfactions have no place in family life, nor that parents ought to make no demands upon their children. The fulfilling of desires is a happy consequence of good family life. Parents properly give innumerable satisfactions to each other and to their children, and children likewise please their parents. That this is so is a matter for gratitude. But to rejoice in the benefits of familial association is quite different from affirming a prudential basis for family life. Husband and wife enter into a covenant of loyalty from which it is hoped joy and happiness will continually spring, but which maintains whether or not these benefits actually accrue. Similarly, parents who take upon themselves responsibility for children may reasonably hope for the joys of affection returned and pride in healthy growth and worthy achievement, but the obligation to love and care for their young holds whether or not these legitimate desires are fulfilled.

PHILIP H. PHENIX
Philosophy

Special Role of the Father *

Is there in the man something analogous, something parallel to maternal instinct? Fathers show parental feeling as well as mothers. Is paternal emotion clear, identifiable, and distinct from maternal emotion? The evidence is scanty and inconclusive, but there is remarkable little to support the notion of a separate fathering instinct. Yet the warmth and passion of some fathers is a striking thing. How shall we interpret it?

Direct observation of paternal behavior leads to some interesting speculations. First, we often see in men, as in women, a tender, solicitous, protective attitude toward a helpless child. A father may act "maternal" too. In his family role as mother's helper, he facilitates the maternal function. In the absence of the mother, he may take over exclusively the maternal responsibility.

Let us examine the man's family behavior at still another level. From one point of view, as the mother mothers the child, so the father mothers the mother. The mother, while caring for the young infant, needs care for herself. In essence, although she is a mother, she still has inside herself something of the dependent child. She requires the solicitous protection of the father, as she previously required the care of her own mother. In actual fact,

* From *The Psychodynamics of Family Life* by Nathan W. Ackerman, M.D., © 1958 by Nathan W. Ackerman, Basic Books, Inc., Publishers, New York. Pp. 162–163.

we may often observe that the protective care of the young mother is divided between her husband and her mother. This view of the father as showing some maternal feeling is admittedly conjectural, but it is the kind of conjecture that receives convincing documentation from direct observation of processes of family interaction.

According to this theory, then, the father, too, is capable of mothering behavior. He may share the parental care of the infant with the mother. He may share the parental care of the young mother with her mother. From these observations we might perhaps evolve the tentative hypothesis that there are biological roots for something like a *basic family feeling,* epitomized in maternal behavior but shared by the father and also by the older child who gives parental care to a younger sibling.

I am inclined to believe that there is no separate fathering instinct. If we speak of something like a maternal instinct, it can be supposed that the father shares this, but his protective parental feeling is organized on a different level by the structure of the family and the structure of society. In this context, "maternal instinct" becomes a theoretical model for a broader form of protective parental urge, a *family emotion,* which may be expressed by man or child as well as by woman. In essence, mothering behavior epitomizes family togetherness, family care, and family loyalty. It expresses the social core of the human species. In this broader sense, maternal feeling is shared with the mother by the father and other siblings. But the mothering behavior of the man is expressed in a different way and at different phases of the child's development.

It should not be forgotten, however, that the young father has within him too a concealed child. He too needs to be cared for; he too seeks mothering from the mother of his child, or from a grandparent. Thus it seems everyone, child, woman, and man, needs mothering. It is the warm embrace of the family group, the essential emotional unity of family, that answers this need. It is only as this need is satisfactorily met that persons may be gradually and wholesomely weaned, that they can grow in strength and face the problems of the larger world with courage and conviction.

In the first phase of the infant's growth, the mother and child are one. The father is a subsidiary figure. He is in the background and serves to facilitate the primary maternal function. His importance as a parent becomes enhanced as the child matures, learns to walk and talk, achieves increasing physical mastery, acquires greater control of his environmental experience, and takes on the characteristics of a social being. The child's interaction with father epitomizes the child's earliest separation from mother and his first adaptation to the "stranger." It symbolizes the child's readiness for expanding his relationships with other family members, including siblings. It prepares the child for progressively wider impact with the outer world, the social universe that extends beyond family. Contact with the first "stranger," the father, personifies the challenge of adaptation to the wider community. The child who fears father also fears the stranger.

The development of an emotional bond with father is the first step in weaning from mother, the first step in integrating an expanding self into the complexities of social organization. Fathers often allude to this transitional phase in a remarkably simple way. They say they feel indifferent or only mildly interested in the infant while he merely feeds and sleeps, but they become vigorously interested when the baby "becomes a person," *i.e.,* after the infant has passed through the vegetative phase, begins to walk and talk, and asserts a place in the family as a social citizen. It is then that the father becomes a more significant parental figure and assumes a role of increasing importance in training of the growing child into society.

Nathan W. Ackerman
Behavioral Sciences

[TO EXERCISE AUTHORITY]

Need for Parental Authority *

One of the greatest weaknesses in modern family life consists in the breakdown of discipline which is involved in the loss of authority. Nearly all observers are worried by the outbreak of violence and lawlessness among the very young, so that we are beginning to use the phrase "The Revolt of the Children." The number of young offenders is so large that we are no longer shocked when we see their faces pictured in the newspapers . . .

Much of our trouble lies in philosophical confusion, especially about such great ideas as equality and freedom. Equality is often claimed by the young as their right, and interpreted as the notion that one person's opinion is as valuable as another's, even if the one is sixteen and ignorant, whereas the other is sixty and experienced. Personal respect is out of date. Many features in our current life, including educational tendencies of wide popularity, encourage the adolescent to suppose that he does not need to look up to anyone, particularly not to his parents. The widespread loss of simple courtesy, which allows young people to be rude in criticism of their elders, may seem to some to be simply bad manners, but it may be, in reality, a symptom of deep moral disorder.

In the older family life, which many are belatedly beginning to appreciate, the sense of order was inherent, and for the children this was psychological good fortune. Perhaps the parents did not make the rules, but they expressed them, and the children usually knew what the rules were. What the child experienced, then, was the extremely beneficent combination of an impersonal order with the personal sense of forgiveness when infractions oc-

* Pages 104–107 in *The Recovery of Family Life* by Elton Trueblood and Pauline Trueblood. Copyright 1953 by Harper & Row, Publishers, Inc.

curred. When the idea of the family has withered, as it has in so many areas today, there is no sin because there is no order, and there is no forgiveness because there are no elders and betters to do the forgiving. Nothing is accepted as having been given or bestowed, but all privileges are accepted ungraciously as natural rights. This is bound to lead to moral confusion, for it is essential to the good life that things should be given and received. The art of receiving requires as much moral development as does the art of living, and may be more difficult to achieve.

Much of our present failure in family life is the fault of parents who have adopted uncritically a false and empty notion of freedom. The more critical we become the more we realize that freedom, far from being a necessary good, is highly ambiguous and variable in value. The freedom which means the absence of all restraint is far from valuable and leads straight to brutishness of many kinds. The fortunate child is not the one who grows up in a world which has neither rules nor boundaries. The child needs boundaries, with an area of freedom within the boundaries, if he is to develop any sense of security. The playground is more enjoyable in the long run if it has a fence around it. The child needs parents to make some big decisions which relieve the very young from burdens for which their experience has not prepared them. The immense value of rules and regulations is that they relieve the immature individual of the intolerable burden of responsibility involved in the practice of unlimited choice.

The modern father, if he is to contribute his rightful share to the reconstruction of our total society and fulfill his parental vocation, must accept the burden of authority. Within his little kingdom he must take a position of responsibility and thus help to overcome the prevalent notion of moral anarchy. He must resist the superficial notion of equality. He ought to know more than his child knows; he ought to be wiser; he ought to make decisions that are unchallenged. Then when he wisely gives more freedom and helps to develop initiative by degrees, these are more likely to be appreciated than abused. He will have the grace to forgive as well as the courage to admit failure on occa-

sion, but he will never forget that the role of father is different
from the role of child. He will not abdicate.

ELTON and PAULINE TRUEBLOOD
Philosophy

Parents Under Divine Authority *

It is said that parents must exercise authority over their children. This statement is true enough in itself. But it must not be
taken to mean that in their dealings with them they will want to
build up a kind of domestic hierarchy, dangling before them a
traditional or invented picture of superiority and inferiority. For
sooner or later children will always revolt either mildly or vio-
lently against this type of procedure. Nor must it mean that when
the parents say "authority" they merely have in view their own
will, standpoint and advantage. For eventually children will see
through this and react with a corresponding rebellious defence
of their own interests. Again, it must not mean that on the pre-
text of parental authority scope is given to a primitive and otherwise concealed desire to dictate and command. For consciously
or unconsciously the child will quickly detect its spuriousness
and will thus be unable to learn the meaning of true authority. In
contrast to all these counterfeits true parental authority is a
wholly unspectacular, unintentional and hence unobtrusive manner of life and conduct. It is exercised as the children realize
that the parents, like themselves, stand under an authority, *i.e.,*
that they live under an immediate and unconditional majesty and
power. It is thus exercised as this is fundamentally true. For in
the last resort authority, too, cannot be exercised but only at-
tested, namely, by those who themselves know and respect its
divine basis, because ultimately only God Himself is and has
authority. Attention, respect and obedience are aroused in children by the fact that the parents themselves live out this attitude

* From Karl Barth, *Church Dogmatics,* Vol. III, Part 4: *The Doctrine
of Creation,* trans. A. T. Mackay, *et al.* (Edinburgh: T. & T. Clark, 1961),
pp. 279–280.

as their own characteristic way of life, and that therefore all direct parental intimations and directives can be for them the illuminating disclosure of a higher and indeed a supreme will which is for parents themselves the final criterion. The honour and obligation of parents is to be an authority in this sense.

KARL BARTH
Theology

Exploring the Issues

According to Malinowski the core of marriage in primitive societies has been a commitment to parenthood.[1] This may not be as true of contemporary marriages in nonprimitive societies, but there is much evidence that the desire to reproduce is far more than a biological drive. There is a real sense in which many adults, especially women, do not feel "complete" until they produce a child. The ancient idea of a man being immortal in his offspring is reflected in this psychic component of contemporary man. For the male this is the provision of an heir; for the female it is evidence of her fruitfulness.[2]

Because the ancient Hebrews thought of immortality not so much as individual survival after death but as living on in one's children, children, particularly sons, were looked upon as a gift from God. "Like the arrows in the hands of a warrior are the sons of one's youth. Happy is the man who has his quiver full of them!" (Psalm 127:4–5) is the poetic rendering of this attitude.

To become a parent is to enter into a new status from which there is no return. In the words of Barth, "Fatherhood and motherhood always confer a *character indelebilis,* introduce an irrevocable turning point in the life of the individual and bring about an indissoluble relationship to a third party, *i.e.,* the child now born." [3] This is the formal stating of the truth that many young parents-to-be are warned of by their friends, "Things will never be the same."

Parents are physically responsible for the birth of a child. When this occurs, it means that a living body has been created, a new person has been produced, and new responsibilities should now be assumed. At the beginning of life these may consist largely of providing for physical and safety needs; later, other considerations, such as personality development, interpersonal relationships, and education, will assume priority. But even much later, when children have left the home and established families of their own, the fact of parenthood still cannot be denied. Even when children have seemingly reversed the roles and have assumed responsibility for the care of aged parents, the *character indelebilis* remains. The status of the creative role, in which parents stand in for God, cannot be canceled by either the passage of time or the debilitation of relationships.

Normally, the contributions of parents to their offspring extend far beyond conception. One of the most important gifts is "sociological identity." [4] At birth the child has only a dependency relationship with its mother and a less definitive relationship with other members of the immediate family. He needs "social placement," [5] *i.e.*, a place within the social environment in which to live. If this is not provided by parents or their substitutes, the infant may actually die from lack of love (emotional marasmus), go insane if totally deprived of love (Fromm), or become a societal derelict without clear purpose, direction, or identity.

These are not mere scare words. The family is essential to the development of a sound emotional life. According to Parsons and Bales,[6] personalities are not "born" but are "made" through the socialization process. Families are "factories" in which human personalities are produced. The family has two irreducible functions: socializing the children and stabilizing the adults. Within the family children establish relationships and learn responsibilities. As they reach adulthood they make commitments to spouses in marriage and to the newborn as parents. Thus, the stabilizing influence of the family persists.

But these values are not won without cost. The Madonna

image of motherhood is often more romantic than realistic. Parents find that the adjustments to the new status have been difficult, and at times extremely traumatic. In one study of thirty-two couples made by Dyer [7] the following reactions to the arrival of the first child were recorded:

Severe crisis 25%
Extensive crisis 28%
Moderate crisis 38%
Slight crisis 9%
No crisis 0%

Previously LeMasters had listed 83 per cent of his families in the Severe and Extensive Crisis categories.[8] "We knew where babies came from, but we didn't know what they were like," was the plaintive cry of one couple.

While there are innumerable facets of the parental role which may be examined with profit, this chapter concerns itself specifically with three concepts which are basic. These requirements of responsible parenthood are:

I. To Plan Conception
II. To Provide Love
III. To Exercise Authority

I. *To Plan Conception*

There are four factors that need consideration in planning for the conception of any child: *a*) the basic issue of world over-population, *b*) the health of the mother, *c*) the health of the child, and *d*) the right of every child to be wanted, loved, cared for and educated. It is scarcely necessary to say much about the first of these. Demographers indicate that if present rates continue, the population of the United States will double in forty years [9] and the world population rise from 3,000,000,000 to 7,000,000,000 by the year 2000.[10] Already in many nations the problem is one of survival, not a matter of parental preference or individual decision. This latter exists, as yet, only in the Western world, and has caused Russell to write, "I am inclined to think that the most important of Western values is the habit of a low birth rate. If this can be spread throughout the world, the rest of what is good in Western life can also be spread." [11]

The problem, then, comes finally and specifically to rest upon the individual couple considering the conception of a child. There are some important considerations to be weighed. What rights does the child have? How will these be safeguarded? Who will represent his interests? The answer is that the parents have the prime responsibility—a trust which they cannot lightly put aside. Hence, it behooves potential parents to think carefully about children *before* conceiving them.

That this does not always happen does not in any way invalidate the premise that it should happen. Dicks graphically points out the difference between the ideal in which conception is regarded as "a mystery beyond our understanding," something to be dealt with "reverently, hopefully and in the fear of God," and what he sees happening all too frequently; namely, "indiscriminate breeding." The need is for both planned parenthood and responsible parenthood.

Obviously, this calls for a high level of emotional maturity. Stokes says, rightly, that one of the strongest tests of maturity is marriage itself. This means that only after the maturity of the couple has been tested and demonstrated by marriage are they ready for parenthood. In a prophetic mood, slightly reminiscent of Orwell's *1984,* he writes:

In the world of that happier tomorrow all planning for children will be a serious and deeply responsible matter. Conception will occur only after the parents have demonstrated that theirs is a compatible marriage. Parents will be educated to undertake the responsibilities and problems of parenthood. Professional advice will be made available to them when required.[12]

There is very little disagreement in America as to the need and wisdom of practicing some form of conception control. Guttmacher, writing as a physician, lists four major reasons why birth control is prescribed by doctors and practiced by married couples. These are "better maternal health, improved child care, financial stability, and family happiness." For many, the real problem, of course, is the choice of the method to be employed.

In the past the only acceptable contraceptive prescription for Roman Catholics has been the "rhythm method," which Roman Catholic theologians have described as "natural." Non-Catholics, on the other hand, have used various "artificial" means, *i.e.,* the use of some device to prevent the sperm from reaching the ovum or the use of the contraceptive pill to prevent conception. The current discussion about this issue within Roman Catholic circles indicates that while there may be no relaxation or change in the Church's officially stated position on the subject, yet in time, with the tacit consent and support of the Church's bishops, artificial contraception may become a near-universal practice.

The Protestant theologian looks at the sexual life of a couple as a whole, not as a series of specific acts. Further, he regards all efforts to prevent conception, including the rhythm method, as having the same purpose and being, therefore, essentially the same, regardless of the method employed. The significance of each act is determined by the total view of sex which each couple holds. As Piper says, "The crucial question, then, is whether a couple is fundamentally ready to recognize parenthood as a divine blessing, but not whether or not each sexual act is performed in conscious awareness of it or with the wish to have children." [13]

Hulme defines the issue quite simply. Either man controls nature, including conception, or man is controlled by nature. Hulme believes that the insights in Genesis about human sexuality indicate that man is intended to subdue nature in all of her manifestations. "And God blessed them, and God said to them, 'Be fruitful and multiply, and fill the earth and subdue it'" (Genesis 1:28). He accurately points out how man is constantly interfering with the forces and patterns of nature in many ways. He does not expect to find in nature any final revelation of the will of God in regard to man's sexual life in general or the personal decision of conception in particular.

II. *To Provide Love*

The psychologist Maslow [14] has developed the theory of hierarchical needs to describe the growing human organism. These needs are briefly described as follows:

—physiological needs (maintenance of life by eating, drinking, and physical functioning),

—safety needs (security from harm, danger, threat of destruction),

—love and belonging needs (necessity of experiencing love, affection, and a sense of belonging),

—esteem needs (assurance of having the respect of others, thus producing self-esteem),

—self-actualization needs (freedom to be one's self and to develop one's own full potential).

The first two of these need levels will normally be met by the family where even the minimal responsibilities of parenthood are accepted unless conditions such as war or extreme poverty prevail. The crux of the growth process is the third need. Whenever unconditional love, warm affection, and family belonging are provided, then the way is cleared for the fourth need; namely, the development of the very important sense of self-esteem. According to Maslow, only about one person in a hundred lives consistently on the fifth level.

The need for a basic sense of security is critical in the life of the newborn child. It is the ground upon which the infant's "sociological identity" will be constructed. In the process by which the child finds his identity, gains maturity, and finally accepts himself as a person of worth, the parent or parent surrogate is the *sine qua non.* "No institutional care . . . ," says Piper, "and no pedagogy, . . . can supply the good the child receives within the parent-child relationship." [15] It must also be stated that where this good influence is lacking or is defective the child may be influenced just as strongly and as permanently in a negative way. The psychiatrist Bergler states flatly that a person's psychical-emotional make-up is set irrevocably by the time he reaches an age somwhere between two and five. From this point on behavior consists of the repetition of these early-acquired patterns. If this is true to any substantive degree, then the truth is underlined that the love and support of parents is absolutely essential to the total salutary development of the child.

To state a child's need is one thing; to answer it is another. There is no way of guaranteeing that this need will be met. But there is a built-in obligation in the parent-child relationship that ideally impels the parent in the direction of total support. This obligation rests upon the fact that the child's existence came about unilaterally. Since he was conceived without his consent, a child has a right to what Phenix describes as "a unilaterally unconditional love of the parents for the child." This concept reinforces the point made earlier that parenthood should be only for the mature.

A family is made up of two parents, both of whom can and must contribute of themselves to their children. The companionship pattern which many young couples choose for themselves quite often conceals and blurs the place of the father in the young family. Ackerman contributes a helpful insight regarding this situation when he defines the father's role as that of "mothering." He tentatively hypothesizes "biological roots for something like a *basic family feeling*" in which the husband "mothers" wife and children much as a mother cares for her child.

During the gestation period a woman's concerns are strongly centered on the child within her body. A man's concerns are nearly always focused on the woman. Quite naturally, since the condition of pregnancy makes the woman vulnerable, like a child, the husband offers his wife the support and protection which a mother could give to her child. Later on, he will (or may) expand this pattern of concern to include the child.

III. *To Exercise Authority*

In a sample study of fifty-six societies, the most common factor was the authority of parents over their children.[16] This is not an unexpected finding in view of the long period of physical dependency which children experience and the socializing process which most parents are often expected to perform. Par-

ental authority involves setting boundaries for acceptable activity
and establishing the movement towards total autonomy in natural
stages or steps. The best kind of authority stems out of the type
of loving concern which has just been discussed.

It isn't necessary in a family for all phases of desirable behavior to be spelled out in detail by parents since much of value
indoctrination takes place at the subconscious level of communication. Where there is essential conformity between high-
level parental principles and practices, a wholesome atmosphere
for child-rearing is present.

If, as is the case, some of the most effective kind of training
comes from unconscious expressions of value systems, then there
is a prime reason for parents to clarify for themselves just what
they do or do not believe in. It is at this point that many parents
find themselves in difficulty. The instability of contemporary life
and the seeming relativity of so many previously accepted standards have robbed many parents of their own sense of confidence
and satisfaction. Some parents "drop out" of their responsible
role when they cannot cope with rapid changes and accept whatever practice is current at the moment. Others try to act in a way
consistent with their values and find that resisting pressures can
be difficult.

Without authority, however, little or no socializing can take
place. Hobbes describes the wicked man as a "child grown
strong." Without parental controls, expectations, training, and
discipline a child might well remain a child, intent throughout
life upon immediate gratification of wants, completely impatient
of any frustrations no matter how necessary or legitimate they
may be.

The authority of parents may be attributed to the will of a
creative God—Barth's point of view. Or it may seem to inhere
in the natural balance of human sexuality and the continued
rythmic cycle of love, birth, and the rearing of children. Or again,
it may be ascribed to the interlocking patterns of human need.
Certainly social structures are normally based on interrelationships of responsibility which may or may not be relationships of
equality. The Truebloods see the confusion of equality and

freedom in the family as a philosophical and moral problem and deplore the loss of the sense of order which allows for discipline, forgiveness, and mutual respect among members.

The existence of authority is a corrollary to the existence of order. Authority then is not arbitrary; this may be only force. But it is the explicit expression of how people are joined together and how they function together in the social order. Barth believes that "ultimately only God Himself is and has authority." Even if this theological viewpoint is not adopted, there is real wisdom in accepting the position that the concept of authority permeates all society. If, for instance, parents admit to living under authority, along with their children, and the children sense this, then there is a chance for a salutary working out in life of all that authority may entail. Surely there is no place in the family for the arbitrary imposition of a parental position upon offspring without reference to the unique and even peculiar needs of the individual child. To be parents whose dictates and lives intertwinedly make for an "illuminating disclosure of a higher and indeed supreme will which is for parents themselves the final criterion," to refer again to Barth, is both "an honour and obligation." In this view, family authority does not become lodged with a particular person; rather it is authority which is applicable equally to all but has particular applications and manifestations according to the roles which persons play within the ordered structure of the family.

SUGGESTIONS FOR DISCUSSION

1. What are the implications of the statement of Julian Huxley: "If the highest good is not quantitative but qualitative, then population increase at some point becomes a threat, and any opposition of principle to birth control becomes immoral"? [17]

2. Since marriage is for the mature, what reactions are there to the plan of a couple to conceive a child in an attempt to save a shaky marriage?

3. Discuss the rights of a newborn child, starting from Question 2 above.

4. Each additional loved one within a family circle—a child,

another child, and a third—increases the responsibility load of parents and multiples the possibility of suffering through anxiety, concern, and loss. What are the implications of this for a couple entering marriage?

5. A doctor may hurt his patient without harming him. In fact, he has healing in mind. In what situations may parents have to function in the same way?

6. What limits to parental authority are sketched out in these lines from Gibran?

> You may give them your love but not your thoughts.
> For they have their own thoughts.
> You may house their bodies but not your souls,
> For their souls dwell in the house of tomorrow, . . .
> You may strive to be like them, but seek not to make
>   them like you.
> For life goes not backward nor tarries with yesterday.*

NOTES

1. Bronislaw Malinowski, *Sex, Culture, and Myth* (London: Rupert Hart-Davis, 1963), p. 42 ff.

2. Otto A. Piper, *The Biblical View of Sex and Marriage* (New York: Charles Scribner's Sons, 1960), pp. 30–31.

3. Karl Barth, *Church Dogmatics,* Vol. III, Part 4: *The Doctrine of Creation,* trans. A. T. Mackay *et al.* (Edinburgh: T. & T. Clark, 1961), p. 277.

4. A phrase of W. J. Goode referred to by Jesse R. Pitts, "The Structural-Functional Approach," *Handbook of Marriage and the Family,* ed. Harold T. Christensen (Chicago: Rand McNally & Company, 1964), p. 72.

5. *Ibid.*

6. Talcott Parsons and Robert F. Bales, *Family, Socialization and Interaction Process* (Glencoe: The Free Press, 1955), p. 17 ff.

7. Everett D. Dyer, "Parenthood as Crisis: A Re-Study," *Marriage and Family Living* XXV (May, 1963), p. 198.

8. E. E. LeMasters, "Parenthood as Crisis," *Marriage and Family Living* XIX (November, 1957), p. 353.

* Reprinted from *The Prophet,* by Kahlil Gibran, with permission of the publisher, Alfred A. Knopf, Inc. Copyright 1923 by Kahlil Gibran; renewal copyright 1951 by Administrators C.T.A. of Kahlil Gibran Estate and Mary G. Gibran.

9. John Clover Monsma, *Religion and Birth Control* (Garden City: Doubleday & Company, Inc., 1963), p. 8.

10. Richard M. Fagley, *The Population Explosion and Christian Responsibility* (New York: Oxford University Press, 1960), p. 18.

11. Bertrand Russell, *New Hopes for a Changing World* (New York: Simon and Schuster, 1951), p. 49.

12. Walter R. Stokes, *Married Love in Today's World* (New York: The Citadel Press, 1962), p. 120.

13. Otto A. Piper, *op. cit.*, p. 147.

14. Abraham Maslow, *Motivation and Personality* (New York: Harper & Brothers, 1954), p. 80 ff.

15. Otto A. Piper, *op. cit.*, p. 127.

16. Morris Zelditch, Jr., "Role Differentiation in the Nuclear Family: A Comparative Study," Talcott Parsons and Robert F. Bales, *Family, Socialization and Interaction Process* (Glencoe: The Free Press, 1955), pp. 307–352.

17. Julian Huxley, *New Bottles for New Wine* (New York: Harper & Brothers, 1957), pp. 103–104.

CHAPTER **7**

Faith Within the Family

The Experts Speak

[CONTRIBUTIONS OF RELIGION TO THE FAMILY]

Symbolism of the Altar *

Someone has said that marriage can be holy wedlock or un-holy deadlock. Certain it is that lovers who meet at the altar, even when that meeting is little more than ritual, join each other in consecrating themselves to each other's happiness. It is a moment of victory, and a moment of faith. There are none who can show just grounds for their not being married, and they are convinced that this is "the finest thing that ever happened." Life is really beginning now. With the approval of the state, in the presence of friends and loved ones, and in the spirit of love, they publicly accept the private and social responsibility of their love.

* From Peter A. Bertocci, *The Human Venture in Sex, Love and Marriage* (New York: Association Press, 1949), pp. 116–118.

There is a symbolism about a church wedding in particular that is inspiring to contemplate, even when many of those present do not take religion seriously. Here are the parents, the relatives, the friends, gathered to express their affection and good will, their joy in what is being achieved, and their hopes for the future. They all stand at the altar, for, in a real sense, whatever happens to these two will happen to them also; they "stand behind" the couple as they consecrate themselves.

Those who are already married, the mothers and fathers, witness the dedication with a special solemnity. There is a "full" quietness as the ceremony takes place. While the parents watch their children, pride and apprehension mingle. They know in a more intimate way the habits and hopes in each life, and they pray that these two will realize their dream.

Every public wedding means at least this much. Two persons meet in the presence of those who care and are married in the name of the Commonwealth. But let us assume that they stand in the presence of God as he is conceived in the Hebrew-Christian tradition, the loving Father dedicated to the creative growth of his children. Our lovers now stand quietly and humbly in the belief that this marriage is God's adventure too, that he cares what happens to each of them, to their loved ones, friends, and children. Here the symbolism reaches a cosmic meaning. They pray that they will have no other gods before them, that their wedding may be not only an adventure in social living, but a determined effort to hold each other up before God, serving, worshiping, and creating. Such a wedding is, indeed, a uniquely human symbol. How better bring together all that the human venture on earth can signifiy? Such wedlock is holy. It is an experience apart, an act supremely different, for it dedicates human love to love at its best.

If a man's religion is the tie that binds him to the Source of Supreme Values, his marriage is the tie which at once binds him more responsibly to God and man, for this person he loves is loved of God and of her parents and friends, and the children that will come are God's concern, his concern, and the concern of relatives and society. *Thou shalt love the Lord thy God with all thy heart, with all thy soul, with all thy mind, and thy beloved as his child!* Let two persons love each other in this spirit, let them *will* the kind of love in which the God of mercy and creative joy can participate, and they will stand at a cosmic altar the rest of their lives.

It does make a difference at what altar two lovers stand now and throughout their lives. How much difference, and what quality of life is sought by two lovers, depends upon the kind of God (or philosophy of life) to which they devote their wills. Any two persons need to be as clear about such basic convictions as they can be. Ultimately, they need to know in what kind of reality they believe their love and their lives take root. . . .

Peter A. Bertocci
Theology

Resources of Faith *

In developing adequacy in themselves and in their children religious families have important spiritual resources. First, they know that the goal of life is not to avoid suffering, pain, or disaster, but to overcome them. Some infantile people may expect that because of their piety God will (or should) protect them and theirs from tragedy. Truly religious people see as the end of life not the avoidance of suffering but the attainment of righteousness. Far from expecting divine protection, they know that those who stand for ideals often arouse opposition that brings upon them even more suffering. Even greater is the anguish that results when they see the noblest ideals nailed to human iniquity. Religion helps mainly, not by protection from suffering but by providing strength to overcome it. Religion in its essence means, not shelter from, but triumph over, tragedy.

A second advantage of the religious family is the realization that the most important things of life cannot be lost. When some

* Reprinted by permission of the publisher, from Evelyn M. Duvall and Reuben Hill, *Being Married* (Lexington, Mass.: D. C. Heath and Company, 1960), pp. 428–429.

families have lost their money they have lost "everything." Financial loss can be serious in a religious family, but the most valuable things of life remain untouched. In some families the death of a loved one may mean the loss of the very center of their lives. For a religious family the loss and the grief are quite as great, but love remains and can be redirected to others who may need it. Such spiritual values do not protect from tragedy. But when tragedy does strike, a religious family meets it with built-in resources. It is these spiritual stabilizers that provide the peace and the joy that the world cannot give, and the world cannot take away.

A third resource is worthy commitments. Stated in a more familiar terminology these commitments include love, concern for the common good, respect for the individual, sound personal integration, and the abundant life interpreted in terms of personality development and spiritual needs. A religious family seeks not only to live its commitments but also to build them into the culture of which it is a part. Religious commitments mean primarily, not shelter and protection, but getting out into the stream of life with all its crosscurrents of evil and good, and learning about it from first hand contacts. Children are not to be sheltered and coddled, but enlisted—an enlistment that includes a careful training that is often arduous and painful. People who are at home in a world of evils and goods no longer have to "solve" problems by concealing them, nor do they panic when serious dangers emerge. An awareness of positive resources gives substance to their faith, and experienced understanding gives effectiveness to their efforts. The survival of civilization may well depend upon religious families who see the need and do their job.

Finally, a religious family, although it lives by spiritual insights and draws upon divine resources, also lives intimately in the world. It can nourish itself only as it shares its strengths with others. As the church is a center of religion in the community, so a religious family is a center of spiritual power among its neighbors and friends. Religious families are the arteries and veins of society that derive their sustenance from the spiritual nourishment that they channel to others. As such they are the bulwarks of society and the means for its nourishment and strength.

EVELYN M. DUVALL and REUBEN HILL
Marriage and Family Life

[PRACTICE OF RELIGION BY THE FAMILY]

Possibilities in Family Worship *

The problem of family worship seems, in the modern world, almost insoluble. We might suppose that our labor-saving devices would give us more time for the great undertakings, but somehow they almost never do. We are well aware of the beauty of the older practice in many families, according to which the father, at the beginning or the end of the day, would read, in the presence of all, a considerable passage of Scripture, after which there would be vocal prayer, sometimes with the participation of all members of the circle. How can we do this now, with children rushing for the school bus, perhaps on different schedules, and with the father often leaving home while it is still dark on winter mornings? A few may still succeed in keeping the pattern of the family altar, but it is fruitless to try to urge it upon all. It simply will not be done. A counsel of perfection may actually be harmful since, when it seems impossible, many conclude that there is *nothing* that they can do and act accordingly.

The part of wisdom is to see what may reasonably be expected of the average modern family and emphasize that with all our power. The point at which most families could begin is grace before meal. Most families, if they really try, can have at least one unhurried and peaceful meal in the day as an entire family. If your family pattern is such that this proves to be impossible, it may be right to consider a basic change in work or location,

* Pages 117–120 in *The Recovery of Family Life* by Elton Trueblood and Pauline Trueblood. Copyright 1953 by Harper & Row, Publishers, Inc.

for the common meal is central. If the one good family meal of the day can be eaten in peace and order, however simple, and if it can be preceded by prayer that is not perfunctory, a great start is already made toward making the home the beneficent religious institution which it ought always to be.

Grace before meat may take many valid forms. Sometimes it ought to be silent prayer, as all sit with heads reverently bowed, each encouraged to make his own prayer. Sometimes a grace ought to be sung or familiar words repeated. Do not suppose that the vocal prayer should be limited to the father of the house. Children as young as four or five can learn to share profitably, even by composing spontaneous prayers on the spot. On other occasions, great classics of prayer may be read with profit. It is one mark of a devout home to have near the dining table a shelf of devotional volumes, including Bible and Prayer Book. Even young children can learn to use these reverently and if the reading is not perfect we need not mind, for we remember that God has chosen what is weak in the world to shame the strong. What is of central importance is that the enterprise must always be genuine and one way of assuring this is to avoid the deadly dullness of always doing it in the same way. We must seek variety deliberately, both in materials and in participation.

The table is the center of the home! Ordinarily there are many beds, but only one *board*. The idea that a meal may be a sacred occasion is so deeply rooted in many religious traditions that it cannot be accidental or of passing significance. The forms of the sacred meal most familiar to us are the Jewish Passover and the Christian love feast, of which the Eucharist is a formalized vestige, but these are not the only examples in religious history. Of especial significance to all Christians is the fact that, according to the gospel record, the Risen Christ was recognized by the disciples at the moment that they began to share in the ordinary meal. (Luke 24:31–35) This leads to the hope that every common meal may be, if we are sufficiently sensitive, a time when we are conscious of the real presence of our Lord. Undoubtedly He is always present, but in many situations we are blind to the presence in the midst. The breaking of bread is potentially such a holy act, that it becomes the means by which we see that to which we are otherwise blind. Of this we may be sure; any child who has, day in and day out, over a period of years, shared in a genuine time of reverence at the family table, has something built into his life that he is not likely to lose, whatever periods of perplexity he may experience in subsequent years.

All the world religions have made much of the great occasions, such as seed time and harvest, as well as birth, marriage and death. In its own way, a particular family can do this and inaugurate its own festivals, whether gay or solemn. The birth of a new baby may be the occasion of a tremendous spiritual experience on the part of the older brothers and sisters. And death, in the family as in the world, must be met within the context of a faith which, far from denying our grief, expresses and thereby ennobles it. In our own situation we found that, when grandfather died, the distance was too great for any of us to go to the funeral, so our little company gathered around the study fire at the same time as the funeral two thousand miles away, and we find that the experience is something for which we shall be forever grateful. The New Testament phrase, "the church that is in thy house," took on a new and vital meaning for us.

Birthdays, the start of long journeys, homecomings, graduations, new jobs, the completion of a new house—all these are the stuff of which the religion of the home may be made. Religion is not something separated from ordinary life, but the way in which common life may be made sacred. God, we believe, is not primarily interested in religion, but in *living,* not primarily in churches, but in *people*. If we can believe that a home is potentially as much a sanctuary as any ecclesiastical building can ever be, we are well on the way to the recovery of family life which our generation so sorely needs.

ELTON and PAULINE TRUEBLOOD
Philosophy

Value of Corporate Worship *

When two married people share the same faith, and have a sense of spiritual unity, it is natural for them to want to express this experience by meeting regularly for worship with other like-minded people. By sharing their own personal religion with others they are better able to sustain and increase their faith than if they kept it to themselves. Belonging to the wider fellowship gives them also the security of an anchorage. When their faith is strong, they can help to strengthen others. When their faith is weak, others can help to strengthen them.

We tend to think of the Church as an institution, and we are justified in doing so. But the real continuing life of the Church is made possible only because it is a fellowship of Christian families. It is such families, generating a spirit of loyalty and devotion to Christ, and transmitting that spirit to the children in their midst, who have made possible the transition of the faith from one generation to another.

Our acceptance, as married couples, of church loyalty signifies our taking of the torch from those who bore it in the past and our passing it on to those who will bear it in the future. We belong to a Christian church because we believe that the world is the better and sweeter because of the Christian interpretation of truth and the Christian way of life. Week by week, as we attend worship, we renew our allegiance to that truth and seek to learn better how to live that life.

It is important to see clearly that the real meaning of our association with the Church is that it is an act of loyalty. It is pleasant for us if we like the church building and enjoy the sermons of the preacher and consider the music good. But these are not the reasons why we attend. We do not go to church to be entertained. We go because we do not desire Christianity, and all that it stands for, to perish from the earth; and that is exactly what could happen, in the course of a generation, if we as a

* From *Whom God Hath Joined,* by David R. Mace, Ph.D. The Westminster Press. Copyright 1953, by W. L. Jenkins. Used by permission. Pp. 81–82.

married couple stopped going to church and everyone else followed our example.

Much the best way to fulfill your church loyalty is to make a clear-cut decision that you will attend worship together regularly every Sunday. To go now and then, in an erratic way, is ultimately harder than to go always. Decide that this is an appointment which is going to be kept with unfailing regularity. Such a decision makes the issue clear to your friends; and it sets an example to your children which they will follow without question. From such regular weekly attendance at worship all the other church loyalties will naturally spring. Plant your anchor firmly by binding this decision upon yourselves and you will never be able to drift into forgetfulness of your duties and privileges as Christians.

DAVID R. MACE
Marriage and Family Life

Witness of Family Faith *

In a true family, children learn that there is one God. They learn it first from their parents, and from the disciplined and thoughtful obedience parents and children alike pay to the same God. Parents who force on a child an obedience they are not willing to accept equally for themselves are committing one of the deepest offences of family life, for they are giving to their child a false view of the one God who rules over all life and in whose will is our peace.

In a true family, children learn what love and judgment mean, for a family ideally is a society in which all bear common pain and share common grief, and all give and receive equally of love.

In a true family, children learn, little by little, how to be free; they practise how to make the choices life requires of them, within the protection of loving concern and watchful care.

. . . .

* From *The Lambeth Conference, 1958* (London: S.P.C.K. and Greenwich, Conn.: The Seabury Press, 1958), pp. 151–153.

In a true family, children learn how to accept themselves and, in time, how to accept others on the same basis; for membership in a family comes not by earning it nor buying it, nor is it given only to those who deserve it. Like life itself and the grace of God, it comes without deserving; and the self-acceptance of healthy childhood is a precious preparation for a humane and tolerant manhood.

In a true family, children learn how to be themselves, in true individuality, and how to accept others in their equally true individuality, with patience and kindness.

Of such qualities is a true family made. To bear witness to these things is part of the vocation of a Christian family in our society. In that society, sympathetic to its good influences, critical of, or resistant to, its unwholesome influences, the truly Christian home should be salt and leaven. To be this it has to be sure of itself and of its basis in the will of God and the Gospel.

Such a home is the one place where Christians can live by the Gospel, as they cannot fully do in a society where other sanctions come in. The marks of "living by the Gospel" are the care of each for other, the value set on persons for their own sake without regard to merit or demerit, to success or failure. Where there is this warm understanding and love there is both freedom and responsibility. Each member feels free to be himself. This sense of freedom is one of the marks of a Christian in the world —all too rarely found in Church or in society.

. . . Well ordered, free, family life of this sort is nearer to the Kingdom of God than anything men and women are likely to experience in this life. It is the best that society and Church can give to young people. There are no substitutes for such homes. They are made and sustained when their life is integrated in Christ, reproducing his passion for social justice, his discerning care and astringent love, and are enfolded in the larger family of his Church.

LAMBETH CONFERENCE

[INTERFAITH MARRIAGES AND THE FAMILY]

Problem of Interfaith Marriage *

The problems of any interfaith marriage are relative. They are relative to the personalities involved, to their personal capacity for handling complex problems. Such marriages are also relative to the degree of meaning that the two persons attach to religion. An interfaith marriage would mean one thing to a couple who were only nominally church members; it would mean quite another to a couple who were very devout. Interfaith marriage is also relative to the degree of difference between the two persons' point of view. It would be one thing for, say, a Baptist and a Methodist, but quite another for a Jew and a Roman Catholic.

In an interfaith marriage a couple may become acutely aware of a fact that often escapes young people; namely, that marriage does not occur in a vacuum. It is not merely a matter of two persons being in love and living together as husband and wife. Interfaith marriage, like any marriage, occurs in a societal milieu. There are other people involved. There are other institutions involved. For example, there are typically two sets of parents who are interested in the new marriage and the children who may be born to it. The parents of each spouse are usually interested in having that person remain close to the parental family's practices, beliefs, and rituals. This interest is often intensified when grandchildren are born. In addition to parents there are friends, other relatives, clergymen, all of whom may be interested and some of whom may bring pressure to bear upon the young couple. Families visit and are visited. Grandchildren are accepted wholeheartedly, accepted reluctantly, or rejected. Parents either attend the wedding or they refuse to attend. They accept the child-in-law of different faith enthusiastically or at least

* From *A Christian Interpretation of Marriage,* by Henry A. Bowman. © 1959, by W. L. Jenkins, The Westminster Press. Used by permission. Pp. 84–86.

graciously, or they may take every opportunity to snipe at the young couple and say, "I told you so."

The problem of having common friends is one that every couple must work out. In the interfaith marriage it is sometimes more than ordinarily difficult. This difficulty is intensified if the husband and wife attend different churches. It is intensified further if they live in a community where there is prejudice against a minority group to which one of them belongs.

Many an interfaith couple can make a successful marital adjustment together but find new difficulty when a child is born. This poses the problem of the child's religious training and eventual church affiliation. A small child can hardly be trained in two faiths and attend two church schools simultaneously. A choice must be made. Which parent's church will be favored? Some persons suggest that the solution for this dilemma is to let the child make his own choice when he is old enough to do so. Granting that each individual should have freedom of choice in this connection, to do it with a child, as is often suggested, may be more easily said than done. It is in a way like saying that the child will be left to choose his own language, or his own mores and folkways, or the country of which he will be a citizen. The child in his earlier years must either be given some religious training, in which case he will be biased; or he must be allowed to grow up without any religious training, in which case he will have an inadequate basis upon which to make a choice. This statement is, of course, oversimplified. Some couples do work out the problem by letting the child choose. Nonetheless, the problem involved in doing so should not be underestimated.

Another complication to which some interfaith couples are subject is what might be termed "focal points." Conflict is normal in marriage. In all marriages there tend to be points of tension and conflict—more, of course, in some marriages than in others. These tensions and conflicts may be handled by the couple successfully or unsuccessfully, constructively or destructively. When they are handled unsuccessfully, there may emerge a general pattern of incompatibility of which there are numerous component and contributing elements. They often fasten on the more conspicuous elements, for example, sex, money, in-laws, and explain their marital difficulties in terms of these. One element that may readily be made such a focal point in marriage is a religious difference. For instance, the couple may overlook the fact that their problems are being caused by a number of personality traits, situational factors, fatigue, pressures of various sorts, and feel that if they were only of the same faith things would be different. Or one spouse may go even farther and say, "If you were not a Catholic (or Jew or whatever it may be), our marriage wouldn't be in trouble."

. . . .

If interfaith marriage were only a matter of faith as the term implies, it would be one thing, and many couples who are now struggling with it might well be able to cope with it. But interfaith marriage usually also involves practice. This could involve things as varied as infant Baptism, communion by drinking or by intinction, the eating of meat on Friday, the day of the week considered to be the Sabbath, the acceptance of divorce, the wearing of a sacred medal, kneeling or standing to pray during church service. Difference in practice, especially when accompanied by a degree of insistence or pressure on one side or the other, can lead to conflict.

HENRY A. BOWMAN
Marriage and Family Life

Proposed Solution for the Problem *

Sufficient has been said to suggest the idea that a mixed marriage is not a good thing. Let us proceed briefly to summarize why:

1. A mixed marriage lacks a commonly held and articulated basis of ideas, purposes, and motivations.
2. A mixed marriage lacks the resources of marital health

* Pages 88–91 in *If You Marry Outside Your Faith* by James A. Pike. Copyright 1954, 1962 by Harper & Row, Publishers, Inc.

provided by common worship and common involvement in
the most significant of all possible interests.

3. A mixed marriage robs the parents of a common relationship with their children on the deepest level; namely of
   spiritual life.

4. In a mixed marriage one of the parents—and sometimes
   both—are robbed of the opportunity of bringing to their
   children the best spiritual heritage that he or she knows,
   being barred from discharging this most important aspect
   of parental responsibility.

5. A mixed marriage (if one of the parties is a Roman Catholic) disenables one of the parties from following his conscience in regard to the planning of parenthood.

THE "COMMON IDEALS" SOLUTION

As devastating as all of these factors—when marshaled—may
look to an outsider, they may well not be strong enough to down
the hopes of those whose love is strong and genuine. So there is
generally a "last-ditch" improvisation designed to present a hopeful prospect. This particular improvisation is heard on the lips
of "mixed" couples of all types.

Case 16. We have plenty of common ground under our feet:
We have our love, we have our ideals; we know what we want
out of life, we think that we can bring fine things to our children. And all this though we are of different religions.

Taking this doubtless sincere statement at its face value, what
it really means is this: We have a common religion, the particular religious labels we bear are secondary to us. Though the
couple might find difficulty in stating what these "ideals" are,
difficulty in defining what the purposes of life are, if they really
mean that Roman Catholicism, Presbyterianism, Judaism, or
what not, is not to be the guiding norm of their lives nor the
heritage given their children, then there are several important
questions for them to consider: Is the new religion which they
have invented ("our ideals," "our purposes," "fine things")
really profound and meaningful, and will it abide not only dur-

ing the sunny periods of life but during the crises? In adopting a view of life which is in effect a rejecting or subordination of their own religious heritages, do they have a really better way of life than these heritages represent? In what religious ceremony for their marriage and with what continuity of worship during their marriage (and with their children) will they appropriately express and deepen these convictions?

THE TRUE SOLUTION

In most cases these questions cannot be answered satisfactorily. But nevertheless in the rebellion which this attitude expresses, and in their desire to do something new and creative in order to provide a common basis for the marriage, the couple is feeling after what is in fact the true solution, . . .

Let us first begin by asking this question: Why are people what they are religiously? More often than not people are what they are because of what they were born. Now of all the reasons to hold to a particular religious faith this is the least convincing. Actually it would have been quite possible for the couple under consideration to have been born "totem-pole" worshipers; the fact that they were born such would not prove the validity of their position. The fact that one's parents are of a particular religious faith proves little also. One's parents can be wrong—and in fact most people of marriageable age have already decided that their parents are wrong in a number of particulars. So why not religiously? This is a good question to ask under any circumstances as a young person approaches adult life, but it is an especially good question to ask at the time of marriage. For now a new unit of society is being created and one which will be autonomous to a considerable degree. In the Bible which Roman Catholics and other Christians alike read is this word: "A man shall leave father or mother and cleave to his wife." Next to God and one's religious loyalty, loyalty to one's spouse is the first loyalty. Parents come second; and after the children are born, the children come second and the parents are third in the priority scale of allegiance. (Were this a general book on marriage counseling this point would be stressed for several pages.)

The solution, in a nutshell, is this: each of the parties, forgetting what he or she was born and forgetting what his parents are, should rethink his or her religious position in terms of what each really believes and what Church most nearly represents that actual belief. Naturally the religious allegiances in which the two are now actually involved should be given serious consideration in the study, but the search need not be limited to them. If it so happens that both parties can come to convictions which are represented by the same Church allegiance then there will be no mixed marriage. And that is the end of the problem.

It is important at the outset to state what the above paragraph does *not* mean. It does not mean that one should seek to persuade himself of the truth of the other's position or yield to it in order to simplify things. This is to make one of the parties into an adjective and leave the other a noun, and in fact to deify one of the two parties. This subjugation of the spirit of one to the other is bound to have difficult psychological consequences in all aspects of the marriage—beyond the question of religion proper. If, however, this honest reconsideration leads both to conviction as to a faith that happens to be already that of one of the two parties, both should have the humility to make possible the conversion of the heretofore outsider to this faith without any sense of having "yielded" to the other. In no case should one yield to the other; both should yield to the claims of truth as they have worked it out through honest study, soul searching and decision. Any other solution does violence to the integrity of one or the other of the parties. Too easy a victory here will be paid for in the end.

JAMES A. PIKE
Theology

Exploring the Issues

A frequently used advertisement carries the statement: "The family that prays together, stays together." If this is only a reference to a specific devotional practice, it hardly possesses validity. But if it is a reflection of a basic attitude towards life, then it is referring to the kind of religious expression that sustains marital and family living.

This support is needed at a time when the modern family is struggling for survival in a difficult, tempestuous world. Such diverse elements as war, poverty, the mass media, automation, urban decay, moral and sexual revolutions may combine at any given moment to contribute to the stress and tension which families face. In the midst of this quandary many people are asking seriously, some doubtfully, "What does religion have to offer the modern family?"

According to the Methodist *Discipline* religion has a great deal to give to the family. It says explicitly: "Religion and the family naturally belong together. What religion is to accomplish, it can do best in the family. What the family must do, it cannot do without religion. Religion and the family are natural allies." [1]

But religion needs definition. The *Discipline* gives this description of a Christian family:

A Christian family is one in which parents so live the Christian life and practice the presence of God that children come to accept God as the greatest reality of life.

A Christian family is one in which each member is accepted and respected as a person having sacred worth.

A Christian family is one that seeks to bring every member into the Christian way of living.

A Christian family is one that accepts the responsibility of worship and instruction to the end of developing the spiritual life of each person.

A Christian family is one that manifests a faith in God, observes daily prayer and grace at meals, is committed to behavior in keeping with Christian ideals for family relations, community life, and national and world citizenship.[2]

But not all men of faith are found within the formal structures of religious communities. Religious faith can be defined in such narrow terms that only a very limited number of individuals or groups qualify as "true believers." It is necessary and proper to recognize as genuine that style of religious life which is described in the "short formula" of Paul Tillich: "Faith is the state of being grasped by an ultimate concern."[3]

This view states that religion can take many different forms. After pointing out that finite formulas, rituals, codes and institutions cannot possibly contain or confine the infinite, Phenix provides a succinct, meaningful definition of the person of faith. He writes: "A religious person is one who in intention and in deed is devoted to the supreme, the infinite, the perfect, the true, the completely excellent, regardless of the words, acts, or institutions through which he expresses his dedication."[4]

This quality of commitment cannot help but influence a family for good, and, through the family, touch the lives and the structures of the social group. The private devotions and the personal inner discipline of the religious man will normally be expressed in specific actions in concrete situations. It was this kind of faith that once "turned the world upside down"; it is a much-needed factor in the irresolute climate of the day.

The place of religious faith within the family is discussed under three headings:

I. Contributions of Religion to the Family
II. Practice of Religion by the Family
III. Interfaith Marriages and the Family

I. Contributions of Religion to the Family

The basic contributions of religious faith to two individuals planning marriage will usually have been made long since—in childhood. Consciously and unconsciously in the home environment many ideas about life will have been evaluated. Attitudes will have been formed, values accepted, levels of aspiration established, and vocational goals adopted. Some essential questions will have been raised for at least preliminary examination. Is the universe hostile or friendly? What is the value of man? Am I my brother's keeper? Is there a God who cares?

But one significant experience which still lies ahead for those contemplating marriage is the ceremony itself. What contributions can a religious service make to the two who participate in it? Is there any value, other than that of sentiment or tradition, which is attached to this act?

It is easier for a Roman Catholic to answer this question positively than it is for a Protestant. The Roman Church teaches that marriage is a divine sacrament which specifically and effectually conveys the gracious gifts of God to the couple concerned. The Protestant believes that marriage is a rite of the church which by and in itself conveys no sacramental gift. But through the rite of marriage a new status is conferred upon the couple. This status comes by virtue of a covenant entered into by the two persons concerned.

Status is not something which may be secured by signing a contract. The wedding ceremony is not actually a contract though it may have some outward similarities to one. For a contract is subject to cancellation and it may have a terminal date written into it. Status is normally a gift which is secured by a covenant of commitment. In Judeo-Christian thinking the relationship of two married persons is much like that achieved by the covenant between Jehovah and Israel, between Christ and the church.

This covenant relationship with its mutual bestowal of gifts upon one another, including the status or state of being married, is brought about by the commitments declared to one another on the occasion. Whether it is a large or small wedding, there are many persons and interests represented. In the witnesses (and guests if it is a public service) are represented the family and friends and especially society. In the ceremony, whether it be civil or religious, is seen the stability of law and the historic, traditional ways in which people covenant together. And the presence of the clergyman symbolizes the presence and the involvement of God.

Bertocci points out the religious significance of such an event even for the nonreligious person. And for those who are religious, who believe "that this marriage is God's adventure, too," then "the symbolism reaches a cosmic significance." For Bertocci believes that it does matter which altar a man stands before and who it is that he seeks to bless him. In a religious service the couple are reminded again of the "valid offer of the great and real blessings that by God's will the Church has to share with the spouses" [5] if and as they continue in the fellowship of believers.

It must be added that the emphasis upon a religious wedding service does not detract from either the validity or the significance of a civil ceremony. Couples appearing in a justice court to be married have also experienced the pull of their physical and psychic natures and are "in love" with each other. The public declaration of their commitment to live together as man and wife gives their relationship the status of a permanent, a legal, and a spiritual relationship. A religious service does not make any marriage more valid; it simply focuses on the religious elements of life relationships and encourages their practice. Some of the more significant ways in which these religious practices contribute to the wedded life of the couple are noted by Duvall and Hill.

II. *Practice of Religion by the Family*

Since religion is relational, it has movement within it. So religion in marriage should normally be expected to produce active and vital expressions of faith. One of the more elemental of these is the sharing of a common devotional or prayer life by the members of the family. This normally centers around the common experience of the family each day. The Truebloods suggest that the best time is probably the evening meal. Traditionally meals have had sacred connotations in both Jewish and Christian cultures. But sometimes in contemporary society evenings shared by the entire family seem rather scarce. The Truebloods go so far as to say that if the family finds it impossible to share one quiet, orderly meal in common each day, then perhaps a change in work or work location should be considered. The family schedule should be built to incorporate and preserve those aspects of obvious value to the family's well-being. One of these, often neglected, is "the responsibility of worship."

The Protestant mentality and doctrinal interpretations have often combined to make attendance at public worship an open option. In comparison with non-Protestant groups there has been little discipline exercised or imposed. As a result some of the values of worship have been so neglected that they can be missed entirely unless a specific point is made of ascertaining their value. Mace is very explicit in his encouragement of public or Sunday worship by couples and their families. "A home that calls itself Christian," he writes, "will acknowledge its allegiance to Christ. This it will do first by worship." [6] And again, "We go [to church] because we do not desire Christianity, and all that it stands for, to perish from the earth."

The focus is on self-discipline, personal commitment, and contribution to others, all elements in responsible living. Too often, Protestants have neglected the values inherent in the orderly progression of Sundays through their lives and have not received the inestimable stabilizing influences which regular worship can put into a marriage. Oftentimes the realization comes too late, when the marriage is dying or dead, that valuable resources were left untouched. The sustaining power of the Christian community is a vital force for marital health.

Part of the tragedy of keeping apart from this community is that some of the potential for social good which lies within each family unit may be lost. The world needs the gifts which good families can supply. The statement of the Lambeth Conference stresses the vital importance of the contributions which such families can make. Each "true family" has a call "to bear witness" to all of the good within it; each "truly Christian home should be salt and leaven." "There are no substitutes for such homes."

These convictions could not be expressed in much stronger language. The level of expectation for the religiously oriented family is high; it is based on the New Testament adage: "Every

one to whom much is given, of him will much be required."
(Luke 12:48) Mace writes very simply and directly, "It [the
Christian home] does not tell others what they should be; it
shows them what they could be." [7]

III. *Interfaith Marriages and the Family*

If a family is to live this kind of religious life and make this
kind of a contribution, it must function as a unit. "If a house
[family] is divided against itself, that house will not be able to
stand." (Mark 3:25) This raises one of the more difficult problems in a religiously pluralistic society; namely, the interfaith or
mixed marriage.

Any discussion of such interfaith marriages must take place
within the context of a marked new flexibility in this area on the
part of the Roman Catholic Church. Following Vatican II, a new
openness has developed, where once there was doctrinaire rigid-
ity. In any specific instance, much will depend on the bishop of
the diocese, since he is permitted a great deal of flexibility in the
way in which he interprets the new regulations, and his parish
clergy will tend to follow his lead. There can be little doubt,
however, that the demands on the faithful which have frequently
introduced strain and tension into the interfaith marriage will
lessen as time goes by. As of this writing, however, the rhythm
method is still the only form of contraception officially permitted
by the Church. And its bishops have made it clear that they do
not favor mixed marriages. Still, in America there are some very
powerful forces which serve to bring about interfaith marriages.
It should be noted that currently in the United States, conserva-
tive estimates are that one out of five marriages is between a
Roman Catholic and a Protestant.[8]

The first of these powerful forces is simply that America is
very clearly religiously pluralistic. There are many differing religious traditions represented in the culture. The second is that
Americans are highly mobile with approximately one-fifth of the
population changing addresses every year. Furthermore, social,
economic, and educational mobility factors are continually at
work eroding the cultural enclaves and putting people in contact

with those of different religious persuasions. And in the third place, a growing secularization of attitudes, a position of relativism in relation to religious absolutes and ecclesiastical authority, and a growing sense of rapprochement between the religious communities have contributed further to lowering the barriers.

Another significant fact is that men and women entering interfaith marriages are working out successful relationships. In 1938, a study was made in Maryland involving the parents of 12,000 young people to determine their religious affiliation and whether or not they were living together. The results revealed that where:

—both parents were Roman Catholic only 6.4 per cent were separated;
—both parents were Protestant only 6.8 per cent were separated;
—parents were of different faiths over 15 per cent were separated;
—parents had no religious affiliation 16.7 per cent were separated.[9]

In short, where there was no religious faith or where there was a mixed religious situation there was about two and one-quarter times as much marital breakup as in a religiously united family. Statistics like these help to explain why churchmen have so earnestly encouraged their communicants to stay within the fold in their marriage relationships.

A study by Burchinal and Chancellor [10] presents a different picture, one which reflects the changing religious atmosphere. It summarizes data from 72,485 Iowa marriages, covering the years 1953–1959. The survival rate as indicated below shows a remarkable similarity in most religiously oriented marriages. Only when one moves into the "unspecified Protestant" category, a reference to the "unchurched," does any major divergence appear.

Both Catholic 96.2%
Presbyterian-Protestant 94.6%
Both Lutheran 94.1%

Both Protestant (smaller groups) 94.0%
Lutheran-Protestant 93.0%
Methodist-Protestant 92.9%
Both Methodists 91.4%
Both Presbyterians 91.0%
Catholic-Lutheran 90.5%
Baptist-Protestant 90.5%
Catholic-Presbyterian 89.8%
Both Baptist 89.8%
Catholic-Protestant (smaller groups) 89.1%
AVERAGE FOR TOTAL POPULATION ... 87.6%
Catholic-Methodist 83.8%
Unspecified Protestant-Protestant 82.7%
Catholic-Baptist 81.6%
Both unspecified Protestant 35.0%
Catholic-unspecified Protestant 28.7%

Two findings of importance for this study can be seen at once. Except for Catholic-Methodist, Catholic-Baptist, and Catholic-unspecified Protestant marriages, Catholics marrying Protestants have a better than average chance of marital survival. Second, the difference between same-faith marriages and interfaith marriages is not so great as to be considered very significant. For example, a Catholic-Presbyterian marriage has almost as good a chance for survival as a marriage between two Presbyterians. And all of the following are within two percentage points of one another: both Methodist, both Presbyterian, Catholic-Lutheran, Baptist-Protestant, Catholic-Presbyterian, and both Baptist. A clear conclusion, based upon this Iowa study, is that some of the sweeping generalizations of the past are no longer applicable.

This does not mean that the interfaith marriage can now be recommended as a pattern which presents no unusual difficulties. Bowman describes some of the specific problems which can arise to plague the interfaith couple; problems which reinforce the plea of the church official or parish clergyman to avoid this pattern of marriage. He points to the possible negative involvement of parents (two sets), and grandparents, and family friends, and family clergymen, and general acquaintances—all of whom feel a vested interest in the marriage. These persons can accept openly or tentatively, or with thinly veiled hostility, a new spouse or a new child, or they can reject such interlopers out of hand. And at times it may be extremely difficult for such a couple to find common friends, or even to live happily together without such friends in a community with strong religious prejudices.

The answer to the problem, provided by the couple involved, is usually expressed in words like this, "We are in love and therefore we will work it out all right." But "love" does not automatically deal with, nor compensate for, such items as hurt parents, a missing or inadequate worship life together, the dilemma of baptism and subsequent instruction for a child, the problems inherent in dietary practices peculiar to a religious culture, and many more. The answer is not to be found in a retreat from religious practices in order to avoid conflict. The result of this action, very often, is to push religious convictions and practices out of sight and out of mind with consequent loss.

The solution proposed by Pike employs just the opposite approach. Pike says that religion must be taken very seriously. He says that the two persons involved must approach God and the religious life afresh, with an anticipation of new experiences and new insights. For the moment they must lay aside their own religious preconceptions and be open to the possibility of change. They must visit the churches and inform themselves of the teachings and practices of a number of denominations. This requires a careful, mature examination of those options which can provide some of the values discussed above. Hopefully, a consensual agreement can be reached that will allow for a wholesome and united religious life together.

Another very welcome answer is presented in a new book, *Protestant–Catholic Marriages Can Succeed,* written by a couple involved in a very happy interfaith marriage. Their recommendation, lived out in their own marriage, is that each person should stay, and grow, in his own church. They present four "simple rules":

1. Each partner must resolve to be active within his church.

2. At no time and under no circumstances should either partner speak with disrespect of the beliefs of the other.
3. Each partner should go out of his way to encourage the other in church activities.
4. Each partner should encourage the other to help in those missions of the church which they can do together: living concern for your fellow human being.[11]

As the time of marriage approaches, there is usually a great deal of thought that goes into planning, thought which more often focuses on the wedding than on the marriage itself. It would be most salutary if each couple, well before the day of the wedding, could sit down and think through together what their religious faith means to them as individuals and, potentially, can mean to them as a wedded couple. If some of the anguished soul-searching felt by the interfaith pair as they re-evaluate their religious commitments were to be experienced by partners of the same faith, there might be some marriages postponed until some serious discrepancies in viewpoint, in practice, or in intent could be worked out; indeed, some postponements might even become permanent.

At the beginning of this study marriage was defined as "commitment." This word is often used to describe the relationship between God and man. If an individual in his religious life has experienced what it means to give himself wholly over to Another in total commitment, perhaps it can be assumed that he has a deeper understanding of the meaning of the word and its application to the man-woman relationship than if he had never thought through his loyalties in such depth.

SUGGESTIONS FOR DISCUSSION

1. Some members of the group have chosen to have a religious service; others may have elected a civil ceremony. In either case, are there members who will share what they expect the event to mean?
2. Evaluate the four "resources of faith" which Duvall and Hill outline.

3. What reactions are there to the Truebloods' depiction of family worship? What have been some of the group members' experiences in their own childhood homes?

4. What interfaith marriages are group members personally acquainted with? What has been observed? What judgments have been reached?

5. Are there any options in the interfaith marriage situation other than those suggested by Pike?

6. What validity is there in the last paragraph of the commentary above starting with: "At the beginning of this study . . ."?

NOTES

1. *Doctrines and Disciplines of the Methodist Church* (Nashville: The Methodist Publishing House, 1957), p. 708.

2. *Ibid.*

3. Paul Tillich, *Systematic Theology,* III (Chicago: University of Chicago Press, 1963), p. 130.

4. Philip H. Phenix, *Education and the Common Good* (New York: Harper & Brothers, 1961), p. 241.

5. Otto Piper, *The Biblical View of Sex and Marriage* (New York: Charles Scribner's Sons, 1960), p. 171.

6. David R. Mace, *Whom God Hath Joined* (Philadelphia: The Westminster Press, 1953), p. 88.

7. *Ibid.,* p. 89.

8. Paul and Jeanne Simon, *Protestant-Catholic Marriages Can Succeed* (New York: Association Press, 1967), p. 26. Entire book is recommended.

9. Howard M. Bell, *Youth Tell Their Story* (Washington, D.C.: American Council on Education, 1938), p. 21.

10. Lee G. Burchinal and Loren E. Chancellor, "Survival Rates Among Religiously Homogamous and Interreligious Marriages," *Social Forces* IV (May, 1963), pp. 353–362.

11. Paul and Jeanne Simon, *op. cit.,* pp. 49–50.

CHAPTER 8

The Problem of Money

The Experts Speak

[AS SYMBOL AND INSTRUMENT]

Money as a Marital Weapon *

In our money world, a young couple's personal relationships are constantly being tested as they move from the warmth of the honeymoon stage into the stage of practical planning to meet their current needs and to acquire a cushion of assets. They may expect a rise in income and a corresponding rise in expenditures. Generally unanticipated, however, is also a rise in temper and tension. The temper flare-ups may not necessarily stem from money matters, as such, but money nonetheless often precipitates them.

* From Frances Lomas Feldman, *The Family in a Money World* (New York: Family Service Association of America, 1957), pp. 31–33.

221

The way each marital partner deals with strain or conflict is determined, in large measure, by their personality development, their emotional maturity, and the mutual expectations of the two persons. Economic problems, therefore, may serve as a safety valve for releasing outbursts of feeling related to issues other than money. Economic problems may also be used as a vehicle for provoking negative feelings and attitudes in the partner or for provoking disagreements and quarrels. Such displacement of feeling onto money matters, if allowed to proceed without understanding or control, may spell unhappiness or even disaster for the marriage.

Money itself does not bring happiness. Nor does its limited availability inevitably bring unhappiness. Its absence may produce anxiety and tension, but the reasonably well-integrated man and woman will develop devices for dealing with this absence, without directing negative feelings toward themselves or each other. But attitudes and feelings are very much entwined with money. Money is a powerful symbol, representing both love and protection, and the gratification of normal dependency needs. It is an equally powerful means of gratifying infantile wishes and of expressing hostility.

Because money has such deeply personal meaning to everyone, since life cannot be maintained without it, there is a natural tendency to think of money problems as the cause of much marital conflict. It is true, of course, that an unexpected loss of the husband's job or a reduction in his income may create tensions for both husband and wife. Strain may arise, too, if the husband's work involves him in travel and long periods away from home. But if the marital partners are reasonably well-integrated persons, they usually can move together toward making an effective adjustment. They may adopt measures for financial retrenchment until more income becomes available; they may utilize personal or community resources to tide them over; they may take steps to find other, more satisfactory jobs; or, if the latter is not practical, they may adapt themselves to the reality limitations and work out acceptable compromises within these limitations.

The immature, hostile, or generally unhappy person, when confronted with such practical problems, has difficulty in finding a satisfactory solution to his problems and in making the necessary readjustment. If the spouse is also immature or demanding, their separate and combined feelings serve to exaggerate the negative aspects of their partnership and to add to their discord.

Money is used in a variety of ways by both marital partners to exacerbate marital discord. One partner often uses his own ingrained habits of spending as a means of attacking the other. For example, a husband may be controlling about money, holding his wife rigidly to a tight budget or doling out an "allowance" to her. Actually, this may be a role expectation, culturally determined. He may come from a home in which his father, like others in his social circle, was the authoritative, thrifty provider. Such controlled disbursement of money, on the other hand, may stem from the husband's recollections of hunger and deprivation in his youth.

To certain neurotic husbands, money may be an unconscious symbol of masculinity and power. The wife's retaliation against his money behavior may take several forms. She may spend money wastefully as a way of expressing hostility toward him or as a means of maintaining a dominant role. She may make no effort to operate within the budget he has prescribed, or she may respond by setting limits of her own in meeting his sexual, physical, or psychological needs. She may even bring charges against him of inadequate support.

Some women often irrationally apply family or social standards for the purpose of attacking their husbands' inadequacy in earnings. Other women with insatiable dependency needs displace their feelings onto material things and make excessive demands on their husbands. The husband's need to placate or hold a demanding wife may result in overspending and accumulation of debts, and both husband and wife may use money to "buy" the other's love.

FRANCES LOMAS FELDMAN
Economist

Money as a Constructive Tool *

The best investment that people, especially young persons, can make is in themselves. Money spent to improve one's self is money saved in the most secure of all banks. After a certain reserve has been set aside for such things as unemployment and accidents, money earned can probably be more advantageously spent than saved. Until one has reached the age of thirty, this is almost certainly true. When one is relatively young, there are so many things worth knowing, so many books worth reading, so many places worth visiting, so much recreation worth enjoying— in short, so many suitable investments that wise spending can be at least as virtuous as saving. Every boy and girl lives to learn that dollars grow smaller and that larger expenditures bring decreasing satisfactions as one grows older. The admonition to spend wisely and grow rich is offered as a provocation more than as an invitation.

DAVID F. JORDAN
and EDWARD F. WILLETT
Economists

[AS PURSUIT AND GOAL]

The Fueling of Desire †

Marketers, then, are striving to promote upward mobility—at least at the consuming level—for solid, business reasons. Should this be considered a healthy or unhealthy factor? One hesitates

---

* From David F. Jordan and Edward F. Willett, *Managing Personal Finances,* Third ed., © 1951. Reprinted by permission of Prentice-Hall, Inc. Pp. 7–8.

† From Vance Packard, *The Status Seekers* (New York: David McKay Co., Inc. 1959), pp. 317–318.

to draw any decisive conclusions; but in either case the conclusions are depressing.

On the positive side, there is the fact that the marketers, by promoting status striving through the purchase of goods, are giving people the sense that they are getting ahead. This, at the lower levels, is largely a consumption gain. But should we deprive people who are stuck in their jobs of even this psychological satisfaction? If we can't give them a fair chance at making their livelihood in a creative way that offers them the opportunities to advance, should we take away from them—to return to the Roman parallel—their circuses?

On the other hand, what do we do to people when we constantly hold up to them success symbols of a higher class and invite them to strive for the symbols? Does this increase class consciousness in a way that could become dangerous in an economic turndown? And, in this constant conversion of luxuries into necessities, are we pushing people to the point where their expectations are so high—and they live so close to the brink of insolvency—that even a mild prolonged belt-tightening would leave them in an ugly mood? Further, by encouraging people constantly to pursue the emblems of success, and causing them to equate possessions with status, what are we doing to their emotions and their sense of values? Economist Robert Lekachman has observed: "We can only guess at the tensions and anxieties generated."

VANCE PACKARD
Sociologist

Happiness or Things *

It should be appreciated at the outset that the acquisition of money is not the goal of life. But it must be admitted that money is important in attaining objectives. Perhaps it would be well to

* From Elvin F. Donaldson and John K. Pfahl, *Personal Finance,* Third Edition. Copyright © 1961. The Ronald Press Company, New York. Pp. 4–6.

pause briefly to consider just what this life is about. Philosophies state that happiness is the goal. Certainly this is a worthy purpose, and one with which there is little disagreement. How to attain a happy life is the problem which confronts everyone. Considering the differences which exist among human beings, it is understandable that the paths leading to this goal might be many and varied. The artist finds happiness in pursuits different from those followed by businessmen. But there are certain basic qualities, the possession of which makes for anyone's happiness.

You should seek happiness day by day, as you go along. A large sum of money is not requisite for such happiness. In fact, the responsibilities which usually go with material wealth may cause unhappiness. Although the goods and services which money can buy often bring enjoyment, much happiness comes from things for which no money at all is spent. Healthy people are usually happy regardless of whether or not they have much money. The lack of money causes many people to worry, but when they acquire it they do not necessarily stop worrying. Worry is a cause of much unhappiness, and it does not necessarily require money to keep one's self from worrying.

You have probably heard the old saying that anticipation is greater than realization. Many people have found out at one time or another that the pleasure derived from working toward a particular goal was greater than that experienced when the objective had been realized. It does not necessarily take money to strive for certain objectives. In fact, the absence of money may in itself be the reason why certain goals are attempted. The objective may be a better position, or more money, or it may be some goal which does not necessarily pay off in money, such as painting a picture, writing a book, or winning a race.

A great deal of happiness can be attained without spending money for it. Furthermore, the value of money to the individual is realized through the enjoyment he receives through spending, saving, or giving that money away. For many, happiness results from proper living and judicious spending of money.

The problem of money is uppermost in the minds of many

people from the time they assume responsibilities until they die. Furthermore, someone else must be concerned about individuals in a financial way before they are born, during their childhood, and after they are dead, since it costs a considerable amount of money to be born, a far larger amount to be reared, and a not inconsiderable sum to be respectably buried. As adults, the greater part of the day is devoted to the pursuit of some form of work for the purpose of earning money. Much of the remaining time, not consumed by sleeping, is given to the spending of at least part of this money. The more fortunate find it necessary to allow a little time for the difficult task of investing part of their money. Truly, this quest for money is what causes the wheels of life to turn.

ELVIN F. DONALDSON
and JOHN K. PFAHL
Educators—Finance

[AS SECURITY AND SATISFACTION]

Managed Spending *

Poor management of family finances can also cause a good deal of avoidable domestic friction. A sound financial structure in family management is second in importance only to the soundness of the sexual adjustment. The family income should be carefully budgeted. The standard of living should always be kept safely inside available income. Worry over indebtedness is a real domestic hazard and can generally be avoided by wise planning and disciplined spending. Sometimes this means a radical change in premarital spending habits. If so, the change should be ac-

* From Walter R. Stokes, *Married Love in Today's World* (New York: The Citadel Press, 1962), page 86.

cepted in good spirit and observed faithfully. Carelessness and indifference are sure to result in irritation and discord.

WALTER R. STOKES
Psychiatrist

Gaining Through Spending *

The things contributing to the achievement of more satisfactory living may be divided into two groups according to whether or not they are of a physical nature. Tangible things, which fall in the first group, include articles such as clothing and furniture, books and boats, and skis and skates. Intangible things, which constitute the second group, include education and travel, and involve concepts such as beauty, culture, appreciation, and vision. Money is decidedly overvalued if its possession is preferred to the satisfactions that the ownership of such tangible and intangible things can afford.

The brilliant John Ruskin, who was an economist as well as an author and artist, wrote, "There is no wealth but Life." The modern economists are inclined to regard wealth more impersonally in terms of money and property. If wealth is life more than it is property, then the things that make life more complete are the things that make the owner wealthier. To the intelligent individual, wealth is measured more in terms of satisfaction than in terms of dollar values.

Any expenditure that gives an adequate return of satisfaction to the spender is a good investment, regardless of whether the money is spent for the purchase of a bond or of an article for the home. One hundred dollars paid for a good bond will provide an income of three dollars a year, but the same money invested in a good bed will provide a degree of comfort and satisfaction far beyond the value of three dollars a year. People who are able

* From David F. Jordan and Edward F. Willett, *Managing Personal Finances*, Third ed., © 1951. Reprinted by permission of Prentice-Hall, Inc. Pp. 2–4.

and willing to pay more than the minimum for many of the necessities of life will be amply rewarded in many instances. A comfortable pair of shoes and an accurate watch are investments of the highest grade. An ample supply of self-confidence-producing clothing is an investment in the "gilt-edge" category.

In the rather prosaic field of home furnishings may be found dividend payers that outrank good bonds as investments. A good reading lamp, a comfortable chair, a serviceable radio, and a small library of interesting books can be obtained for prices that are in no way proportionate to their values. In view of the considerable portion of life that is devoted to sleep, one would have difficulty in finding a better investment than a bed that is conducive to strength-restoring slumber. It is economy of the falsest kind to limit expenditures for articles that add so much to the wealth that is life, and that are available to persons of even limited incomes.

DAVID F. JORDAN and EDWARD F. WILLETT
Economists

[AS GIFT AND TRUST]

Choice of Values *

Only the slow development of satisfactions which are not expensive, and the discovery of a pattern of life that fits individual needs and abilities, will lead to real happiness. The problem of the consumer is ultimately not an economic one but a religious one. . . . He needs information and the habit of insisting on having adequate information. He needs a clear awareness of his own potential and the power to set his sights on realizable goals. But most of all, he needs to know what things are really important in his life, and to have the maturity to face the fact that

* From James N. Morgan, *Consumer Economics,* © 1955. Reprinted by permission of Prentice-Hall, Inc., Englewood Cliffs, N. J. Pp. 427–428.

choices involve giving up some things for others. Whether you choose to call this religious maturity, mental health, or rational behavior, it involves many choices not customarily regarded as in the realm of economics.

This does not mean that you must conform to anyone's idea of what is best. One consideration though must certainly be, other things being equal, that there are some reasons for conformity if only to make your neighbors more comfortable. Neither does it mean that anything you happen to decide you want will make you happy. There is a moral order in the universe, and there are other people around. Some types of activity tend to lead to harmony with others, and to increase the "general welfare," and others do not.

JAMES N. MORGAN
Economist

The Nature of Sharing *

God has imparted to man the capability of acquiring and possessing goods and of freely disposing of them. Thereby man is enabled to assert himself not only as the master of his possession, but also as God's child in a world of things. On the same basis man is also capable of sharing his goods with others, and he has an innate urge so to act toward those in need. That urge does not manifest itself continuously. It is remarkable, nevertheless, that it should be found in all men, notwithstanding the fact that people act so frequently in a selfish manner and deprive others of what they have or need. Yet there are situations where a man feels that he ought to help another person who is in need, that is to say, lacks goods which we consider indispensable for a true life. In primitive society such helpful action is performed almost instinctively by sharing all the available goods and by taking care of special needs. Judaism and Christianity have strongly emphasized the value of giving, for thereby man is enabled to co-

* From Otto A. Piper, *The Christian Meaning of Money* (Englewood Cliffs: Prentice-Hall, Inc., 1965, paperback), pp. 87–89.

operate with God in his redemptive work. By means of sharing men are brought together in the most intimate way; namely, in the awareness of their common origin in God's creation. The ability to share enlists all the goods which one is able to possess, not just material things, but also health, leisure time, physical capacity, knowledge and so on.

Yet in our modern economy the predominance of money creates a special problem. On the one hand, people are particularly reluctant to part with their money. On the other, the impression prevails that the giving of money is the only way of sharing. Just the contrary is true, however. People in need are especially grateful for personal utterances, above all, when we show sympathetic understanding and friendship. Notwithstanding its impersonal character, however, money proves to be an extremely convenient means of sharing. It enables people to bring help across wide distances, where formerly geography placed an unsurmountable obstacle into the way of those willing to share. It is also capable of providing effecting help in instances where one lacks time or ability to help personally. Far from spurning this mode of assistance, we should be grateful to God for granting us this mode of helping.

Giving help by means of money is not a specifically Christian way of handling money. It is an aspect of human nature. It is not surprising, therefore, that very often "Christian" appeals for funds differ in no respect from the non-Christian way of soliciting money for a thousand good, bad and indifferent causes. It is regrettable, nevertheless, that frequently Christian congregations and denominations are proud of, and satisfied with, the statistics of monetary contributions. For God is not interested in the quantity of money we give. Rather, when He laid the will to help into man's heart, He did so because He had chosen man to carry out the divine purpose here on earth. This means that whatever help we give must never be a merely temporary relief for a person's material need. Rather, true sharing is an event by which the structure of human history is affected. The rule of the powers of evil is thereby broken at one point of human relationships.

The goal to be reached by means of Christian giving is the full realization of man's constructive ability. Since man is made to be sensitive to other people's sufferings and wants, it is not surprising that appeals for the benefit of hungry, orphaned or crippled children, ailing war invalids or permanently disabled persons will always meet with a sympathetic response. But God is not primarily concerned with rendering people happy. Rather, he wants them to become truly human. That is the reason why the evangelistic and educational work of the church and its community life are so important. Thereby, material life becomes a means by which personal relations are established between giver and recipient. The follower of Jesus is called upon to realize the fellowship of men. This is done most effectively by serving those in need. Yet much of our giving is condescending. We contribute from our affluence, and we expect the recipients of our gifts to accept them on our terms. True fellowship, however, is possible only when we allow the specific needs of the others to determine the kind of relief to be given. We must adjust our way of helping to the specific situation in which the recipient finds himself. While not all of our giving can be of a personal character, every Christian should have at least one person or one cause for whom or which he cares in a personal way. Here lies one of the specific difficulties that confront Christian giving in our time.

The end which God has in mind with us is not in the first place to rid this world of all material ills. God wants to humanize this world. For the former end it would be sufficient to mobilize the financial resources of mankind. For his own end God brings people together in such a way that through the difference of their conditions they might supplement each other and thus have an opportunity for effective service.

OTTO A. PIPER
Theology

[AS PUZZLE AND PROMISE]

Pieces of Budget *

The following list of items is suggested to help you both to record your expenditures of the past and to budget those of the future.

A. INCOME TAXES (federal, state, and local)
These are usually deducted in advance, so that you look upon your income only as your take-home pay. Yet you should certainly know what your income taxes amount to, at least for the record.

B. FOOD
You may want to divide this into two items, groceries and meals out, or you may not. Your groceries are likely to include some items that actually are not foods, such as cigarettes, soaps, detergents, and brooms, as well as sales taxes . . .

C. HOUSING
This includes a number of items, some of which you may want to keep separate, such as:
1. Rent or payments on the mortgage.
2. Real estate taxes.
3. Insurance on the house and furnishings, including not only fire, but liability and other types.
4. Upkeep and repairs, including the plumbing bills, etc.
5. Utilities. These usually include gas, electricity, water, and telephone. If you buy coal or oil, include these . . .

* Reprinted by permission of the publisher, from Evelyn M. Duvall and Reuben Hill, *Being Married* (Lexington, Mass.: D. C. Heath and Company, 1960), pp. 241–243.

D. HOUSEHOLD
  1. Certain items of purchase, such as linens, dishes, refrigerators, washers, and the installment payments on same . . .
  2. Certain services, such as baby sitters, and repairs on the equipment, such as the vacuum cleaner or the TV set.
  3. Miscellaneous items.

E. CLOTHING
  1. Purchases, including shoes and hats.
  2. Laundry, cleaning, and repairs.

F. TRANSPORTATION
  1. The car. The payments on your car will, of course, be known exactly in advance. Gas and oil in "normal" months when there are no special trips, can be reliably estimated. Licenses and insurance can be known exactly but likely will be heavily bunched in certain months. Repairs are the item most difficult to estimate in advance.
  2. Other transportation. This will be big only if you must commute regularly some distance to your work by public transportation . . .

G. HEALTH AND MEDICAL EXPENSES
  1. With hospitalization insurance you can take much of the uncertainty out of your budget. Sickness and accident insurance and company health plans may come as a fringe benefit to further reduce your risks and costs.
  2. Doctors' bills are more likely to be unpredictable, except in obstetrics cases where almost the exact cost can be known and planned for in advance.
  3. Dental bills are often a large unknown, especially when your family has increased in size . . .

H. LIFE INSURANCE
This can, of course, be exactly known and planned for in advance. Any uncertainties are likely to be on the favorable side in the form of dividends that help your budget.

I. PERSONAL EXPENSES

1. Allowances for each member of the family old enough to spend his own money.
2. Grooming. With haircuts and permanents, this can amount to considerable money.
3. Dues. Include not only membership in volunteer organizations, but also any union dues, even if deducted in advance.

J. RECREATION AND EDUCATION

1. Ordinary recreation: movies, shows, entertainments, and the like, unless they come out of personal allowances.
2. Vacation. This can come to a sizable sum, and usually all at one time. Either you must save up for it in advance or go into debt for it.
3. Books, magazines, daily papers, tuition for courses, etc.

K. DONATIONS

1. Gifts to individuals, especially around Christmas, but also for such events as weddings.
2. Gifts to agencies and causes, such as church, community chest, the Red Cross, and YMCA. Barring special emergencies and appeals you should be able to predict this with considerable accuracy.

L. SAVINGS

Money deposited in a checking account to be used for expenses is, of course, not saved. Savings will ordinarily be of two kinds.
1. Temporary savings for specific purposes, such as having a baby, vacations, making the down payment on a house or a car, which you expect to use up.
2. Investment, which is money saved for the purpose of producing income on a relatively permanent and continuous basis.

M. OTHER

This is, of course, a catch-all for items not included elsewhere.

Some of the above items will not be applicable to your budget. Therefore you should make your own list and use it as a basis of both recording and planning your own expenditures.

EVELYN M. DUVALL and REUBEN HILL
Marriage and Family Life

Exploring the Issues

The title of this chapter is a deliberate attempt to call attention to the fact that money in marriage often is a problem, and sometimes can be a very troublesome one. There are many studies and surveys which indicate this, some of which point out that it takes longer for many couples to find a good monetary adjustment than it does for them to find a good sexual adjustment. While money problems are often symptoms of basic conflicts in other areas of living, they can and do play a major disruptive role of their own.

It is not difficult to see why this is so. Money plays a very significant role in all but the most primitive societies. Most adults handle money every day they live. In the United States money— its gain or loss, use or misuse, sufficiency or lack—is an engrossing subject of daily conversation. Most people live in a money world.

The discussion of money problems in this chapter goes well beyond the content of billfold or purse. It also includes possessions and material things of all kinds. Philosophically, the problem of money means coming to terms with the total lure and power of materialism in a society steadily growing more affluent.

The accumulation of things as opposed to the pursuit of values is a choice each married couple must ultimately make.

These choices are not made any easier by the structure of society. It is a "cut-flower" civilization, to employ Trueblood's phrase, within which new families are forming, a civilization cut off from its roots in which fewer and fewer persons can find and maintain any viable relationship with the natural world. More and more objects, including food, are the products of man and his machines rather than the products of the earth itself. Man is becoming alienated from his source.

Paul Tillich notes how the configurations of most objects in and of the home have no intrinsic relation to their true nature. Colors, lines, and shapes are simply applied to materials giving them what he terms "an alleged beauty." He writes insightfully of the primal understanding of things in these words:

> The primitive magical interpretation of reality is based on an experience of the intrinsic power of things. For the primitive man things have a kind of numinous or sacral quality. This gives them a tremendous significance for his whole existence. He feels them always as forces capable of fulfilling or destroying, of shattering or saving, his life. He approaches them with ritualistic methods. Even when he tries to use them, he is bound to their power, their wilfulness, and their protection. He is a part of them, having a limited power of his own but no superiority in principle. He himself is a smaller or greater power among a system of powers to which he must adapt himself.
>
> All this changes when the system of powers is replaced by the correlation of self and world, of subjectivity and objectivity. Man becomes an epistemological, legal, and moral center, and things become objects of his knowledge, his work, and his use. They become "things" in the proper sense of the word—mere objects, without subjectivity, without power, of their own. They lose their numinous power, their sacral quality. They are no longer able to fulfil and to save, nor are they able to destroy and to pervert. Nothing divine and nothing demonic is left in them. They have become means for the personality and have ceased to be ends in themselves.[1]

While man cannot, and perhaps should not, go back to any primitive perceptions of the nature of things, his almost complete separation from nature has produced this deep sense of alienation and forlornness. Essentially, it is a denial that man is part of the natural world of matter as well as being also above it. It is a denial of the Biblical insight that "the Lord God formed man of the dust of the ground." (Genesis 2:7)

Erich Fromm similarly points out the depths of this alienation by enumerating many of the things that are used without any understanding of their nature or function. He lists the telephone, radio, phonograph, and other machines that are operated with a button or switch. They are as much of a mystery to the average man of today as they would be to a primitive man. "We consume," he concludes, "as we produce, without any concrete relatedness to the objects with which we deal; we live in a world of things, and our only connection with them is that we know how to manipulate or to consume them." [2]

Some of the deep concerns of the young people of today in relation to the preservation of the natural environment are undoubtedly rooted in the foreignness of so much of what they normally come in contact with. Man needs to be at home in the world of things, the world about him.

Man's need to work also throws him into conflict with his environment. His satisfaction with himself is often equated closely with his satisfaction at work. If he is to reach Maslow's level of self-esteem (cf. Ch. 6), he needs to be contented in his labor life. The average man is bored with too much leisure, chafes under an extended vacation, is driven to distraction by unemployment, and often holds more than one job just to fill up his time. He may also have a hobby and one or more participation pursuits going at the same time. Most people need work almost as much as they need food. Only if this work satisfactorily relates him to the world of things will he be a fulfilled person. Or, to put it another way, only if he makes and uses money in ways which meet his inner needs will he be happy in this money world.

The problem of money will be examined briefly:

I. As Symbol and Instrument
II. As Pursuit and Goal

III. As Security and Satisfaction
IV. As Gift and Trust
V. As Puzzle and Promise

I. *As Symbol and Instrument*

Money is more than metal and paper; it is power of many different sorts. The currency itself is oftentimes of little intrinsic value. The silver content of so-called silver coins in this country has been sharply reduced. A paper bill may run from $1 up to $10,000 in face value, yet actually be worth only a few pennies. Money is a symbol. It stands for bullion in a vault, confidence in a government, the power to buy and to own. With money an individual can exercise a degree of control over others, over his own environment and even over his own destiny. It is neutral only in theory; normally it is so identified with the psychological needs of the possessor or would-be possessor that it already has a character. Its spending merely acts as a confirmation of this fact.

Money may cover up a multitude of sins and omissions. It brings invitations to society's inner gatherings and presentations in foreign courts. Money cracks open exclusive enclaves wherever they may be found. Deficiencies in formal education are overlooked, poor manners are not mentioned, a notable lack of aesthetic interests or ethical values need not be an impediment— if one has money. Money is a symbol so universally known, accepted, loved and passionately desired that it may easily be substituted for wisdom, breeding and taste with few to criticize the exchange.

In marriage money may be a symbol, and sometimes even a substitute, for love. Feldman interprets just how it is used as a destructive weapon within a marriage relationship when it becomes a sharp-edged tool used to express personal unhappiness, emotional imbalance or a desire to dominate. The person who feels angry, neglected, or abused may quite instinctively retaliate with whatever power leverage may be closest at hand. Quite often this is money. And if, as Feldman suggests, money has status power especially for the male, then the attack strikes at the particularly sensitive area of the masculine self-image. Un-resolved conflict in this area, particularly if much of this is on the unconscious level and there is little or no awareness of what is going on, can and will continue to produce serious misunder-standings and perhaps permanent ego and marital damage.

Jordan and Willett point out, on the positive side, how money may be deliberately invested in the personal life of an individ-ual. Its existence as an instrument is recognized and conscious use is made of this fact. Money should not be saved; this is a non-dynamic concept. It should rather be spent or invested for those values and things which people have in mind when they *save* money.

Theodor Reik has a very insightful contribution to make in the analysis of money as symbol.[3] He says that a home sym-bolically is an extension of a woman's body. Thus she is present and even on display when her house is entered, even though she may not be there physically at the moment. Thus, many women have what appears to the masculine mind to be an overweening and, at times, irrational interest in their home. It really should not be too hard to understand, says Reik. It is only showing a very natural interest in their own bodies.

II. *As Pursuit and Goal*

The quality of economic pressures which young couples face can be symbolized by that brainchild of American ingenuity, the credit card, which, on demand, produces instant debt for its user. The card is generally available to all who are considered to be potential purchasers of luxury items. On the other hand, credit is rarely available to the very poor for the essentials of life.

Americans are now oriented toward *buying* and *using,* rather than *producing* and *saving* as in previous times. Furthermore, this consumption is seldom based on absolute needs but rather on contrived ones. For example, an inexpensive car might well satisfy the need for transportation. But in the common mind the more expensive transportation is better. This "judgment by price tag" is a mark of today's culture.

The automobile is a highly mobile symbol of achievement.

The fancy home and the exclusive residential district serve the same purpose. No wonder Duvall writes of "the high cost of impressing others." Carefully conditioned by advertising, people purchase things in order to sustain, improve or embellish the status and rank which they have chosen for themselves in their particular subculture. The process is commonly labeled "conspicuous consumption." To buy and to discard, even to waste, is not an uncommon thing. The phrases, "planned obsolescence," "this year's model," and "the new, improved version" help identify the program of planned waste in the American industrial economy.

Competitive buying can no longer be described as simply "keeping up with the Joneses." As Piper says, "Advertising, originally meant to direct people to the source where their real needs would be satisfied, has now become a veritable art of persuading unwilling customers by means of half truths, exaggerated promises and flattery to believe that the good advertised is absolutely necessary for their happiness or health." [4]

David Hamilton succinctly describes what is going on by a comparison with the customs of the old Kwakiutl Indian of the Pacific Northwest:

The Northwest Indians, in the course of a potlatch feast, not only gave away commodities in huge quantities to their invited guests but even resorted to public destruction of commodities to demonstrate their indifference to economic wealth. The chief who gave the potlatch demonstrated his prowess by putting on such a wasteful display. The point of the display was to convince the guests that the chief had such vast possessions that he could be indifferent to them.

We read about these customs and are astounded that such public waste could be unrecognized by the Kwakiutl Indians. But we have the same kind of waste in our own culture. At the same time that we pay allegiance to the Puritan virtues of thrift and abstinence, we also feel the necessity of placing our wealth and economic success on public display. The miser receives censure equal to that heaped upon the prodigal. . . . To pay attention to money expenditure with an eye to curbing wasteful expenditure implies impoverishment and, hence, low status. People are embarrassed if others receive the impression that they cannot "afford to pay" on a level commensurate with their accepted status position.[5]

In the New Testament Jesus personifies money and material things as "Mammon," a "supreme earthly power that vies with God for control of mankind." [6] It is not necessary to go as far as this in theologizing the problem to see the tremendous influence exerted on personal lives by the power of the material.

But this influence is not in and of itself bad. The New Testament is often incorrectly quoted as saying that "money is the root of all evil"; the accurate rendering refers to "the *love* of money" as the radical element in human evil. The right to possess is clearly stipulated in the words "Thou shalt not steal," and is just as clearly defended in the rest of Biblical teaching. Problems arise when the right to possession becomes a form of obsession.

Vance Packard refers to the marketers at work in the advertising industry. The terrible fallacy in this business is that psychic (*i.e.* spiritual) hungers are being proffered material food. A single and yet classic example is the effort to satisfy the person's need for love by an abundance of material gifts, items taken down from a shelf in some store.

Donaldson and Pfahl suggest that the choice had better be made between tangible items (money and goods) and intangible values (happiness and pleasure). It is patently impossible to satisfy emotional needs with things. As these men put it, "Although the goods and services which money can buy often bring enjoyment, much happiness comes from things for which no money at all is spent." These are things which are valued for other reasons than their monetary state.

Life can be a headlong pursuit after money and things and thus a pursuit that never satisfies and never can. Or it can be the taking of pleasure in what money can provide for one's self, one's family or for others. "There is great gain in godliness with contentment" is a sage New Testament adage. (I Timothy 6:6)

III. *As Security and Satisfaction*

A sound approach to money handling is to ask the question, "How shall it be spent?" People should spend for the things which will provide a sense of security. This requires both a point of view about values and a listing of needs. Actually, a budget need be no mysterious thing. It consists of an enumeration of legitimate needs in priority categories.

Spending can be impulsive.[7] This may provide a host of minor satisfactions of the moment, but rarely anything of any permanent value. Furthermore, if the money were really needed for something else, then the end result will only be irritation and frustration.

Spending can be compulsive.[7] The compulsive spender is usually well over his budget and most often his income. His financial condition is a harassment in his life, not a source of satisfaction nor a base of security. Like the alcoholic or the chronic gambler, he cannot help himself.

Spending can be competitive.[7] This is buying because others do, not because there is a need justifiable in light of the income and/or budget. It stems out of a need for peer approval. It is the mark of the "other directed person" of David Riesman.

Stokes is primarily concerned about sexual adjustment—about securing the best sexual foundation possible for each particular marriage. It is noteworthy, then, that he takes time out to speak about the need for the sound financial undergirding of marriage. He regards this as "second in importance only to the soundness of the sexual adjustment."

Jordan and Willett in clear language and using simple illustrations point out how satisfaction and security can be gained by spending, even for saving. It is noteworthy that intangible values rate high on their list of significant items for which to spend money.

The author's own married life has always included what he has termed "buying memories." These memories have been purchased on occasion by taking money budgeted for other items and—at times when it was especially needed to renew the channels of love and communication—spending it for a week-end together at some special place of beauty and seclusion. In each instance it was something that "we could not afford." But the decision to go was based on a more pressing value judgment; namely, that "we could not afford *not* to go." The result has been to develop feelings of closeness and memories of sharing that have made continuous contributions to the marriage through the years, far exceeding the financial expenditures. The question was decided on the basis of value priorities.

IV. *As Gift and Trust*

In a world of materialism man has largely lost the sense of matter being a creation of God and His gift entrusted to man. Yet the insights of the opening chapters of Genesis point both to a Creator and to a trust. "And the Lord God planted a garden in Eden, in the east; and there he put the man whom he had formed . . ." (Genesis 2:8) "The Lord God took the man and put him in the garden of Eden to till it and keep it." (Genesis 2:15)

Man has dismissed the Creator and has ravished the earth. Yet now in the new thrust toward nature, man may be able to sense again the natural world and all its components as a gift and a trust bestowed.

Morgan speaks of a "moral order in the universe," and refers to "other people around." The very crowding of the earth has in a sense given the death blow to the unfettered individualism of the day. One can only "do his own thing" to the extent that it doesn't impinge on the action of another who may be engaged in the same exercise. The accretion of goods is granted by God to man, says Piper. So is the right to possess and to dispose of them. But unless the principle of trusteeship or of stewardship comes into play, there can only be expected greater confusion, aggrandizement, and tension.

Money must be used "to humanize this world." Any other use is not worthy of man.

The individual couple must come to terms with the power of money, acknowledge it as a force, and then seek to employ it for the service of others. This calls for a commitment in depth. There are other options, of course. The most grievous is to see envy and greed spawning a host of evil offspring too horrible to contemplate.

V. *As Puzzle and Promise*

This chapter is not intended to furnish a detailed budget to fit each family. The determination of this must be worked out in each situation. Duvall provides an excellent summation of those items which should be taken into account in any soundly constructed budget. When the puzzle pieces are put together, there is a promise of economic strength and stability which can serve as an excellent economic base for a satisfying marriage.

SUGGESTIONS FOR DISCUSSION

1. How acceptable is it if the wife joins her husband in the labor market to help get settled, to find satisfaction in work, or to escape household chores?
2. What is foreseen as the most formidable economic problem in each approaching marriage?
3. What changes in family routines and marital attitudes might occur if it were understood that man's chief personal satisfaction comes from his labor life, woman's from her love life?
4. What attention should be given at the early stages of marriage to major items such as insurance, investment programs, the drawing up of wills, and the like?
5. What reaction is there to the idea of "buying memories"?

NOTES

1. Paul Tillich, *The Protestant Era* (Chicago: University of Chicago Press, 1948), p. 120.
2. Erich Fromm, *The Sane Society* (New York: Rinehart, 1955), p. 134.
3. Theodor Reik, *Of Love and Lust* (New York: Grove Press, Inc., 1949, paperback), p. 477.
4. Otto Piper, *The Christian Meaning of Money* (Englewood Cliffs: Prentice-Hall, Inc., 1965, paperback), p. 19.

5. David Hamilton, *The Consumer in our Economy* (Boston: Houghton Mifflin Company, 1962), pp. 130–131.

6. Otto Piper, *op. cit.,* pp. 28–29.

7. Evelyn M. Duvall and Reuben Hill, *Being Married* (New York: Association Press, 1960), pp. 245–246.

For Further Study

For Further Study

BAILEY, DERRICK SHERWIN. *Sexual Relations in Christian Thought*. New York: Harper & Brothers, 1959.
————. *Sexual Ethics: A Christian View*. New York: The Macmillan Company, 1962, 1963. Paperback.
BOWMAN, HENRY A. *A Christian Interpretation of Marriage*. Philadelphia: The Westminster Press, 1959.
BRITISH COUNCIL OF CHURCHES. *Sex and Morality*. Philadelphia: The Fortress Press, 1966.
CHRISTENSEN, HAROLD T., ed. *Handbook of Marriage and the Family*. Chicago: Rand McNally & Company, 1964.
COLE, WILLIAM GRAHAM. *Sex and Love in the Bible*. New York: Association Press, 1959.
DOELY, SARAH BENTLEY. *Women's Liberation and the Church*. New York: Association Press, 1971.
DUVALL, EVELYN MILLIS. *Why Wait Till Marriage?* New York: Association Press, 1965.
———— and REUBEN HILL. *Being Married*. New York: Association Press, 1960.
EHRMANN, WINSTON. *Premarital Dating Behavior*. New York: Bantam Books, 1960.
ELLIS, ALBERT. *Sex Without Guilt*. New York: Lyle Stuart, 1958, 1966.
FELDMAN, FRANCES L. *The Family in a Money World*. New York: The Family Service Association of America, 1957.
FRIEDAN, BETTY. *The Feminine Mystique*. New York: Dell Publishing Co., 1963.
FROMM, ERICH. *The Art of Loving*. New York: Bantam Books, 1963.

249

HATHORN, RABAN, WILLIAM H. GENNÉ, and MORDECAI BRILL. *Marriage: An Interfaith Guide for All Couples.* New York: Association Press, 1970.

HOFFMAN, RANDALL W. and ROBERT PLUTCHIK. *Small Group Discussion in Orientation and Teaching.* New York: G. P. Putnam's Sons, 1959.

KIRKENDALL, LESTER A. *Premarital Intercourse and Interpersonal Relationships.* New York: The Julian Press, 1961.

MACE, DAVID R. *Success in Marriage.* New York: Abingdon Press, 1958.

———. *Whom God Hath Joined.* Philadelphia: The Westminster Press, 1953.

MEAD, MARGARET. *Male and Female.* New York: William Morrow & Co., 1949; New American Library of World Literature, Inc., 1949.

MORRIS, J. K. *Premarital Counseling.* Englewood Cliffs: Prentice-Hall, Inc., 1960.

PETERSON, JAMES A. *Toward a Successful Marriage.* New York: Charles Scribner's Sons, 1960.

PIPER, OTTO A. *The Biblical View of Sex and Marriage.* New York: Charles Scribner's Sons, 1960.

———. *The Christian Meaning of Money.* Englewood Cliffs: Prentice-Hall, Inc., 1965.

REIK, THEODOR. *Of Love and Lust.* New York: Farrar, Straus & Giroux, Inc., 1957.

REISS, IRA L. *Premarital Sexual Standards in America.* Illinois: The Free Press of Glencoe, 1960.

RUTLEDGE, AARON L. *Pre-Marital Counseling.* Cambridge: Schenkman Publishing Company, Inc., 1966.

SIMON, PAUL and JEANNE. *Protestant-Catholic Marriages Can Succeed.* New York: Association Press, 1967.

STOKES, WALTER R. *Married Love in Today's World.* New York: The Citadel Press, 1962.

THIELICKE, HELMUT. *The Ethics of Sex.* Translated by John W. Doberstein. New York: Harper & Row, 1964.

TRUEBLOOD, ELTON and PAULINE. *The Recovery of Family Life.* New York: Harper & Brothers, 1953.

WOOD, JR., FREDERIC C. *Sex and the New Morality.* New York: Association Press, 1968.

WYNN, J. C., ed. *Sex, Family and Society in Theological Focus.* New York: Association Press, 1966.

————, ed. *Sexual Ethics and Christian Responsibility: Some Divergent Views.* New York: Association Press, 1970.